MW01278188

Valuing Health Systems

Thank you for choosing a SAGE product! If you have any comment, observation or feedback, I would like to personally hear from you. Please write to me at <u>contactceo@sagepub.in</u>

—Vivek Mehra, Managing Director and CEO,
SAGE Publications India Pvt Ltd, New Delhi

Bulk Sales

SAGE India offers special discounts for purchase of books in bulk. We also make available special imprints and excerpts from our books on demand.

For orders and enquiries, write to us at

Marketing Department
SAGE Publications India Pvt Ltd
B1/I-1, Mohan Cooperative Industrial Area
Mathura Road, Post Bag 7
New Delhi 110044, India
E-mail us at <u>marketing@sagepub.in</u>

Get to know more about SAGE, be invited to SAGE events, get on our mailing list. Write today to <u>marketing@sagepub.in</u>

This book is also available as an e-book.

Valuing Health Systems

A Framework for Low and Middle Income Countries

Charles Collins
Andrew Green

www.sagepublications.com
Los Angeles • London • New Delhi • Singapore • Washington DC

First published in 2014 by

SAGE Publications India Pvt Ltd
B1/I-1 Mohan Cooperative Industrial Area
Mathura Road, New Delhi 110 044, India
www.sagepub.in

SAGE Publications Inc
2455 Teller Road
Thousand Oaks, California 91320, USA

SAGE Publications Ltd
1 Oliver's Yard, 55 City Road
London EC1Y 1SP, United Kingdom

SAGE Publications Asia-Pacific Pte Ltd
3 Church Street
#10-04 Samsung Hub
Singapore 049483

Published by Vivek Mehra for SAGE Publications India Pvt Ltd, typeset in 10/12 Berkeley by Tantla Composition Pvt Ltd, Chandigarh and printed at Sai Print-O-Pack Pvt Ltd, New Delhi.

Library of Congress Cataloging-in-Publication Data

Collins, Charles, 1949–
  Valuing health systems: a framework for low and middle income countries/ Charles Collins and Andrew Green.
      pages cm
  Includes bibliographical references and index.
  1. Medical care—Developing countries.   2. Medical ethics—Developing countries.   3. Medical policy—Developing countries.   I. Green, Andrew, 1952– II. Title.
  RA441.C65   362.109172'4–dc23   2013   2012047334

ISBN: 978-81-321-0724-8 (HB)

The SAGE Team: Sharel Simon, Shreya Lall, Nand Kumar Jha and Dally Verghese
Cover Artwork: Andrew Green

Contents

Tables

Figures

Boxes

Abbreviations

AG	Andrew Green
ARV	Antiretroviral
CC	Charles Collins
CHW	Community Health Worker
CMS	Cooperative Medical Scheme
COPD	Chronic Obstructive Pulmonary Disease
CSDH	Commission on Social Determinants of Health
CT	Computerised Tomography
DALY	Disability Adjusted Life Year
DfID	Department for International Development (UK)
DHA	District Health Authority
DRC	Democratic Republic of the Congo
DRG	Diagnosis Related Group
GAVI	Global Alliance for Vaccines and Immunisation
GDP	Gross Domestic Product
GHI	Global Health Initiative
GNP	Gross National Product
GPPP	Global Public Private Partnership
GRIPP	Getting Research Into Policy and Practice
HIC	High Income Country
HIS	Health Information System
HIV/AIDS	Human Immunodeficiency Virus/Acquired Immuno-deficiency Syndrome
HQ	Headquarters
IAH	Inter-sectoral Action for Health
ILO	International Labour Organisation
IMF	International Monetary Fund
IT	Information Technology
ITN	Insecticide Treated Bed-net
LMICs	Low and Middle Income Countries
MDG	Millennium Development Goal

MoH	Ministry of Health
MSF	Médecins Sans Frontières
NCMS	New Cooperative Medical Scheme
NGOs	Non-governmental Organisations
NHS	National Health Service
NICE	National Institute for Health and Clinical Excellence
NTD	Neglected Tropical Disease
OECD	Organisation for Economic Cooperation and Development
PEPFAR	President's Emergency Plan for AIDS Relief
PHC	Primary Health Care
ppp	Purchasing Power Parity
PRSP	Poverty Reduction Strategy Paper
QALY	Quality Adjusted Life Year
RCT	Randomised Controlled Trial
SWAp	Sector Wide Approach
TB	Tuberculosis
Tk	Taka (Currency of Bangladesh)
UK	United Kingdom
UMIC	Upper Middle Income Country
UN	United Nations
UNDP	United Nations Development Programme
UNICEF	United Nations Children's Fund
US or USA	United States of America
USAID	United States Agency for International Development
WHO	World Health Organization
WHR	World Health Report

Acknowledgements

There are many people whose ideas have influenced us in the writing of this book; it is impossible to name them all. In the course of our work over many years in the area of health systems of low and middle income countries, we have met many health staff at levels of the system and service users and we owe much to them for their insights. Students on courses in many institutions—but particularly the Nuffield Centre for International Health and Development (University of Leeds) and the Liverpool School of Tropical Medicine (University of Liverpool)—have been a major source of ideas, information, encouragement and useful criticism. The same can be said of colleagues from a range of different organisations, including the late Carol Barker, Nancy Gerein, Lucy Gilson, Miguel Angel Gonzalez-Block, Andrew Long, Tim Martineau, Di McIntyre, Anne Mills, Tolib Mirzoev, James Newell, Mayeh Omar, Shenglan Tang and Goran Tomson. Of course, we do not ascribe the particular views of this book to them and take full responsibility for its content.

Lastly, we wish to thank our families. For CC, Yan has given support and encouragement and many thanks to Marisol, Catherine—and their partners—and Xiao for being who they are. For AG, Mary continues to provide both a test bed where ideas can be grounded, and a major support. Laura, Chris and Martin, and their partners and, in the next generation, Leon, Layla and Dylan, are a constant reminder of the important and genuinely valuable things in life.

1

Setting the Scene

The title of this book was carefully chosen with a deliberate double meaning. In what follows, we hope to persuade you of two central propositions. First that to improve health, we have to get a better understanding of the complexity of the different forces and elements that are present in and shape a country's endeavours to improve health—what we will be calling the health system. In this sense, we want you to recognise the value of your own health system and hence the importance of understanding its nature. The second proposition is that there are many different ways to configure these elements—to shape the health system—and that values play a major role in the architecture of the health system. The design of the one that currently exists in your society was not driven, we argue, by technical considerations alone but was also heavily influenced by the values of those with power within this health system and the broader society. We will not be arguing that we should remove the influence of values; indeed, we think it would be impossible to do this. Rather, we would like to persuade you to recognise the role of these values. One important theme throughout the book is the recognition of the range of values that each of us hold and how they affect the workings of a health system. We will present our own values and try to persuade you how they may be furthered through the health system.

This book has been germinating for some years and, even after a decision to write it, has taken time to come to fruition. Over the last 28–40 years, we have both been working on and in health systems in low and middle income countries (LMICs) as public servants, academic researchers and consultants. When we started, the term *health system* was not used. It is only in the last decade or so that it has begun to be used widely. Indeed, our work in this field would not originally have been seen as 'health systems work'. Charles Collins' (CC's) focus was originally on health management and Andrew Green's (AG's) on health planning and policy. However, we have always recognised the connections that exist within the different elements of 'the health system' and indeed our previous collaborations have allowed us to explore these from our different foci and perspectives.

As we both approach the evening of our careers in this field, we increasingly find ourselves reflecting on the lack of an analysis that explored the wide picture of health systems and that deliberately exposed the value base of these health systems. Slightly nervously, we decided we should try to build on our previous work and develop a new analysis of this beast, the health system. We need quickly to qualify the above by recognising the excellent work that has been done by other analysts, both as individuals and through organisations such as the World Health Organization (WHO); we will be drawing heavily on this work. However, we have not seen an analysis that deliberately examines the way in which values permeate these health systems and that argues for both greater recognition and place for these values in decisions about changes to health systems. This is the challenge we have set for ourselves and which has, as our publisher will attest, taken longer than we originally envisaged.

This book focuses on the health systems of LMICs. This is not to suggest that we do not think high income countries do not face similar challenges in the design of their health systems or that they are any less value-driven—they are. However, there are two reasons for this focus. Perhaps most pragmatically, our previous work and interest has focused on this group of countries; as such, it is natural that we draw particularly on this experience. More importantly, however, these countries, though each unique, share many characteristics that make the study of their health systems particularly urgent. Their categorisation, in terms of their income levels, immediately points to the low levels of resourcing available to them for their health systems. This, when coupled with the high levels and changing types of ill-health that they face, places particular demands on their health systems. These challenges are compounded by wider contextual issues ranging from political fragility through to increasing urbanisation. Such pressures are here now; other pressures are currently less obvious but are increasingly recognised as occurring in the future yet needing responses now—in particular, the pressures from climate change and the increasingly globalised nature of the world. On top of these broad contextual factors, a number of these countries have introduced reforms to their health systems over the last two decades, such as new funding mechanisms, a greater public–private mix and decentralisation. These have often been the result of pressure from external agencies. The appropriateness of a number of these 'reforms' is now being questioned and health system leaders are seeking to adjust or replace them. In making these adjustments, we argue, a holistic analysis of the health system, its internal interactions and the underlying values is critical; we attempt to contribute to this analysis in this book. Though the book focuses on LMICs, we do however believe that there are many lessons that high income health system architects can learn from the experience of such countries, not least because the consequences of ill-judged reforms are often particularly palpable in such stark environments.

So, we are trying in this book to set out such a holistic analysis and at the same time demonstrate how different values will change the nature of the prescriptive measures. We said earlier that there is a range of values and each reader will have their own (though they may not explicitly recognise them). We, of course, also have our own and in Chapter 2 we set these out, fully recognising that a number of readers will not share these values. However, we believe that it is both essential and indeed in the spirit of the approach of the book and our own values that we are clear as to our own starting point. If you, as a reader, having read Chapter 2, do not share these, we would still ask you to persevere and read the book, not in the hope that we will change your mind—this book does not attempt to evangelise as to particular values—but in the hope that you will recognise the importance of values in health system design through this particular exemplar.

As you will soon realise, our values (and particularly, but not solely, that of equity) lead us to assert a lead role for the state—as a policy leader and mediator, as a financer and as a provider of services in our interpretation of a good health system. As such we focus on the role of the public sector within the analysis. We do examine the role of other actors, but we do this predominantly from the perspective of the public sector and certainly in terms of action by the public sector.

We also recognise that much health system analysis has focused on the provision of health services. This is despite a recognition by many (though in some cases, tokenistic) of the importance of the wider determinants of health and ill health. We have attempted, though we recognise the difficulty of this, to reflect in the book on how, practically, the development of a more balanced view of the sets of activities across a range of sectors can be influenced by health system leaders. This inter-sectoral approach is much more, we believe, than multi-sectoralism, in which a range of activities occur in parallel. A genuine *health* rather than *health care* system needs to find ways of breaking down the verticalist mentality and engaging in integrated inter-sectoral action, whilst recognising the reality of different aims of different sectors.

There are times in this book that we have used terms such as *sector* and *system* without a clear definition. Although we attempt to pin these down in Chapter 2, we recognise this is not always possible and that the term *sector*, for example, may be used by us due to popular parlance when *system* may in fact be more correct. Another challenge surrounds the two terms of *state* and *public sector*. In some cases we use these two terms interchangeably, although we try to use the former when we are referring to the paramount legal authority and sovereignty in a given territory and the latter when we are referring to its roles and range of services (such as health care). We recognise the elusive nature of such definitions and indeed recognise that we ourselves may not always be consistent in their use in this book. This reflects another challenge for both us and for health system analysts—the challenge of language. We increasingly have recognised, as we developed this book, that use of language can be a significant barrier to shared understanding of the health system. Frequently we have found colleagues working in specialised parts of the health system using the same words as ourselves, but with different meaning. As another writer put it in a different context, we are divided by a common language. For example, terms such as *integration* and *public–private mix* are often used by system analysts and programme managers differently, leading to confusion. Even our basic values, such as equity, can be apparently shared until tested against real policies only to discover that the interpretation is different. We do not claim to have a monopoly of truth on definitions of terms but we believe, as part of the development of a common analytical framework, that it is important for analysts to be clear as to how *they* use the terms. As such we try, in what follows, to be clear about our own use of these terms. In attempting such clarity, we have avoided some terms such as *partnership* which, we believe, gives an unnecessary emotive tone to interrelationships between health system actors. We also avoid the term *stewardship* which we feel is a rather vague term; instead, we try to refer to more precise activities such as promoting values, strategic health planning and policymaking.

We fully recognise that we have not covered every aspect of the health system in equal depth. The health system is an immense and complex beast and we have had to prioritise. There are various aspects that you may feel deserve greater coverage, such as human resource policies or quality of care. But we have had to make decisions as to where to draw the line and we have done this, in part on the basis of the existence of other texts that deal more fully than we ever can, with these topics.

In the preceding pages, we have referred to *you*—our reader. We should perhaps explain who we hope *you* will be! Whilst we would love to see a wider readership of this book, we have had, as our target audience, a particular set of people. First, and most importantly, we hope that those people who have a role in designing health systems will see the value of this book. We do not, however, associate this only with individuals who have the words 'health system' in their job title. As will become clear in the book, we believe that a wide variety of individuals and institutions are, and should be, involved in the moulding of the health system. Whilst planners and policy analysts are perhaps the most obvious group, we also see professional leaders, experts in disease control, health managers, health care providers, policy advocates and international agencies as having critical roles. Though we place particular emphasis on the public sector, we also hope that readership will not be restricted to public servants and that civil society organisations and even the private-for-profit sector will gain something from the book in terms of understanding how they may, or may not, fit within a wider health system. We also hope that readership will go beyond the health service sector and that other sectors with an influence on health will be interested in understanding how this complex jigsaw fits together. We also hope that students from a variety of disciplines will use this book as they develop skills for their future professional life. As we have suggested above, different disciplines view the health system from different perspectives. Though these different viewpoints can be enriching, they can also lead to confusion and suspicion. We would like to see all students in the health field have a basic understanding of how a health system fits together and how values affect this. We hope this book will help in this. Given the above diverse potential readership, we have tried, as far as we are able, to make the book accessible and 'non-academic'. We have kept academic references to a minimum—whilst trying to acknowledge those people whose ideas we are drawing on and suggesting further reading where appropriate. We apologise if we have made any mistakes in this respect. One of the challenges in writing this book stems from the already large and growing volume of academic and grey literature on health systems (propelled both by a genuine desire to understand the detailed workings of a part of the system and in part, unfortunately, by academic drivers of advancement). This is already forcing analysts to become specialists in particular areas (such as financing or policy processes) with the danger of a loss of a holistic overview. It also means that inevitably specialists in particular fields will find our analysis of their area of interest superficial. We would ask them to see this book as not attempting to give deep coverage of each aspect of a health system but to place it within a wider whole. To use a medical analogy, we see the book as a text on general practice rather than a text for a particular specialism. At the end of this chapter, we provide some key background texts that may be helpful accompaniments to this book.[1] We have also interspersed the text with examples in boxes to illustrate the points we are making. We have also tried, where possible, to use figures to illustrate concepts or relationships. We often find these more powerful than words in getting key messages across. Sometimes they are used to clarify the differences and relationships between activities. They are then useful in giving an initial starting point for our analysis and understanding and will inevitably be oversimplifications of the situation they are attempting to portray. Sometimes, however, we also use them to show the complexity in the relationship. We hope that they are helpful. We should say that though we stress the interrelatedness between the different elements of the health system that our analysis covers, we are also realists. We do not necessarily expect readers to read the whole book or to read it in the order it is presented. We fully recognise the demands on the time of many of our readers and the need to be selective. As such we have tried to make each chapter as self-standing as possible, though giving cross references to other chapters where appropriate.

The substance of the book starts in Chapter 2 with a broad discussion of what we mean by a health system and how interest in this has emerged over the last two decades against a backdrop of global health policies related to national health systems. We also lay out what we see as the key objectives of a health system and how these relate to the values we espouse for a health system. The chapter also sets out our analytical framework for a health system around which the rest of the book is structured. Chapter 3 starts by defining governance in terms of power and authority and states what we understand by good governance. This is then developed through an understanding of what we refer to as the proactive state and related issues of accountability, decentralisation, inter-sectoral action for health, participatory governance, ethical conduct, regulation and information transparency and accessibility. These issues raise questions about how power and authority are exercised within a health system and how these relate to the predominant ideologies and values within a health system. Underpinning this are critical issues as to *who* makes decisions and the distribution of this power. Of course, these issues permeate all the other processes that we discuss within the book—hence its position at the beginning of the book. This chapter is followed in Chapter 4 by a discussion of the potential mechanisms, and implications of these, for generating resources for health care and inter-sectoral action for health. The means by which finance is raised for this has profound implications for the ability of the health system to achieve its aims and in particular that related to equity. We turn, then, in Chapter 5 to the question as to how the health system uses these resources and, in particular, how it translates its overall objectives into specific policies and plans. We focus in particular on the relationship between planning and policy processes, the wider context within which this occurs, the actors involved (or not) and their values; these influences combine together to produce the policies and plans that (should) guide the health system in its actions and activities. Chapter 5 also discusses issues related to the allocation of funding within the health system and how this, in turn, affects the achievement of system objectives. Chapter 6 focuses on management in the health system; we explain what we mean by it and then cover important thematic issues on management style, the use of evidence in management, management in health systems, the public and private sectors and management in relation to politics. We examine the management of structures, external linkages, resources (finance, staff, logistics) and culture. The key issue throughout this chapter is how values in management are important to meeting health system objectives. The culmination of these health system processes—governance, resource generation, policymaking, planning and management—are the two key activities of inter-sectoral action for health and health service delivery, and they are analysed in Chapter 7. The former is particularly seen through two lenses—legislative and regulatory responsibilities in the health system and health-related advocacy. For health service delivery, five key issues are analysed—health programmes, health projects, scaling up of services, public–private provider roles and relations and the referral system. These issues are analysed against our key values. The final chapter attempts to identify and crystallise the key themes of the book. We conclude by bringing together our suggestions, discussed in the chapters of this book, as to how the capacity of the health system to deliver on its objectives can be strengthened.

Finally, we recognise, as we said above, that our values will not be shared by all readers. By emphasising our own values in this book, we do not claim any moral superiority—far from it. We also recognise that our analysis may be flawed in places. We hope, however, that this book achieves its central aim, to inspire you, our reader, to consider the values that you believe should underpin and permeate the health system and develop your own analysis of how to achieve this. If we realise this, we will feel that we have achieved our aim of showing the value in and the value of our health systems.

Notes and References

1. We suggest a number of key texts which provide a background to the book:

    *   Buse, K., Mays, N. and Walt, G. 2005. *Making Health Policy*. Milton Keynes: Open University Press.
    *   Collins, C. 1994. *Management and Organisation in Developing Health Systems*. Oxford: Oxford University Press (OUP).
    *   Commission on Social Determinants on Health. 2008. *Closing the Gap in a Generation: Health Equity through Action on the Social Determinants of Health Report of the Commission on Social Determinants of Health*. Geneva: WHO. Available at http://whqlibdoc.who.int/publications/2008/9789241563703_eng.pdf (accessed 12 March 2010).
    *   Green, A. 2007. *An Introduction to Health Planning for Developing Health Systems*, Third Edition. Oxford: OUP.
    *   WHO. 2000. *The World Health Report 2000—Health Systems: Improving Performance*. Geneva: WHO.
    *   WHO. 2008. *The World Health Report 2008—Primary Health Care (Now More Than Ever)*. Geneva: WHO. Available at http://www.who.int/whr/2008/en/index.html (accessed 12 March 2010).

2

Health Systems: An Overview

1 Introduction

This book is about health systems and their values. As such this chapter will discuss these terms and set out our own views on the characteristics of a 'good' health system, based on our stated values. However, before doing this, we introduce the policy background to the current international health situation and give an overview of the key health system policy shifts over the last 50 years highlighting the changing nature of health systems.

2 Key Historical Health System Changes and System Policy Initiatives

In this first section, we examine the key policy shifts that relate to health systems and that have occurred in recent years and form the contextual backdrop to the rest of the book.

2.1 Early Developments of Health Systems[1]

Health systems, as collections of services, have, of course, always existed, but it is only relatively recently that there has been organisational analysis or attempts to treat them, in policy terms, as a holistic system. Prior to this period, in Europe, the focus of health care had three key and largely unrelated elements. The most powerful and visible was care provided in hospitals by medical and associated staff. The original development of hospitals was through charitable (often linked to religious organisations or more recently philanthropy) care; the responsibility of the state for such care is a more recent development—often through local authorities. Alongside hospital care, a variety of professional (and non-professional) workers provided care in what became (more or less) organised into a primary care system. This included self-care and care provided by what may now be described as 'traditional (that is, non-professional) practitioners'. In many parts of Europe, the organisation of such care was set up by workers' guilds or mutual societies—early forms of insurance—providing access to panels of doctors with either voluntary or, in some cases, compulsory contributions by members and employers. Such primary care ran in parallel to hospital care and the links between these two approaches in the form of formalised patient referral and coordinated approaches is relatively recent. The third arm is that of public health with an initial focus on sanitation, water and the control of infection. Public health was seen as requiring state responsibility, in part because of the difficulty of encouraging or enforcing interventions that might be seen to favour wider society compared to individuals and in part because of the 'public good' nature of such interventions.

The lack of an organised approach to the delivery of health care in Europe can be seen in the lack of systematic relationships between these elements and indeed within them until the 19th century when the state began to take a serious interest in health care provision.

Outside Europe, there were variations in the patterns of development of health services. Within the USA, for example, services based often on charitable care, moved more towards private provision and financing—though the development of safety net provision for the poor and elderly gave the state a significant role for these groups. Within (former) colonies in Africa and Asia, organised health care was initially introduced to provide for the colonisers but gradually extended often through missionary and then government provision. Public health initiatives were largely developed to protect colonisers through *cordon sanitaires*.[2] The precise nature of the emerging system was often a reflection of the pattern in the colonising nation.

The late 19th and 20th centuries saw a number of changes in the delivery, and organisation of the delivery, of this triad of health-related activities. Some can be linked to technological developments (such as the development of anaesthesia, discovery of penicillin or vaccine developments); some to a concern over particular groups (such as the fitness of the military or ability of workers to perform). However, there were also very significant shifts in the *organisation* of health activities.

Two major European policy initiatives provided broad organisational alternatives to a privately (including through charitable institutions) organised and financed set of diverse and fragmented providers.

The first of these was the organisation of health care through social funds raised by contributions collected through the workplace (see Chapter 4 for further discussion of financing of health). What is now known as the Bismarckian model (after its political patron, the then German Chancellor) is a form of insurance based on collective rather than private arrangements and marks a recognition of the potential for social intervention in health care. It is closely associated with, and grew out of, the mutual society/guild approaches outlined above. Such a means of organising health care has, in its current common form, four key features. First, it emphasises the contributions of beneficiaries/members based on their level of income; second, it is compulsory—thus avoiding the difficulties in terms of loss of cross-subsidy caused by opting out by high-income or low-usage members. Third, and related to this, the use of health services is linked to the needs of beneficiaries rather than their level of contribution; and finally, there is a range of potential provider mechanisms, including both state-organised and private. Social insurance approaches to the organisation of the delivery and financing of health care based on this Bismarckian model have been dominant in various parts of the world including Europe (with the notable exception of the UK to which we turn shortly) and Latin America. They also form significant parts of wider health systems in an increasing number of low and middle income countries such as Thailand.

The second and later development based on social rather than private arrangements is that of the UK National Health Service (NHS)—often known as the Beveridge model after its founder. The NHS, set up in 1948, shares the basic social objectives of social insurance systems (and grew out of an insurance-based primary care system) in that its contributions and benefit mechanisms are designed to be needs based. However, the financial underpinning is, as we will see in Chapter 4, drawn from a range of public revenue sources. Furthermore, in its early form, it differed from the Bismarckian model in that both the financing and provision of services were organised directly by the government. Recent policy shifts have led to a more complex set of arrangements both in terms of the direct level of control by the government through intermediary 'trust' organisations and through the use, in certain circumstances, of contracted private providers. However, this second broad social approach has formed the basis of the organisation of health systems in many countries, including former British colonies in Africa and Asia. As we will see, there are variations within these two basic models of social intervention in health care. Furthermore, the mix of these social models with privately managed health systems results in a large set of combinations of health system. However, these two models may be considered key historical policy events in the development of health systems and remained, alongside the third option of a private system, largely unmodified until the major reform period, which we outline below, in the 1990s.

2.2 Primary Health Care

However, prior to this, the next major policy paradigm shift can be seen in the Primary Health Care (PHC) movement, as it became known, initiated in the 1970s but formally linked to the Declaration signed at the WHO/United Nations Children's Fund (UNICEF)-organised conference in Alma Ata (now Almaty) of 1978. The PHC movement had a number of significant features in terms of its policy content, which we discuss below. However, in addition to these, it is worth noting two other important aspects. Though described as a global policy, in reality, its focus was on low income countries and perhaps represents the first major international attempt to respond to the particular needs of such countries. It also marked the emergence of the WHO as a key leader in global health policy formation in the area of health systems (rather than its more traditional role as a public health force). Though it did not use the terminology currently associated with a systems approach, its focus on both the way health care should be delivered and the underlying broad principles demonstrated a clear systems focus.

The PHC policy can be seen at two levels. It specified a collection of service components that any health system should provide based on a new orientation towards the primary level of care, a marked shift from the dominant hospital model. In many ways these components are analogous to the later minimum package policy of the 1990s (see Section 2.3). Perhaps of more lasting interest, however, the PHC policy explicitly laid down clear principles that were seen as paramount foundations for health systems.

First, the PHC approach saw *equity* as a fundamental component of any health goal. Many health systems, and not just those in low income countries, have very inequitable patterns of ill-health. This inequity, and its causes, has been widely discussed in various recent reports relating both to low income countries and rich countries.[3] Whilst widely accepted on paper, the principle that pursuit of equity should be central in any health system faces a number of obstacles to its pursuit. In particular, there are different interpretations of what *equity* actually means. Inherent in the concept of equity[4] is a notion of fairness or justice as a key value. Thus, in a well-used definition, inequity is seen as 'differences in health that are not only unnecessary and avoidable, but in addition unfair and unjust'.[5] This fairness relates to the relationship between needs and resultant service provision. Equity is different from equality, though may be interpreted by some as equivalent; equity requires equal treatment of individuals with similar needs and unequal treatment of individuals who have differing levels or types of need. The concept of vertical and horizontal dimensions of equity illustrates this well.[6] In maternal care, for example, equitable policies would require that all women with a normal pregnancy would receive the same level of antenatal and intra-partum care (the horizontal dimension); however, this care would be less than that provided to a woman who had difficulties in pregnancy such as anaemia or a breech presentation; we would expect such a person to receive more or different services (the vertical dimension). Differences in definition can highlight also whether the focus is on the *provision* of services or their *utilisation*. These differences recognise that inequity does not just occur in terms of health needs and resultant provision of services but also in barriers to the utilisation of such services. Such barriers may arise from a number of sources. Most obvious ones are financial ones such as user charges that clearly affect the poor more heavily than the wealthy, but there are others such as the way in which services are provided that can involve, for example, its cultural sensitivity and gender or race barriers.

The definition we will use is that an equitable distribution of health services is one in which the provision of services is based solely on the relative health needs of individuals and under conditions that do not disadvantage utilisation by the individual in terms of social, economic and political determinants. Equity, as a principle for the organisation of health services, is superficially widely accepted—few are prepared publicly to challenge it. Yet, its active pursuit strikes at the heart of inequality in society and the relationship between individuals and the state. In particular, it relates to the capacity or responsibility of the state to make decisions on behalf of citizens and potentially constrain the activities of individuals for the greater good of the community. Thus, whilst the principle of equity may appear hard to challenge, there are other principles that may be held by some to be equally important and yet run counter to equity. Most obvious is the principle that an individual should be able to choose the type and level of health services; at first sight, such a principle appears reasonable, yet on reflection it carries the potential for significant inequity, particularly in heavily resource-constrained contexts. If wealthy individuals are able to choose the level and type of health care, this raises the possibility, indeed likelihood, that they will use more services than someone with less resources but similar needs.

Taking the logic of an equitable approach to its conclusion would require restrictions to the usage of health care on grounds other than relative need, such as income. Such an approach can be argued for on two grounds. First, where resources are scarce, the utilisation of some health care by richer individuals on a non-needs basis will mean a suboptimal, in equity terms, distribution of these scarce resources. Second, there is a more contentious argument that even where the utilisation of resources by one individual on a non-needs basis does not affect another's utilisation, it can be argued that the relative disparity in access is seen as *unfair*. This argument is more contentious because it may lead to conflict, as a result of the denial of potential health care to an individual, between this value and a fundamental concern to 'save life'. We leave each reader to decide their attitude to these two arguments which will be based on their approach to these values and their specific context.

These different perspectives reflect, at the wider ideological level, different views as to the role of the state as well as other perspectives such as religious beliefs or moral codes. For some, the state has a responsibility to make collective decisions on behalf of its members to protect the vulnerable and disadvantaged, and in doing this, to pursue, where necessary, redistributive policies. For others, the role of the state is to ensure there is an environment in which individuals are as free as possible to pursue their own interests, with minimal concern as to the wider social effects of these actions. The former is associated with a position of equity, the latter with a position of individual choice. Between these two extreme positions that can be associated with socialism and libertarianism, there are a number of variations such as conservatism, liberal democracy, social liberalism, social democracy and environmentalism.[7]

In practice, equity is largely accepted in a tokenistic way with little discussion of its real implications both in terms of the type of health system necessary and more fundamentally in terms of the type of government role in social welfare.[8] The fundamental nature of this debate can, however, be seen to be at the heart of the recent fight over health care reform in the USA.

The second key principle of Alma Ata was that *improvements in health require action across all sectors*—and not solely the health care sector. This is the natural conclusion of the fact that the differing and inequitable health experiences of individuals and social groups result from a wide range of factors including genetics, gender, environment, education, social, political and economic structures, conditions and experiences.

As an illustration, Table 2.1 shows how the under-5 mortality rate varies according to place of residence, income and education. Such inequalities are not confined to LMIC as is well documented in recent work.[9]

Table 2.1

Under-5 mortality rate according to place of residence, income and mothers' education

Deaths per 1000 under-5		Bangladesh (2007)	Colombia (2005)	Egypt (2008)	Philippines (2003)
Place of residence	Rural	77	33	36	52
	Urban	63	23	29	30
Wealth quintile	Lowest	86	39	49	66
	Highest	43	16	19	21
Educational level of mother	Lowest	93	51	44	105
	Highest	52	20	25	29

Source: Derived from WHO. 2010. Table 8.[10]

The early public health advocates of the 19th century recognised these relationships and pushed for strategies related to water, sanitation and housing; where taken up, they were effective. Public health, however, as a profession, has often been overly medicalised, with a focus on prevention through strategies such as immunisation rather than broader inter-sectoral activities. Whilst such strategies aimed at individuals are obviously important, the Alma Ata Declaration urged policymakers to develop broader health promoting strategies in other sectors—what has become known as *multi-sectoralism*. To address the real causes of unequal health experiences, action on these social and economic determinants is critical. This carries huge implications for how we view the responsibilities and make-up of the health system. The Alma Ata Declaration said little about the details of this, other than calling for greater *inter-sectoral* collaboration and, for many countries, this aspect of the PHC strategy was given little priority and health care provision dominated policies and activities. It is important to recognise at this point the difference between multi-sectoralism (where a number of sectors may be involved in parallel activities) and inter-sectoralism (where there are concerted and integrated activities between different sectors).

The third key element of PHC at the Alma Ata Conference focused on a redefinition of the *relationship between health care providers and the wider public*. The development of health services had been characterised by a medical profession that saw its role as interpreter of the scientific basis of medicine/health and gatekeeper to services; indeed the terms medicine and health were, and still are by some, often seen as inter-changeable. The resultant relationship between modern medicine and its users was one that, at its worst, saw the general public as passive recipients of interventions determined and delivered by the medical (and related) professions. This relationship can be challenged on various grounds.

First, at a pragmatic level, such asymmetry of knowledge and power is unlikely to result in effective health behaviour—much of the causes of ill-health, and routes to better health, require the informed involvement of the public. This suggests a need for greater education of the public and willingness (and skills) on the part of health professionals to share (rather than selectively hand down) knowledge.

Second, there are critical decisions about the overall type of health system that calls for the involvement of a range of actors beyond the medical professionals. Such involvement is called for on two grounds. Such groups (such as civil society organisations with a specific interest in particular health problems such as disability) have access to informa-tion that medical professionals may not have (for example, concerning the barriers to utilisation of care) and which can affect the way health care is provided. More fundamentally, however, the design of health sys-tems requires decisions about priorities and approaches which, as we will see, are value-based. As such there are questions about *whose* values should inform these decisions. Alma Ata, perhaps rather naively, sug-gested it should be that of the 'community' suggesting, for some, a single homogenous grouping easily identifiable and willing to participate. Its call for greater 'community' participation[11] in decision-making, however naive, suggested a major shift in power relations—the ramifications of which have seldom been fully systematically explored. In practical terms it led, post Alma Ata, to the setting up of mechanisms such as village health committees in rural health facilities; however, these rarely had any significant decision-making power. The 1980s and beyond also saw a growth in civil society organisations campaigning for particular issues in the health system, both within a national health system and interna-tionally in fora such as the International Conference on Population and Development in Cairo in 1994.

There are important issues related to the roles of communities, their constituent parts and relative powers, in decision-making and the mech-anisms for doing this that we return to in later chapters. These include most particularly the critical questions of how to shift the current bias in the access to state decision-making of particular groups and the nature of the representativeness and accountability of such civil society groups to the constituents they represent, or claim to represent.

The Alma Ata Declaration is also associated with a further principle— that of the need to use *appropriate technology*. This almost self-evident principle was perhaps an indicator of the growing deployment of a range of criteria beyond medical ones (including economics which was beginning to flourish in the health sector) about decisions as to the type of technology to be used by health services. The post–Alma Ata period saw a growth in use of cost-effectiveness analysis techniques in technology assessment (one of the most developed mechanisms for this is the UK National Institute for Health and Clinical Excellence [NICE]);[12] the 1980s saw various health systems adopting policies on medicines ranging from the use of generic (and hence cheaper) brands to the restriction of prescription to centrally determined essential lists. It also, at a wider level, developed into an assessment of the potential relative benefits of investing in primary care levels versus secondary and tertiary care, or investment in different groups of health workers (such as clinical officers compared to doctors).

We can see from the above that the Alma Ata Declaration set out new and explicit values for health systems. It also clearly enunciated a specific approach for the health system in terms of health service delivery and a wider responsibility in broader health promotion.

The period immediately after Alma Ata in the early 1980s was one of optimism in many low income countries and development agencies. However, by the end of that decade there was a growing sense of disillusionment with the progress of the Alma Ata agenda and, as we will see in what follows, the original conception of PHC was, to a large degree, lost in the reforms of the 1990s. See Table 2.2 for a review of the achievements of PHC.

Table 2.2
Thirty years after Alma Ata, what worked and what did not

	What worked?	*What did not work?*
Common global vision of health for all universality and equity	Promoted wide involvement of stakeholders in health problem: focused on the needs of many, reaching scale; pro-poor: overcoming	Health for all and Summit for Children goals not country specific so some countries could achieve easily and others could never achieve; some goals were unreachable as not effective, feasible intervention (e.g. low

Table 2.2 continued

Table 2.2 continued

	What worked?	What did not work?
	the inverse care law; primary care solutions: health service provision and health promotion (supply and demand): the MDGs have revitalised this common vision with inter-sectoral development linkages	birth weight reduction) so pushed the action focus to more specific, achievable interventions; very low investment except for a few specific issues (e.g. some vaccine preventable conditions and even for immunisation funding fell during the 1990s); challenge of competing priorities but perhaps case not communicated clearly to the key audiences
Comprehensive action	Conceptual framework of an integrated health system with inter-sectoral linkages and appropriate technology and essential drugs; successes in some countries persisted with incremental implementation	Conceptual framework of comprehensive health care considered too complex—broken into dichotomies: health or development (inter-sectoral), vertical or horizontal delivery, coverage or quality, facility vs community, mother vs child, central vs decentralised; management and programme tools lacking
Community participation and ownership	Community diagnosis process now embedded in some societies and programmes and revitalised as community action cycle, participatory learning and action leading toward empowerment	Community ownership perceived as slower and less controllable, less measurable; very bottom up, so variable and harder to track and risk that communities may select a priority judged to be inappropriate leading to conflict with professionals rather than partnership
Community workers	Promotion of innovative delivery strategies not just the status quo (e.g. delegation of tasks)	Patchy: lack of consistent supervision and linkages to existing health system, reliance on volunteerism, local cost recovery erratic and mostly for the lowest levels
Collection of data for action	Use of coverage data to drive action, especially for immunication,	Focus on outputs instead of impact (e.g. number of trained community health workers or

Table 2.2 continued

Table 2.2 continued

What worked?	What did not work?
leading to the development of coverage data surveys, the precursor of UNICEFs Multiple Indicator Surveys (MICS)	trained doctors who may not be retained or may not be effective especially without supervision and functional system support)
Innovation for supplies and technology — Developed innovations: cold chain, oral rehydration solution, partogram, vitamin A capsules, salt iodation; essential drug list used in almost every low and middle income country	Technology, even appropriate technology, considered a waste of money compared with other priorities; very low investment in innovative technologies for health in low-resource settings
Environment — Recognition of importance of water and sanitation for health. Some countries placed major emphasis, especially on water	Sanitation and garbage disposal more complex than clean water and has progressed slowly, especially for the poorest countries and rural areas, so inequity has increased
Inter-sectoral action — Some countries convinced agriculture to play on a role in food security, occasionally even household nutrition, but this was rare	Education, agriculture, housing, public works often ignored their role in health and were ignored by health planners. The inter-sectoral concept is good in theory, but in practice each sector has its own agenda and major change is required for effective inter-sectoral collaboration

Source: Reproduced from Lawn et al. 2008 with permission from *The Lancet*.[13]

2.3 Health Sector Reforms

The post–Alma Ata period was a decade of greater global interest in, and optimism about the health systems of low income countries and was accompanied by increasing donor involvement in support to health sectors. One emerging donor was the World Bank whose investment in the health sector had previously been limited. Its obvious financial muscle and growing widening of its role from traditional economic investment to the social sectors, accompanied by internal investment in research and policy functions related to these sectors, saw it occupying a growing global policy role in health; this coincided with a period in which WHO's formal leadership within the UN system of technical health matters was undermined by a crisis of governance and weak leadership. This growing power of the World Bank led to a particular milestone in health systems thinking and policy—the publication in 1993 of their annual World Development Report[14] focusing, on this occasion, on the health sector. This offered the first major analysis of the state of health and health systems of low income countries from the World Bank. The report had two functions—first, it offered a diagnosis of the current situation in low-income countries and concluded that the poor performance being experienced in many such countries was attributable to inappropriate health system structures. Health systems were seen as being bureaucratic, centralised, inefficient and non-responsive to the needs or wants of its populations. Much of their diagnosis is widely accepted as accurate. However, the second function of the report was to set out an agenda for reform. This agenda was based on a belief (we use the term deliberately) that the introduction of market principles and practices into systems that had been largely centrally planned and managed by the state would lead to enhanced efficiency and responsiveness to patient needs. This market paradigm was part of a wider resurgence of neo-liberal ideology in a number of industrialised countries, notably the USA and UK. It was consistent with wider structural adjustment policies (led by the International Monetary Fund [IMF]) aimed at low income countries which attempted to reduce the size and role of the state and substitute it with consumer power through the market mechanism and private provision in a number of fields.

This combination of a new policy paradigm with the financial power and influence of the World Bank led to a decade of 'reforms' promulgated by a number of agencies and governments. They can be divided into three broad areas—the structure and governance of the health system, financing of health care and prioritisation of the use of resources. We look at each of these separately, though they are closely interrelated.

The reforms related to *structure and governance* had various elements. Underpinning them all was a belief that there should be a changed and reduced role in health care for the central state. It was accepted that the inevitability of market failure in the health sector (see Box 4.1 in Chapter 4) would require leadership in policy from the state but that the delivery of health care could, and should, be divested from central authorities to a combination of self-governing public institutions and, where possible, the private sector. The neo-liberal philosophy saw the latter as the ideal in that it was perceived as responding to market signals in a way that generated responsiveness to consumer desires in an efficient manner.

One element of the reform movement is related to decentralisation (which we discuss in more detail in Chapter 3). A key governance issue for any public health system concerns the relationship between the national and more local levels and how decision-making powers are divided between these. The PHC philosophy, with its emphasis on a needs-based approach and participation by communities in decision-making, led to greater interest in district-based systems of health care, though it is important to recognise that this was not in itself new; many low income countries during colonial periods and immediately afterwards had been built around district systems. The World Bank–style neo-liberal reforms also interpreted privatisation as a form of decentralisation. From the 1990s, there has been an increased interest in decentralisation from a number of agencies and health systems.

The second strand of reforms focused on *how health care should be financed*. We examine this in Chapter 4. However, the main thrust of the reforms was, in line with neo-liberal ideology, a shift towards greater personal responsibility for health care finance through user charges and personal insurance mechanisms. The reforms did recognise that market failures associated both with the health sector and with low income country contexts, meant that collective financing through taxation or compulsory social insurance would be necessary for some services (such as public health) and in some countries or for particular groups. Reforms also recognised the need for safety net mechanisms where user charges were used, though the practical design and implementation of these (where the devil often lies) was not detailed.

The final strand related to *priority-setting*. This is in recognition of the low levels of resources available for the health sector in low income countries. Explicit prioritisation was seen as inevitable and, despite the market orientation of the reforms, market mechanisms (Adam Smith's 'invisible hand') were not seen as the tool to do this. Instead, economic appraisal techniques from the now well-established discipline of health economics were proposed to rank interventions on health problems by their cost-effectiveness (with cost per Disability Adjusted Life Year [DALY] as the key indicator). This approach had close similarities to a strategy known as Selective Primary Health Care[15] which had been proposed in the early 1980s as a modification to the more 'comprehensive' PHC strategy of Alma Ata. The result of such ranking was a set of minimum basic or 'essential' health interventions bundled together in a package whose delivery the state was to be encouraged to support.

2.3.1 Criticisms of Reforms

The period of the 1990s saw the introduction of these elements in many low income countries either through donor-funded projects or as part of wider civil service reforms and structural adjustment programmes under the general leadership of the World Bank and IMF. While the specific reform packages differed between countries, there was a remarkable similarity between the broad approaches leading to one of the main criticisms of the reform paradigm—that of 'blueprintism' and a failure to design specific reform packages against the specific needs and contexts of particular national health systems. Other criticisms were levelled against the reform agenda, not on the grounds that reforms were not necessary but on the basis of both the specific reform bundle and the way in which they were introduced. Criticisms of the contents of the reforms included:

- their focus on the delivery of services (as economists would put it—a supply-side rather than demand-side focus) to the almost total exclusion of strategies related to individual or community behaviour, attitudes or participation;
- a failure, even with this service delivery focus, to appreciate the particular contribution of health staff and to recognise the growing crisis in their supply (in part the consequence of the reforms themselves);
- a failure to consider the wider determinants of health—the arguments for multi-sectoralism that PHC had encouraged;
- a failure to critically examine the specific role of the private sector, and its relationship with the public sector, both in terms of mechanisms such as contracting (for example, the transactions costs associated with contracting were largely ignored or underestimated) and regulation;
- the technocratic and disease-focused nature of the prioritisation element of the reforms and their failure both to link to wider participative governance and the danger of reinforcing a vertical approach to public health programmes;
- the assumption that the underlying cause of the failure of health systems was in structural inefficiency; the low levels of finance available to deliver health care was not seen as a major obstacle or indeed a potential cause of the inefficiency.

Underlying this was perhaps a failure of health system reformers to give adequate consideration to the system needs of the services to be provided by the health system. The focus on macro issues such as financing and governance swung the pendulum too far away from consideration of *how* services were to be provided and what was needed to support these services. There is perhaps a useful analogy between the design of the health system that reformers were intent on and architecture. An architect sets out to design a building that meets the needs of its future users. As such, s/he will spend time talking to the clients about their future usage and needs and will then design a structure that accommodates, as far as possible, these needs within a given resource budget. Compromises may need to be made to overcome competing or inconsistent needs of different users. So, it should be with the design of the health system. A good health system designer will find out what is needed from the 'users' of the health system (both the professionals providing services and the people potentially utilising these services) and design to meet, as far as possible, these needs. The resultant overall health system structure (building) will have a number of rooms (services)—some open plan (integrated) and some separate (vertical services) according to their needs, but all sharing a common set of services and framework. The skill of the architect/health system reformer is in finding ways of overcoming and mediating between the competing needs of the different users. Perhaps most obviously in recent years this has been seen in the debate over the 'needs' of vertical disease-control programmes and those of integrated services and how a system can be designed to meet both these needs. The failure of reformers to work in such a bottom-up fashion has led to scepticism and distrust on the part of many health professionals of health system designers. This has been exacerbated by language—both groups use similar language (such as health system) to refer to different concepts.

However, of perhaps even greater concern was the fact that striving for greater efficiency in health care delivery supplanted the goal of equity which lay at the heart of the Alma Ata paradigm. Such concerns were voiced by policy analysts and researchers, but there was little cohesive resistance to the wave of reform; the obvious role for the WHO as the champion of health and equity through PHC was lost given its weakened leadership at the time.

The second set of criticisms related more to the way in which the reforms were designed and introduced. In particular, they were often seen as being externally imposed with little local ownership or leadership. Indeed, at a wider level it is clear that, for any policy change to be successful, there needs to be a critical mass of support within the political, administrative and professional systems. Whilst clearly there *was* some support for the reforms, it is also clear that they were often resisted through 'street level bureaucratic' action.[16] In particular, the public sector that was expected both to manage the reform process and to change its own practices was often disaffected. Indeed, morale in the public sector dipped as a result both of the downsizing and, less obviously, as a result of the implication that the public sector was a second best solution tolerated through the lack of a private sector presence. Such an attitude was symptomised by the introduction of private sector management techniques such as performance-related pay in the public sector and the attempts to develop internal competition (see chapters 6 and 7).

2.3.2 Assumptions Underpinning Reforms

Underlying the reform movement were assumptions about the behaviour of health systems and the potential for the market approach within the particular and varied contexts of low income countries. The basic assumption was that competition enhances efficiency (both generally and within the specific context of the health sector). Competition is seen to drive efficiency in its search for profits; yet there is no a priori reason why profit maximisation will lead to health maximisation—the presumed goal of reforms. There was, and still is, little evidence that profit maximisation for providers *will* result in health maximisation; indeed, the experience of the US health system suggests otherwise. Nor was it evident that the lack of competition was the driver for inefficiency. Closely linked to this is another assumption that the public sector, working under conditions of direct management and planning, is *inevitably* inefficient. The causes of inefficiency were rarely explored; yet it is increasingly recognised that a combination of low levels of resources and the complex aid architecture with parallel financing and accountability structures can in themselves lead to inefficiency. One might have expected, in an evidence-free zone such as this, the use of pilots to test out new approaches. However, pilots were rarely used with reforms often being introduced nationwide.

A third assumption stemming from the market philosophy was that the demand signals in the health sector should come from sick individual patients. However, this fails to take account of the well-recognised market failures related to issues such as information asymmetry and the effect of differential income levels on effective demand. Furthermore, it runs counter to the argument made in the PHC approach of the need to involve *communities* as well as *individuals* (both as sick patients and as healthy individuals) in decision-making—a social rather than individual response to determining the prioritised use of health resources that follows from an equity perspective.

2.3.3 Post-reformism

By the beginning of the new century, the grand experiment was largely over. The mounting criticisms about the particular reforms, the growing self-confidence of national health systems in their ability to self-determine their future and, above all, the recognition that the health experiences of some populations (and particularly those in sub-Saharan Africa) were declining rather than improving led to a gradual movement away from a focus predicated on the market to a more general paradigm of 'health system strengthening'. Of course it would be wrong (and indeed difficult methodologically to prove) to link this failure to health reforms alone. The 1990s saw a number of other factors that affected national health systems' abilities to promote overall health. Most obviously Human Immunodeficiency Virus/Acquired Immunodeficiency Syndrome (HIV/AIDS) and the other two 'big' communicable diseases, malaria and Tuberculosis (TB), had a major impact on both population health and the wider health system context. One particular aspect of this system context was the issue of health professional supply. The focus of the reforms on structures had largely disregarded the implications of these structures on staffing. Indeed, to a large degree, policy attention in the 1990s ignored the growing crisis in health professional supply. However, the increasing mobility of professional staff both between the public and growing private sectors and between low- and high-income health systems led to a serious and increasing shortage of professionals to staff the public sector structures, which continued to be the main source of health care in many countries, particularly for the poor.

Before we leave the reform movement, it is worth summarising briefly on the differences between the two paradigms of reform and PHC. The major elements of PHC are set out in Table 2.3 alongside the related reform components.

Table 2.3
Comparison of health sector reform policies with PHC policies

PHC	Neo-liberal reforms
Equity	Emphasis on user fees with negative equity effects
	Emphasis on efficiency at expense of equity
	Decentralisation potentially led to inter-district inequity
Promotive multi-sectoral focus	Main focus of reforms on *health care provision* rather than inter-sectoral activities
Community participation in decision-making	Focus on participation by sick individuals through market mechanisms
	Governance and structures had potential for community involvement, but in practice, minimal
	Bamako Initiative on financing seen as means of promoting community participation

Table 2.3 continued

Table 2.3 continued

PHC	Neo-liberal reforms
Appropriate technology	Prioritisation focus with economic appraisal on cost per DALY
Basic elements of primary care provision	Minimum or essential list had similarities

Decentralisation was implicit in PHC policies as part of the other principles. Within the neo-liberal reforms, it was often seen as including privatisation of health care.

To complete the picture of the major policy shifts affecting health systems, we turn now to a brief overview of four important trends and initiatives—the growth of globalisation including international public–private initiatives, the Millennium Development Goals movement, the re-emergence of Primary Health Care and the Commission on Social Determinants of Health.

2.4 Globalisation

Globalisation is neither a new phenomenon nor one that is easy to define. In particular, the term covers a variety of international forces and linkages that are often unconnected—at least directly. These include increasing economic and political interdependence, the growth of multilateral and international institutions (both political and commercial) and the spread of, and interplay between, international culture and norms, particularly through travel opportunities and information technology. These international or global trends are increasingly affecting the policies and performance of national health systems; as such it is important to analyse their various effects.

At the economic level, increased economic interdependence and relations are felt in the health system through the growth of international markets, both in health care itself and in the resources that go into the supply of health care. The internationalisation of health care can be seen both in the growth of multinational private health care companies and in the growth of travel for treatment (sometimes known as medical tourism) to which countries such as India and Thailand have responded. International resource markets are not new; pharmaceutical provision in particular has been dominated for years by multinational companies able to capitalise on the commercial benefits of international operations related to relative costs in terms of sourcing, ensuring economies of scale and, in some cases, the opportunities for sidestepping specific national legislative and regulatory hurdles. More recently the increasing globalisation of the market for professional staff has affected the health sector leading to significant (though again not new) migration from low income countries of medical and related staff to high income and more rewarding work environments.

Both these aspects of globalisation can affect national health systems and policies and require international responses. Current international responses have been either weak (for example, in the case of staff migration, restricted to non-binding codes of conduct) or weighted heavily in favour of the economic advantages with less concern about the health effects (as in the case of the World Trade Organisation's activities in encouraging and regulating international trade) and of advantage to richer industrialised countries.[17]

Alongside, and perhaps related to, greater economic interdependence is the growth of political interdependence and institutions. Multilateral and bilateral institutions have been involved in supporting and influencing the health systems of low income countries for many years. The UN family has a number of agencies, often not well inter-coordinated, with an interest in health led, nominally at least, by the WHO. In addition, many industrialised countries have departments with a development remit often particularly focusing on former colonised countries. The power of such agencies is closely related to their financial muscle and the World Bank's role in the 1990s reform movement is a clear example of this. However, finance is not the only source of influence; the WHO, for example, has greater influence than its financial power would suggest, though paradoxically its reliance on extra-budgetary funding may be perceived to restrict its policy independence.

By the late 1990s, however, there was a rapid growth in the number of new forms of international organisations with a specific health remit and which combine different sources of funding. They have been defined as 'a collaborative relationship which transcends national boundaries and brings together at least three parties, among them a corporation (and/or industry association) and an intergovernmental organization, so as to achieve a shared health-creating goal on the basis of a mutually agreed division of labour'.[18] The remit of such Global Public–Private Partnerships (GPPPs), or as they have been more recently renamed Global Health Initiatives (GHIs), is usually a combination of financial (with an objective to 'leverage' money for a particular health cause) and technical objectives. The best known of such organisations include the Global Fund for AIDS, Malaria and TB and the Global Alliance for Vaccines and Immunisation (GAVI); but there are over 100 others. Such organisations were set up to respond to specific global challenges such as AIDS; their success in attracting new money (as opposed to diverting it from existing causes) is debatable, though they do seem to have been able to provide a conduit for private charitable funds such as the Bill and Melinda Gates Foundation. Where they have been successful, they have had significant effects on national health systems; however, this has often been through a form of verticalisation of health care which has been criticised. Buse and Harmer,[19] for example, identify seven habits practised by a number of these that lead to negative effects on the wider health system: skewing national priorities; depriving particular stakeholders of a role in decision-making; inadequate governance practices; inappropriate assumptions of the efficiency of the public and private sectors; insufficient resources to implement partnership activities and pay for alliance costs; wasting resources through inadequate use of recipient country systems and poor harmonisation; and inappropriate incentives to staff working in partnerships. The Global Fund has, in particular, been heavily criticised for developing national initiatives that divert resources from other health care processes and the wider generic health system, though the need to support the wider health system and not just disease-specific programmes is now being more widely recognised. These GHIs have become major actors in the international health systems[20] and yet their accountability to national health systems or to international governance mechanisms such as the WHO are often weak. This aspect of internationalism—the linkages to national accountability—is an important one to which we return in Chapter 3. Linked to this growth in GHIs is the wider issue of aid architecture. The fragmentation of external support to national health systems arising both from traditional multilateral and bilateral donors and GHIs and the negative effects of this became increasingly recognised in the 1990s leading to the Paris Declaration on Aid Effectiveness[21] and attempts through more coordinated approaches such as Sector Wide Approaches (SWAps). This is further discussed in Chapter 4.

The last aspect of globalisation to which we refer here is that of the growth of international civil society movements looking for an alternative approach to health and health systems. Movements such as the People's Health Movement[22] have tapped into national health movements and, through sharing of knowledge and tactics, are becoming increasingly influential in international policy processes.[23] The role of international travel and communications within this growth in power and confidence is important and likely to grow. The increasing sophistication of some of these organisations in advocacy techniques and their ability to gain a place at the international policy table (albeit the lower end) is to be welcomed as a means of allowing a community voice. However, it raises issues analogous to those referred to in Section 2.2 in relation to country civil society organisations, concerning their representativeness and accountability. The above has focused on direct international influences on health policy or care. However, there are other wider international influences on national health systems. A critical one facing the world is the effect of *global economic shifts*. The 2009 recession, for example, hit low income countries both directly in terms of their own economies and also in terms of international aid flows. Economic globalisation is often cited as leading to stronger global economies and the increase in trade as benefiting poorer countries. However, the current approach to such globalisation has been challenged as is well illustrated in the following:

> The economic benefits of recent globalisation have been largely asymmetrical, creating winners losers and growing inequalities between the two. Globalisation's enlarged and deepened markets reward more efficiently countries that already have productive assets (financial, land, physical, institutional and human capital) than they do countries that lack them (typically low- and some middle-income nations). Globalisation's rules favour the already rich (both countries and people within them) because they have greater resources and power to influence the design of those rules.[24]

The political fragility of various states and regions can also have major effects on both the national health systems and those of neighbouring states. In the Eastern Mediterranean Region of the WHO, for example, around half the member countries are currently facing conflict or are affected, particularly through refugee movements, by conflict elsewhere in the region. Political forecasters suggest that such conflict is likely to hit other regions when the effects of environmental degradation and climate change filter through via effects on national supplies of water and other resources.

2.4.1 Millennium Development Goals

By the end of the 1990s, there was, as we have suggested, increasing international concern over the failure of some countries and regions both to develop economically and, within the context of this book, to improve their health situations. The neo-liberal style health reforms were clearly not providing the answer that had been expected. There was also increasing recognition that the low levels of finance available to the health system in many countries were not even sufficient to meet minimum standards, as set out in the WHO Commission on Macroeconomics and Health.[25] Greater international attention was seen to be needed. Interest from industrialised nations in this can be interpreted as a mixture of genuine humanitarian concern, as expressed by popular movements, and self-interest in terms of avoiding political conflict with wider global ramifications and ensuring growth of global markets, seen as essential to continued capitalist growth and minimising spread of public health problems. The millennium provided an opportunity to galvanise political and popular support for renewed attention to development issues and the setting of international *Millennium Development Goals* (see Box 2.1) was the result. These eight goals which had specific quantified targets for achievement by 2015 include three directly related to health, though all the goals have health implications. Mid-term assessments[26] of the progress towards these goals suggest however that some countries, and in particular those in sub-Saharan Africa, are unlikely to meet the targets.

Box 2.1 Millennium development goals
(Health-specific goals in italics)

Eradicate extreme poverty and hunger
Achieve universal primary education
Promote gender equality and empower women
Reduce child mortality
Improve maternal health
Combat HIV/AIDS, malaria and other diseases
Ensure environmental sustainability
Develop a global partnership for development

Source: UN. 2000.[27]

One of the dangers of the Millennium Development Goals however is that it has focused attention on specific diseases and hence vertical responses rather than on the wider integrated health system and indeed on internal national prioritisation as to which are the key health problems within each country.

2.4.2 Renaissance of Primary Health Care

The third and health-specific policy area to which we now turn has clearer links to health systems. The year 2008 saw the 30th anniversary of the Alma Ata Declaration and this was used by the WHO, and its recently appointed Director General, to reassert its leadership of the health field through revitalising and modifying its original PHC vision. The 1990s had seen an almost unnatural silence within agencies such as the WHO over the original PHC strategy, as the health sector reform movement dominated global policy formation.

However, the failures of the neo-liberal reform movement allowed the original paradigm of PHC to re-emerge, albeit with different language and elements contested. The WHO 2008 World Health Report[28] laid out the new PHC policy with a number of important implications for health systems. There are four key features of this policy as summarised in Box 2.2.

Box 2.2 Key reforms of World Health Report 2008

Reforms that ensure that health systems contribute to health equity, social justice and the end of exclusion, primarily by moving towards universal access and social health protection—*universal coverage reforms*

  reforms that reorganize health services around people's needs and expectations, so as to make them more socially relevant and more responsive to the changing world, while producing better outcomes—*service delivery reforms*.

  reforms that secure healthier communities, by integrating public health actions with primary care, by pursuing healthy public policies across sectors and by strengthening national and transnational public health interventions—*public policy reforms*

  reforms that replace disproportionate reliance on command and control on one hand, and laissez-faire disengagement of the state on the other, by the inclusive, participatory, negotiation-based leadership indicated by the complexity of contemporary health systems—*leadership reforms*

Source: Reproduced from WHO. 2008. p. xvi with permission from WHO.[29]

2.4.3 Commission on Social Determinants of Health

The final policy initiative that has clear implications for health systems thinking is that of the Commission on Social Determinants of Health[30] which published its final report in 2008. The report was the result of a number of years' work by a variety of networks of academics and activists and was the first major international attempt to link the wider determinants of health to a policy framework. The original Alma Ata Declaration had recognised these wider influences on health but had not dealt in any detail with the policy implications. The Commission brought the twin issues of wider health determinants and equity together and clearly showed the critical importance of policy in this area. Its foreword, for example, says:

> (The) toxic combination of bad policies, economics, and politics is, in large measure, responsible for the fact that a majority of people in the world do not enjoy the good health that is biologically possible.[31]

Its recommendations were based on three broad principles of action (see Box 2.3).

Box 2.3 Principles of action of the Commission on Social Determinants of Health

1. Improve the conditions of daily life—the circumstances in which people are born, grow, live, work, and age.
2. Tackle the inequitable distribution of power, money and resources—the structural drivers of those conditions of daily life—globally, nationally and locally.
3. Measure the problem, evaluate action, expand the knowledge base, develop a workforce that is trained in the social determinants of health and raise public awareness about the social determinants of health.

Source: Reproduced from CSDH. 2008 with permission from WHO.[32]

Whilst the commission clearly recognised the role of the health system in providing health care services as one of the determinants of health, it also stressed the role of the health system, and the health ministry, in providing leadership for a social determinants of health approach.

This placing of health in the wider policy context and outside the narrow confines of health care brings us back to the challenge for health care providers as to their role, and the appropriate structures within which to exercise this, in the wider health policy processes. We return to this critical issue at various points in the book, but at this point we leave the policy context and turn to discussing what we mean by a health system.

3 Developing a System Framework

We have, in the preceding section, used the term health system on a number of occasions assuming that readers will have a sufficient understanding of the meaning of the term to follow the wider discussion. However, we turn now to examine in more detail what is meant by the term. The term *health system* is relatively new. Its increasing use and underlying approach to health policy is the result of various influences that can be traced to the 1970s and since. Prior to this, policy had focused primarily on the types of interventions to be provided by a health service. This reflected the wider biomedical focus of health policy. Whilst there *were* discussions as to the manner in which such services were provided, the dominant paradigm was of a hospital-based set of interventions, complemented by (weaker) primary health services. The PHC movement of the 1970s challenged this paradigm and opened up questions about the nature of health services, their interrelationships and the linkages to the population and individuals they purported to serve. A second set of influences can be traced to the increasing recognition of a variety of resource pressures including, but not confined to, the underlying financial basis of the provision of health care. This concern over the resource base underpinning services led to increasing interest in the economics of health and health care and the birth of what has become a new discipline—health economics. As a discipline, economics draws heavily on systems thinking, and the 1980s saw, in its increasing influence in health policy circles, an attendant widening of interest away from interventions per se to the broader set of influencing factors and interrelationships. A good example of such thinking can be seen in the relationships between *inputs* (resources such as staff time or medical supplies), *outputs* (such as particular services), *outcomes* (the result of such services in terms of health status change) and the *process* that link these (see Figure 2.1).

A recent example of systems thinking can be seen in Box 2.4. This approach stresses the importance of recognising the potential interrelationships between different parts of the health system in developing specific strategies.

Figure 2.1
Inputs, outputs and outcomes

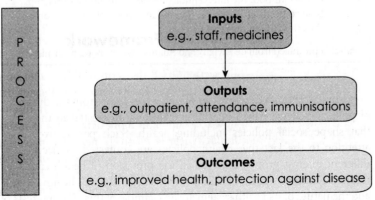

Box 2.4 Ten steps to systems thinking

Ten steps to systems thinking: applying a systems perspective in the design and evaluation of interventions

I. Intervention design

1. **Convene stakeholders:** Identify and convene stakeholders representing each building block, plus selected intervention designers and implementers, users of the health system and representatives of the research community
2. **Collectively brainstorm:** Collectively deliberate on possible system-wide effects of the proposed intervention respecting systems characteristics (feedback, time delays, policy resistance, etc.) and systems dynamics
3. **Conceptualize effects:** Develop a conceptual pathway mapping how the intervention will affect health and the health system through its subsystems
4. **Adapt and redesign:** Adapt and redesign the proposed intervention to optimise synergies and other positive effects while avoiding or minimising any potentially major negative effects

II. Evaluation design

5. **Determine indicators:** Decide on indicators that are important to track in the redesigned intervention (from process to issues to context) across the affected subsystems
6. **Choose methods:** Decide on evaluation methods to best track the indicators
7. **Select design:** Opt for the evaluation design that best manages the methods and fits the nature of the intervention
8. **Develop plan and timeline:** Collectively develop an evaluation plan and timeline by engaging the necessary disciplines
9. **Set a budget:** Determine the budget and scale by considering implications for both the intervention and the evaluation partnership
10. **Source funding:** Assemble funding to support the evaluation *before* the intervention begins

Source: Reproduced from de Savigny and Adam (eds). 2009 with permission.[33]

A similar, though different, set of influences came from the discipline of political science which became increasingly interested in the forces that shape social policies including health. Such perspectives drew attention to the fact that health policies are contested—reflecting the different interest groups involved in the provision of health care. The recent political battles in the USA over President Obama's health reforms and the nature of its health system are an example of this. The interests of the medical profession and the insurance and pharmaceutical industries were clearly exposed alongside the more overt interests in promoting access to health care.

All the above have contributed to the development of a wider view of health and recognition of the complexity of social responses to health and ill-health. The days of seeing such responses as ensuring simple provision of services from a doctor or a hospital were gone, and analysts sought new ways of understanding what became called the *health system*. Such analysis ranged from a wide macro-level view which attempted to incorporate all the constituent parts and forces within a health system which affect the ultimate level of an individual or population's health to a focus on specific aspects of the health system (or perhaps more properly, subsystems) such as health staff.

This invasion by social and political scientists into what had traditionally been the domain of natural scientists and biomedical professionals brought with it a new set of analytical tools. One of these will be widely used in this book—that of the analytical or conceptual framework. A framework is a means of trying to understand the nature of a phenomenon by describing its key features and structuring the interrelationships between them. As such it is an analytical device that may help us to get under the skin of a particular problem. It is usually, though not necessarily, depicted graphically alongside a description and we turn now to health system frameworks.

4 Existing Frameworks for Understanding a Health System

Frameworks are useful to analysts in a number of ways. First, they allow an overview picture of the influences on health and health care responses to ill-health. There is, as we will see, a huge diversity of health systems and such overviews allow the analyst to pick out and assess the key similarities and differences between and influences on them. Without such a typological understanding, it is difficult to develop appropriate and feasible policy. Second, they both set out the obvious interrelationships between the elements and draw attention to other, less obvious interrelations. They may be used also to hone down on a particular aspect, developing within this, a subsystem, as described earlier.

Frameworks have, however, to be treated with caution. Their very strength—the ability to encapsulate key considerations—carries with it accompanying weaknesses. In particular, they can never capture *all* the complexities of a situation; as such there is always a danger of ignoring a key element or relationship. Each framework, inevitably, leans in a particular direction. They also, by their attempts to make sense of the world, may suggest a more rational and ordered view than is the reality; as such they may downplay the messiness of any health system. Their apparent rationalism may also understate the value-laden nature of all health systems, by suggesting a more technocratically driven reality than exists.

Lastly, they also rarely reflect the changing nature of health systems, which is one of the key themes of this book.

There are various frameworks for understanding a health system. An early one was that of Roemer[34] (see Table 2.4), which saw four different types ranging from entrepreneurial to socialist and differentiated by economic levels. He conceptualised the health system to have five major categories (production of resources, organisation of programmes, economic support mechanisms, management methods and delivery of services).

Table 2.4
Roemer's typology of health systems

Economic level (GNP per capita)	Health system policies (market intervention)			
	Entrepreneurial and permissive	Welfare-oriented	Universal and comprehensive	Socialist and centrally planned
Affluent and industrialised	United States	West Germany Canada Japan	Great Britain New Zealand Norway	Soviet Union Czechoslovakia
Developing and transitional	Thailand Philippines South Africa	Brazil Egypt Malaysia	Israel Nicaragua	Cuba North Korea
Very poor	Ghana Bangladesh Nepal	India Burma	Sri Lanka Tanzania	China Vietnam
Resource-rich		Libya Gabon	Kuwait Saudi Arabia	

Source: Reproduced from Roemer, M.I. 1991. *National Health Systems of the World, Vol. 1: The Countries*. Oxford: OUP. By permission of Oxford University Press, Inc.

Mills and Ranson[35] suggest that there are various ways in which classification can be done and list five: the dominant method of financing, the underlying political philosophy, the nature of State interventions, the level of GNP and historical or cultural attributes. They develop what they call a 'map of the health system' (see Figure 2.2).

Figure 2.2
A map of the health system

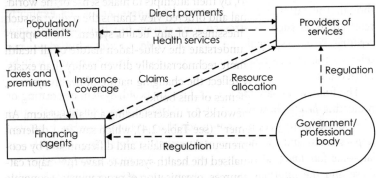

Source: Reproduced from Mills and Ranson. 2012 with permission from Jones and Bartlett Learning.[36]

We do not have the space here, nor intent, to cover all these different frameworks. However, perhaps the currently most widely used approach is that of the WHO. The WHO 2000 World Health Report has its own framework for the health system that set out the relations between functions and objectives (see Figure 2.3) and whose definition of a health system is:

... all the activities whose primary purpose is to promote, restore and maintain health.[37]

Figure 2.3
Relations between functions and objectives of a health system

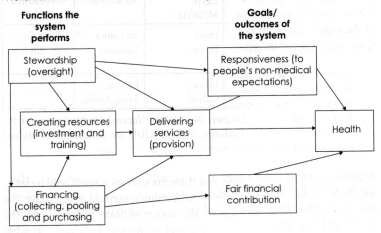

Source: Reproduced from WHO. 2000 with permission from WHO.[38]

Various features of this framework are worth noting. The framework is a mixture of functional activities and value-based goals, though the latter are not necessarily comprehensive or explicitly referred to as such. It stressed four system functions—*stewardship, creating resources, financing and delivering services*—but does not refer to the structures within, or processes by which they will be carried out.

The framework saw the key goal of any health system as creating or protecting *health*; however, it also recognised two related goals—that of responding to people's non-medical expectations—what it termed *responsiveness* and the need to ensure that the financing of health was fair—*the fair financial contributions* goal. The relative weight given to these and the interplay between them are issues to which all health systems need to respond.

Lastly, the framework is firmly focused on health care; there is no reference within it to the wider health agenda, which, as we have seen, is, inevitably, a critical challenge in any policies designed to improve health.

The WHO framework was originally conceived as a conceptual device to help understand and analyse the constituent parts of a health system. However, it was also used to develop a means of assessing the performance of health systems. This was a highly contentious exercise presented initially in the form of a league table measuring the various elements of the system and bringing these together into a single composite indicator allowing ranking in notorious league tables comparing the relative performance both according to the various elements of the framework and giving an overall ranking—necessitating developing relative weightings between the different elements. Following criticisms of the report, the WHO set up a Scientific Peer Review Group to assess these methods.[39,40] Its report

> examined carefully the role of 'league tables' of health-system performance within the HSPA process. It considers that the decision as to whether or not to publish such league tables is ultimately a policy and strategic decision for WHO rather than a technical issue. However, there were serious technical questions raised about the WHR 2000 methodology relating to the weights used in the composite index, the scaling of the component indicators, and the treatment of missing data.[41]

A more recent addition to the framework has been the concept within the WHO of building blocks for health systems (see Figure 2.4). Note also within this framework the addition of improved efficiency as a goal of the health system.

Figure 2.4
Health system framework

The WHO health system framework

System building blocks

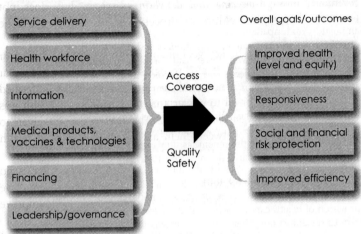

Source: Reproduced from WHO. 2007 with permission from WHO.[42]

Common to all the different approaches to classifying health systems is recognition of the diversity of the different health systems that exist. A good illustration of these differences is given in Box 2.5.

Box 2.5 Illustrations of the structure of health systems

Tanzania (GNI per capita $440)
The public sector plays a leading role in the Tanzanian health system, with the government owning approximately 64% of all health facilities and covering all levels of health care, from primary to tertiary.[43] Relative to neighbouring countries, the public system is quite decentralised, with public services managed at the district level. Mission (church) services are a very important source of care outside the main towns, providing the same number of hospitals as the government, and are subsidized by the state. Private doctors practice in the main cities, and there is a large informal sector of traditional practitioners and drug sellers. The majority of health expenditure flows through government; most of the remainder consists of out-of-pocket expenditure. A national health insurance funding provides health insurance coverage to government workers, a parallel scheme covers formal-sector employees, and a number of community-based insurance schemes also exist. Nevertheless, the coverage of insurance schemes is still limited.

Box 2.5 continued

Box 2.5 *continued*

India (GNI per capita $1,070)

The public sector health system in India is large in absolute terms, providing all levels of care. Health care is, in general, a state-level function with central government involved mainly in overall policy and specific disease control programs. There is also a very large formal private sector, providing both ambulatory and inpatient care, and an even larger informal sector consisting of unlicensed and unqualified practitioners and drug sellers. A compulsory state insurance system covers lower paid, formal-sector workers and another scheme covers government workers. Numerous community-based health schemes exist, some with an insurance component. A new health insurance scheme was launched by the government of India in 2008, covering first-level hospital care for the 300 million people who live below the poverty line. By the end of 2009, only a small percentage of the target population had been reached[44] but the scheme is now expanding rapidly. Several new state insurance schemes are offering access to tertiary-level care for the poor.

Mexico (GNI per capita $9,980)

Both the public and private sectors play an important role in financing and provision of health care in Mexico. Formal-sector employees are covered by various social insurance institutions, whereas the poor receive care through government facilities or private providers (allopathic or traditional). There is very little interaction between public and private sectors, in the form of regulation or contracting for service delivery. Concern about duplication and waste of resources between the three subsystems—social security, other government and private—and lack of protection against increasing health-care costs (especially for the poor has led to reforms based on decentralisation, managed market principles and a new voluntary insurance scheme for the uninsured, which over time is gradually extending its population and service coverage).[45] In 2007, 27% of the Mexican population remained uninsured.

Thailand (GNI per capita $2,840)

Both the public and private sectors have major roles in the Thai health system providing all levels of care. There is widespread use of the private sector, especially for outpatient care. Compulsory social insurance covers those in formal employment and finances care provided by public and private hospitals (chosen by the insured). Civil servants have their own medical benefit scheme which pays for care at public and private hospitals. The remaining part of the population—who formerly could get a low-income card exempting them from fees if they were poor, purchase a voluntary health insurance card, or pay out of pocket for care—are now part of a universal coverage arrangement in which they register at a local facility and can then access a wide range of health care benefits.[46]

Source: Reproduced from Mills and Ranson. 2012 with permission from Jones and Bartlett Learning.[47]

Note: Gross National Income (GNI) is in 2008 dollars.

The above has set out a number of different ways of viewing the health system. Each of these has emerged at a particular point in time, has brought out key features of the health system and has been developed to serve specific purposes. We do not have any major criticisms of any of these; our own analysis of the health system seeks to build on these frameworks, adjusting their content to portray the importance we attach to the values that underpin the health system. We seek to bring out also the importance of context, stakeholders, health need and the processes that result in the delivery of health services and inter-sectoral action for health to meet these needs. We call this a value-based health system framework and now turn to explaining it in the next section.

5 Building a Value-based Health System Framework

We turn now to the framework of the health system that underlies the rest of the book and in this section we introduce its elements and interrelationships. In doing so, we will show the basic elements and some of the critical issues in a health system together with the values we express in this book. We begin by identifying the values that we consider to be important for the health system, which then allows us to interpret its objectives. Essential to understanding the objectives of the health system is the difference between a health and a health *care* system. We then move on to discuss the elements of the health system. As we have seen in the preceding section, these constituent elements may be looked at in different ways but we analyse it here in terms of resources, stakeholders/health system members and processes. Lastly we emphasise the importance of context; the health system does not operate in a vacuum but interrelates with a political, economic and social context.

In presenting this analysis of the health system, we need to emphasise three points. First, our use of the term 'system' suggests that the different parts are interrelated, with changes to one part having implications for the others. It also implies interdependency between the parts in that for one part to work effectively it requires other parts to exist and help it. This suggests the need for integration and compatibility between the parts. However, we need to recognise that this is not always the case in practice. In fact, we frequently find fragmentation and disjuncture in the relations between the parts. Second, using the term *system* implies that there is an intention or purpose in *why* the parts interact; the underlying values and objectives. However, stakeholders have different interests and values that can conflict. Domination and conflict can be as much a part of a health system as collaboration and harmony. Last, there is a danger with using frameworks such as this, in that the necessary oversimplification of the different elements is interpreted by the reader as universal statements. They should be seen rather as tendencies that will play out differently in different contexts; the framework is an analytical device to help understand the likely tendencies.

Our framework which we develop in the following sections is set out diagrammatically in Figure 2.5.

We introduce Figure 2.5 first by a short overview.

The system should be designed to respond to the needs of its members and exists within a wider context. It includes a number of processes, all underpinned by the governance of the system. Actors are those individuals and institutions that attempt to influence this governance. The outputs of the health system are both health services and inter-sectoral action for health, which should be designed to meet the three objectives of the health system. The whole system rests on and is permeated by values. We start by examining these values.

5.1 Values

In the last chapter we explained our concern that the role of values in analysing health systems had not been sufficiently recognised; indeed, our interest in the place of values in the health system is reflected in the book title.[48]

The health system relies heavily on technical approaches and professional attitudes and training. It deals with issues which can be 'life and death'. In such a situation it is easy to assume either technocratic neutrality ('science will provide the appropriate answers') or a common interest and set of underpinning shared values. However, we argue both that values need to lie alongside scientific evidence and that there is no single set of accepted values. As such, in analysing any aspect of the health system, it is essential to identify the driving values.[49] We are here using the term *values* to represent the beliefs of individuals and groups as to what is important and worthy of pursuit. They are strongly influenced by the interests of the individuals and groups in society. Brought together, they form the basis of an ideology and agenda for political action to remould society in the light of these beliefs. For example, socialism is based on values of common worth and a responsibility of individuals and society to respond to social needs; this contrasts with libertarianism that sees individual choice and freedom as paramount. Individuals and groups may also share values but give different weight to their importance. Thus, there may be hierarchies

Figure 2.5
A 'valued' health system framework

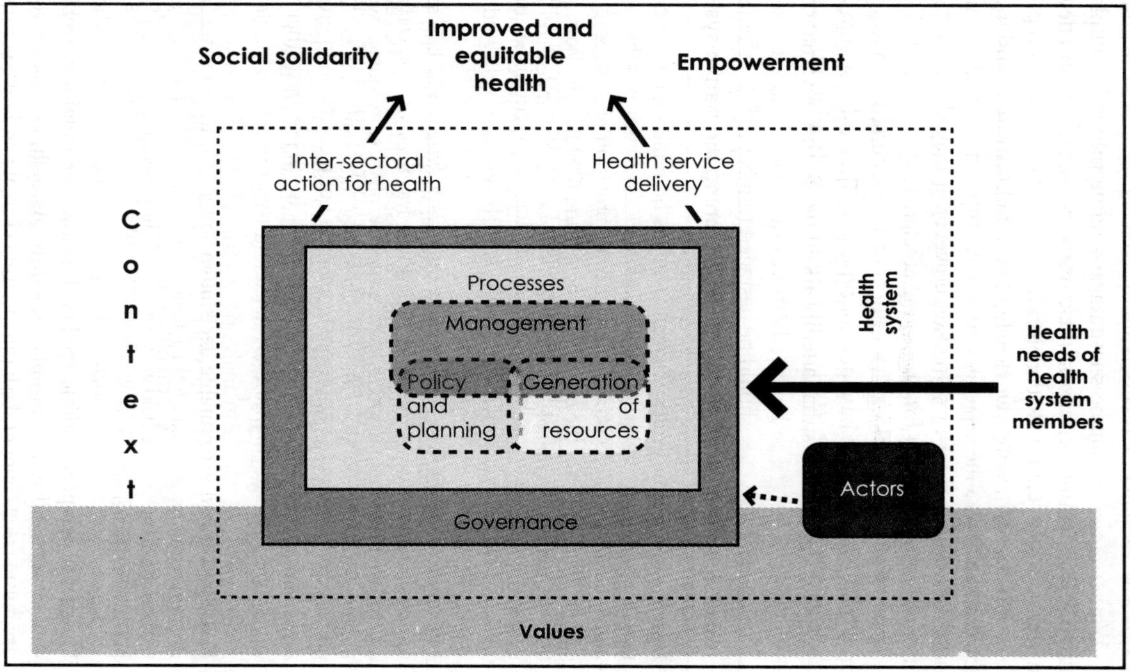

Social solidarity

Improved and equitable health

Empowerment

Inter-sectoral action for health

Health service delivery

Health needs of health system members

Health system

Processes

Management

Generation of resources

Policy and planning

Governance

Actors

Values

C o n t e x t

of values with some being seen as overriding. One approach to analysis of this hierarchy, for example, divides such views into world views, principled views and causal beliefs[50] with one end being exemplified by religious beliefs and the other by beliefs based on evidence.

We here refer to values as leading to guiding principles that are not testable in scientific or rational discussion but which, combined with scientific evidence, provide the basis for action or influence the approach to action. As such, some values may be seen not only as an end in themselves but also as a means to an end. For example, accountability may be viewed as desirable for its own sake; however, it may also be seen as an important precondition for promoting efficiency.

Box 2.6 sets out the four key values—each expressed as one or more principles on which we base our conception of the health system in this book. We examine each of these in turn in more detail in the following points.

Box 2.6 Values and principles underpinning the health system

Equity and right to health: That all members have the right to attain the maximum level of health (defined in its broadest sense) possible within individual biological constraints; this includes provision of services to mitigate, as far as possible, the effects of ill-health and disability. It also requires that the resources available to the health system will be funded according to ability to contribute and used to provide services which are distributed amongst members on the basis of health need.

Efficiency: That resources available to the health system will be used in the most efficient way possible, to achieve the system objectives, within an accepted ethical framework. In particular, use of these resources will be informed by evidence about the effectiveness of interventions in achieving the system objectives in a manner consistent with other values. These interventions include both activities in the health system and in other systems for which the health system may advocate.

Participative and accountable decision-making: That decision-making in the health system is based on the balanced involvement of stakeholders and that decision-makers are held accountable for these decisions, through transparent and participative processes.

Long-term perspective: That the health system is equally responsible for both current and future members of society. As such, decisions made today must take account of the future needs of current and future generations alongside the current needs of the current members. It also implies that the health system needs to be responsive to the wider long-term environmental needs and as such have minimum negative environmental effects.

5.1.1 Equity and the Right to Health

The way we define health has an influence on the way we interpret the health system. A broad, rather than restricted, medical definition of health is to be found in the position taken by the WHO (see Box 2.7). The Constitution also sees health as a fundamental human right. We adhere to these two positions. In so doing, we recognise the importance of health and the health system and also the need to take action in society against all those constraints that limit health. This includes more than improving access to good quality health care but action on inequity and the social determinants to health.

Maximisation of health gains does not necessarily equate with a focus on life-threatening health problems. The broad view of health that we espouse recognises the importance of caring and responding to non-treatable or non-life threatening but debilitating conditions, and clearly one of the key issues for any decision-makers is the interpretation of the relative importance of these different aspects of health. Such decisions are ultimately value-driven.

Box 2.7 Excerpt from the Constitution of the World Health Organization

... the following principles are basic to the happiness, harmonious relations and security of all peoples:

Health is a state of complete physical, mental and social well-being and not merely the absence of disease or infirmity.
The enjoyment of the highest attainable standard of health is one of the fundamental rights of every human being without distinction of race, religion, political belief, economic or social condition.

Source: Reproduced with permission from WHO.[51]

The right to health raises difficult issues. Whilst few would argue with it as broad principle, its very breadth makes it hard to operationalise.[52] In particular, it needs to be reconciled with the fact that inevitably there are inadequate resources in any health system for full attainment of these rights by all people. Given this reality, it is important to balance it with a principle that can be used to determine the relative pursuit of this right by different groups. Without such a principle, it is almost inevitable that the powerful and well-resourced members of society have a disproportionate move towards such full health, and we consider this to be wrong. We have already referred on several occasions to the principle of equity. We have also pointed out that its definition is often murky. It should be, we suggest, a requirement of all health policies that they incorporate a clear and measurable definition of equity. The work of the Equity Gauge movement[53] gives useful pointers towards this. Without such a focus on equity, policy can be dominated by the average which masks the needy. This can be illustrated, for example, in relation to Millennium Development Goals (MDGs) where a drive to attain the overall MDG target may result in a focus on those groups who are easiest to reach and therefore potentially the least needy.[54] In Section 2.2 we gave the definition of equity that we follow here. One of the important aspects of equity is the difference between equity and equality. The concept of equity incorporates the essential idea that some people receive fewer resources than others to respond to the different levels of need. It is in this simple and, on reflection, obvious characteristic that resistance to equity lies.

5.1.2 Efficiency

The 1980s, and the growth of the discipline of health economics, brought out more explicitly a principle which is not new—that resources should not be wasted but used to their full potential. The rationale for this is simple—such wasted resources could be used to provide other services. Within this simple and incontestable concept lies the more subtle concept that underpins the wider use of the principle of efficiency. This is that resources should be used in ways that promote the objectives of the health system. Most obviously this suggests a need to ensure maximisation of wider health gains as part of the movement towards the attainment of health rights. This suggests not only avoidance of 'waste' but that resources should be shifted to activities with higher gains. This might, for example, imply that resources be shifted from hospitals to primary care. It can also mean the need to develop an inter-sectoral approach to health to focus on the wider determinants of health if greater gains were seen to be achievable through such a route. Closely related, then, to efficiency is the concept of effectiveness. This refers to the ability of a given intervention to deliver desired objectives and includes notions of feasibility and appropriateness of the services related, for example, to delivery issues such as continuity of care.

However, it is important to recognise that our operationalisation of efficiency (and effectiveness) will depend heavily on our conceptualisation of health, as discussed above. As such we argue that efficiency should not solely relate to maximisation of health gains but should also refer to the distribution of these gains—the equity dimension. This is a critical issue in terms of the functioning of the health system and its decision-making. For example, some economic appraisal techniques used to assess efficiency have focused on a reduction in mortality or reduction in disease incidence, downplaying or ignoring other health effects and in particular the equity dimension. We will argue that techniques such as these, which make decisions between alternative uses of resources, inevitably carry with them a number of implicit values that need to be made explicit and tested against the core values of the health system.

We have also used the term *within an accepted ethical framework*. Of course, all of our principles and values constitute an ethical framework. However, we are here particularly referring to ethical standards concerning health care provision. This includes, most obviously, procedures in areas such as abortion, organ transplant, cloning and right to die policies but also enters into areas such as compulsory testing for communicable disease, required supervision of treatment in areas such as TB, withholding of treatment for 'self-inflicted', such as tobacco-related illness. We are not ethicists and we do not presume to be able to define or indeed discuss in any detail this area but we recognise that it is essential that there are clearly accepted clinical guidelines developed by a combination of professional representatives and the wider health system members. Such guidelines, though professionally led, are bound to be influenced by social norms including any dominant religious values (such as the Catholic position on use of condoms) suggesting the need for clear transparency concerning the make-up of the body determining the ethical codes.

Efficiency, therefore, needs to be related to the other key principles and in particular (but not solely) the concept of equity. Implicit, therefore, within the concept of efficiency are the wider objectives of the health system. If these are simply defined as maximising health, then there is a danger of a clash between equity and efficiency principles. However, by defining health gains to incorporate an equitable dimension, as we propose in the goals of the health system, this clash can be avoided.

As will be apparent from the above, we do not see efficiency as a value that can be isolated from other values and particularly the right to health and equity.

5.1.3 Participative and Accountable Decision-making

The reality for most health systems is that there is a small elite group of people and institutions who make decisions. We believe that this decision-making needs to be opened up to allow participation by all members of the health system. We use the term health system members to reinforce our view that the health system belongs to all those resident within a country. Various terms are often used, including actors and stakeholders, and we return to these in later chapters, but they both refer to subsets of the wider 'membership'[55] that we are referring to. We also use this term rather than that of patients to include both users and non-users of health services.

We believe that such members (and not solely current users) have rights to influence the shape of *their* health system. Given the current social structures in different societies, it is essential that such involvement is seen as balanced and democratic (in its widest interpretation). Such participation has also, we argue, to be based on, and consistent with, the other key values. This caveat is important to ensure that the rights of minorities in such processes are not overwhelmed by a populist majority. As such, any health system needs to consider both the relative rights of different members to such participation and the mechanisms by which it will occur. Improving participation as outlined here is also linked to the objective of empowerment and we refer to this below.

There are other reasons for participative decision-making but these are primarily instrumental. They are based on arguments of pragmatism—health care decisions will be more effective if they have taken account of the views of the (potential) users and, whilst clearly an important means of achieving effective health systems, is not a value as such.

We fully recognise that, practically, the depth of the practice and interest in participation by different groups and individuals will vary. We are not naïve believers in total citizen control of the health system. However, it is important not only that the principle of participation is clear but also that the inevitable delegation of decision-making to policymakers, planners, managers and service deliverers is done through clear and accountable mechanisms that spell out the relative delegated powers of these groups. These mechanisms give authority to decision-makers to take decisions on behalf of the wider society or health system. Their authority should be derived from this link to the wider society. This leads us to another key ingredient for this value—their accountability back to society. Chapter 3 looks more closely at the governance of the health system and accountability mechanisms including the importance of transparency in decision-making as a means of ensuring accountability but which can pose challenges for governance structures and the speed of decision-making. Accountability mechanisms also absorb resources and as such trade-offs may have to be made between this and the efficiency principle.

5.1.4 Long-term Perspective

We believe that the health system is responsible for both current and future members of society. We argue that decision-makers should give equal weight to the future needs of both current and future generations alongside the current needs of the current members. However, the short-term perspective of both society[56] and decision-makers (and particularly politicians conscious of their electoral vulnerability) means that the inevitably competing priorities between investment in the present and future health are skewed towards the former. Techniques such as economic appraisal can reinforce this position, in a seemingly technocratic manner, as we will see in Chapter 5, through the use of discount rates. One of the roles, we suggest, for the health system is to ensure that a clear voice is given to the needs of future health system members in decisions about the health system.

Closely linked to our belief in the importance of a long-term perspective is the need for the health system to be responsive to the wider long-term environmental needs, and as such have minimum negative environmental effects consistent with pursuit of its other objectives.

5.1.5 Role of Values in the Health System

As we examine the different elements of the health system, we will frequently return to the importance of these values and their associated principles. An underlying theme in the book is that values underpin, and are expressed in, the different parts of the health system. For example, different values will lead to different types of governance, financing and mechanisms and criteria to set priorities. Values are also held by the different actors and stakeholders.

Clearly, however, values alone cannot drive decision-making. Values have to be seen alongside evidence (including, but not solely, from scientific research) and judgement. The three are complementary and all are necessary.

There has been an emphasis in recent years on policymakers adopting a more evidence-informed process of decision-making. Whilst this is clearly desirable, it is important to recognise both that there are different forms of evidence and that evidence *alone* is insufficient for decision-making.

Within the formal research world, evidence can range from complex randomised control trials which answer questions about efficacy of particular interventions through to qualitative studies that illuminate our understanding of why particular situations arise. Both are important sources of evidence. Alongside this, we have to recognise that we all draw on personal experience as evidence. Indeed, it is likely that many decision-makers may give greater weight to their own experience than to the findings of formal research. All these types of evidence however are attempts to empirically understand both the current situation and the potential effects of changes (through, for example, new interventions such as new medicines). Furthermore, no evidence is applicable to all situations. It is frequently, if not always, context-specific. Evidence is also always based on population samples that inevitably can never fully be representative.[57]

Science can provide answers to questions about causes and effects— why a health problem occurs or what the effect of an intervention may mean. It cannot, however, tell decision-makers what to do. There are various reasons for this. First, given the uncertainty over evidence that we have argued above, the robustness of the evidence needs to be assessed. Second, there may be several pieces of evidence each suggesting the need for different forms of action. Lastly, each piece of evidence needs to be held up against the values which give meaning to the relative importance of a specific health problem or the effects that science has predicted.

The combination of evidence and values is not easy and requires the third component—judgement. Whilst many of the management and planning processes explored in this book provide a framework for such judgement, in the end it is the responsibility of the decision-maker to apply his/her judgement for combining the evidence and the desired values, and where necessary to mediate in terms of potential tensions and trade-offs in pursuit of the health system objectives. The source of such judgement is complex and involves individual ethical frameworks (showing a complex interrelationship between values and judgement), training in decision-making (such as through management or leadership courses) and personal experience.

This judgement leads to decisions through policy, planning and management processes and resultant activities aimed at meeting the health system objectives. This complex set of relationships is shown diagrammatically in Figure 2.6.

We need to recognise the potential tension and contradiction around the values driving the health system. Different stakeholders espouse different values; indeed, individual stakeholders may well find that their own values are 'contradictory with each other' in terms of reactions to specific policies and their own hierarchy of values is needed to form a personal view as to the desired policy. This is inevitably a contested arena. While many would agree with the values we have put forward, there are others who would promote different values and/or give secondary importance or tokenistic recognition to values such as equity. In their statements and actions, stakeholders can express quite different and occasionally contradictory values. For example, health may not be seen as a right but as a good for individual consumption traded in a market place of private providers. We have seen how neo-liberalism adopts market values associated with efficiency (narrowly defined), consumer choice, competition and monetary incentives. Values of monetary gain can also be seen in corruption and unprincipled conduct in the health system.

Figure 2.6
Objective, values, evidence and judgement

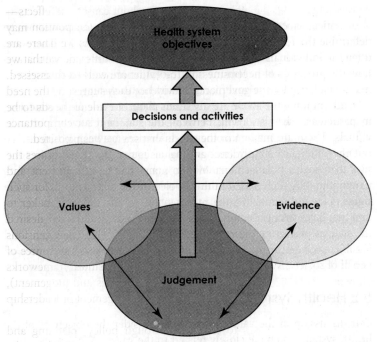

Values associated with political loyalty and exchange can penetrate into the health system leading to it becoming a tool of political patronage. Some professional perspectives can also mark out relations of domination both within and between professions and, in the case of the medical profession, lead to a medical interpretation of health and the dominance of a curative medical approach in the health system. Furthermore, values and approaches that equate sophisticated and high technology with a sought after modernisation and development can lead to a misallocation of resources and a failure to recognise the importance of primary health care and inter-sectoral action for health.

In many respects, the values that emerge as the dominant ones in a health system reflect an issue of political governance. There are likely to be tensions between different stakeholders and values. How these tensions are resolved involves two processes of governance—hegemony and resolution. Hegemony in the health system rests on the emergence of political coalitions that are able to support and develop their own set of coherent values and achieve their dominance in the health system. The resolution of tensions also depends on the extent to which governance within the system is able to mediate between different interests and beliefs through agreements and possibly political concessions.

A critical aspect of both these processes is where the power lies to determine the relative importance of different values. As we have seen, different individuals and organisations will have different values and how the processes of hegemony and resolution are worked through is a major challenge for the governance in any health system.

Underpinning the above are questions about the role of the state and, in particular, the relationship between the state and society and individuals. There are major ideological differences between positions. To put the difference simply (recognising of course that it is more complex than such a polarised formulation), one view sees the individual as paramount—in such a view, the key role of the state is to protect the rights of the individual to pursue their interests. This differs from a position that gives stronger emphasis on the wider society and see the role of the state as protecting the vulnerable and as such, where necessary and feasible, taking distributive action across society and making choices on behalf of society. We, in this book, take the latter position.[58]

5.2 Health System Objectives

Our discussion of the values leads us to consider the objectives of the health system which are closely related to the values. We propose three objectives which a health system should strive to attain (see Box 2.8).

The first and paramount objective is that of promoting and maintaining the health of members[59] equitably. Within this objective, there are two points to which we would draw attention. First, although health is seen as paramount, it is essential that its *equitable distribution* is part of this. Without this qualification, there is the danger that health

---

Box 2.8 Health system objectives

The key objective of the health system is:

- to promote and maintain the health of its members equitably to their full biological and social potential

There are two secondary objectives:

- To promote social solidarity amongst health system members
- To empower health system members in terms of decisions about their own health, the wider health system and society

maximisation may be pursued in ways, as we have seen, that are non-equitable (for example, prioritisation may be given to easily achieved health gains amongst the urban middle classes instead of more difficult health gains amongst the poor).

Second, we use the term *health* here in its broadest definition (as set out by the WHO). This means that we are as concerned about the social and mental well-being of members as their physical health. This wider definition requires the health system not only to attempt to redress biological problems but also to provide supportive measures where biomedical challenges exist in order that individuals can achieve their full social potential. As such an individual with an incurable disability would be entitled to rehabilitative measures to support him/her in their social functioning.

The second objective is the promotion of social solidarity and cohesion. The health system can have wider impact beyond those of health gain and empowerment. It can also be seen as a social institution with wider social effects. As such, we see a health system as having a role over and beyond the production of health and also contributing to social cohesion within society. In part, this is the rationale for an equity dimension—the recognition of the social, rather than solely individual, nature of health.

The third, and closely related, explicit objective of a health system is the empowerment of the health system members. The concept of empowerment draws on ideas such as those of Amartya Sen[60] who sees a range of factors including political, economic and social as a major constraint to development. Indeed, he sees freedom from such constraints both as a means to and an end of development. In this way he radically shifts the objectives of development away from economic growth per se (though he recognises its importance) to more social objectives. In an analogous way, we propose that such empowerment should be an intrinsic objective of the health system and part of a health experience. We believe that this is resonant with the holistic WHO definition of health. We recognise also that such empowerment is an instrumental element of health promotion in itself—the task of health promotion *has* to include the active participation of an empowered individual, but here we are concerned with it as an end in itself.

Our framework, as set out in and elaborated on below, highlights these objectives. It is however important to note that there may be other objectives held by different actors just as we have already noted that there may be other values. These are sometimes hidden and sometimes not. Examples of such motives are the political motive of generation of full employment or that of profit-making in private health facilities. Such alternative objectives may conflict with the three core ones proposed above.

5.3 Scope of the Health System

We turn now to the scope of what we mean by a system. First, there is a critical issue as to whether we are referring to a *health* or a *health care* system. As we have argued, health and ill-health are the products of a wide variety of factors encompassing all areas of life. Factors other than health care, such as education, income, security, road safety and availability of quality water are critical for health. This poses an important challenge for those responsible for national health policy—how to ensure a 'joined-up approach' to health, given the various interests of agencies and institutions who have, alongside their prime objectives, an effect (positive or negative) on health. It is generally assumed that the health ministry of a national government, or its equivalent at lower decentralised levels, is responsible for setting and overseeing implementation of health policy. However, in practice, such organisations have little power or influence over public agencies operating in other sectors and on private sector institutions. Furthermore, the professional leaders of such health ministries are likely to have had a more medically focused training and experience within the health *care* field. As such the policy and implementation focus of health ministries remains largely on health care provision. The Alma Ata Declaration called for greater inter-sectoral collaboration, but the many (such as institutional) barriers to this often prove difficult to surmount and ministries retreat into working in the areas over which they do have control.[61] However, given the complex interplay of factors affecting health, the challenge remains as to how to achieve effective inter-sectoralism acting on the social determinants of health along the lines set out by the WHO Commission of that name as discussed earlier.[62]

This has implications for our understanding of the term *health system* itself. The WHO's definition of a health system refers to a *primary* purpose of improving health, but this does not help at a practical level, particularly given the WHO's own broad definition of health as set out in Box 2.7. Thus, though water may be needed for industry and agriculture, its provision also has a key health objective. An education system also has an ultimate aim of allowing the participants to maximise their personal potential which is clearly related to their social and mental health *in its widest interpretation*. The practical difficulties, however, of organising activities that may share a similar aim but have different characteristics in terms of their delivery (water versus health care, for example) suggest that institutional arrangements are likely to continue to be guided by the *type of activity* rather than its ultimate *goal*. We see a health system as one in which the primary purpose is improving health but which may do this both through delivery of services but also through action which impinges on other sectors that may influence health positively or negatively. Such actions may include legislation and regulation on the activities of other sectors and advocacy to persuade them to health promotive activities. Box 2.9 sets out our definition of a good health system.

Box 2.9 Definition of a good health system

A good health system is one that has access to a level of resources commensurate with the national level of income and uses these resources in the most efficient way to ensure an equitable and maximised level of health that is sustainable over the long term and that empowers the health system members in areas concerning their health and contributes towards wider social cohesion and mores.

Second, in our use of the term *health system* we are encompassing all activities by any institution that has the purported primary purpose of improving health. We deliberately include the term 'purported' as we recognise that for private-for-profit providers of health care, their primary purpose is profit generation with the provision of health care as their means of achieving this. However, in most such cases, the purported objective is the promotion of health and, as such, we include these.

In using the term *health system* we are aware that, for many, their term of choice is health *sector*. Indeed these terms have been, and still are, often used interchangeably and loosely. At times we have bowed to popular usage and referred to sector and not system, as in the case of inter-sectoral action and health sector reform. We will attempt, however, other than this exception, to use the term *sector* to refer to parts of the health system such as the public or private sectors.

5.4 Delivery of Health Services and Inter-sectoral Action for Health

Within the health system, various terms concerning the nature and aims of the systems' activities are often used loosely and in an overlapping manner; for example, terms such as public health, health promotion, health prevention and advocacy. The linguistic difficulties are further complicated by the fact that different writers make assumptions about the scope or area of operation of the term. Thus, for some, health promotion refers to activities related to improving an individual's health through education to change personal behaviour. To others, it refers to a wider social health improvement through actions such as policy or legislative activity on the determinants of ill-health such as income inequalities, housing or education. We are not concerned here with the linguistic differences but in capturing the key differences that will then affect the focus and strategies of the health system. We suggest various books that provide deeper insights into the details of these.[63]

Box 2.10 sets out the way we are using these key terms in this book.

Box 2.10 Health system activities

The most obvious activity of the health system is the provision of health services—*Health Services Delivery*. A variety of *health services* are provided within the health system aimed at individuals. These are often divided into preventive and curative services, but we would include a third category of 'carative' or palliative services aimed at supporting and minimising pain for those with incurable disease such as some cancers and AIDS.

The dividing line between curative and preventive activities is not always clear as some of the former result in prevention of further problems.[64] For example, the early detection and treatment of infectious diseases, such as TB, prevents wider transmission to others.

Some preventive activities may be aimed at individuals; these may be either done through activities provided directly to the individual (such as immunisation or screening for disease) or carried out through wider activities (such as health education aimed at changing behaviour). Other preventive activities may be carried out through acting on the prime causes of ill-health. Such activities range from interventions such as spraying larvicide on standing water to prevent mosquito breeding to road safety measures, improving the access to good quality water, enhancing levels of literacy and reducing poverty. Some of these (such as spraying) are often seen as the responsibility of the health system; in some cases, the health system may do this in collaboration with other sectors (such as jointly providing schools health education) or working collaboratively on issues such as road safety with the transport sector.

The health system may also attempt to influence the activities of other systems that have health implications. This may be done through a variety of means including legislation and regulation (for example, on food quality), or through research and advocacy that attempts to persuade other organisations to carry out health promoting activities and minimise health-detrimental activities. The Ministry of Health may, for example, try to persuade the agriculture ministry to emphasise the production of healthy foods in pursuit of enhanced nutrition. We refer to these as *Inter-sectoral Action for Health* taken by an organisation to attempt to achieve change in another organisation outside the health system.

5.5 Health System Members, Stakeholders and Actors

We have used various terms up to now to describe the individuals and organisations who are involved to greater or lesser degrees in the health system. We suggest that there are three overlapping terms that describe different attributes of individuals or organisations in relation to the health system. These are illustrated in Figure 2.7.

Figure 2.7
Interrelationships between members, stakeholders and actors

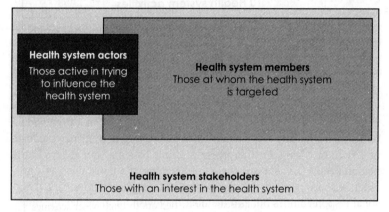

We have already introduced the idea of *health system members* as the target group for whom the health system is operating—the potential health beneficiaries of the system. Health system members are individual residents of the country. They, as members, have a right to participate in its decision-making. However, they may not actually be able to do this under current decision-making processes or they may have no interest in so doing. *Stakeholders* are those with a stake or interest in the system. They clearly include health system members whose prime interest is promotion of their health. However, the stakeholder group also includes others such as health providers and funders and other bodies that have an interest in the policies and activities of the health system. They may be both individuals (such as doctors) and organisations (such as advocacy Non-governmental Organisations [NGOs]). These include organisations that see the activities of the health system as acting against their interest perhaps through affecting their profits. Cigarette companies, for example, are stakeholders in the health system in a negative sense. It is important to recognise that many of these stakeholders will have employees who are individual members of the health system and there may, as a result, be differences between the views of these employees and those of the organisation itself. For example, a private hospital may seek restrictions on the roles of the public sector whilst its lower income employees may not be able to afford such private care and seek a strong public sector.

The last group are the *actors*. These are those individuals, groups and organisations who are actively involved in the processes of the health system—whether effectively or not. They are, almost by definition, all stakeholders. However, they are not necessarily all health system members (for example, foreign donors may have significant influence on the health system). Nor conversely are all health system members actors in that they may not wish to influence policy. Our framework uses the term actors as the group that is active in attempting to influence decision-making in the health system. Our approach in this book is to advocate for a greater role for members as effective actors in the health system. It is important to recognise that individuals may wear more than one of these hats. A nurse is a stakeholder in that s/he is interested in the way the health system which employs her operates; s/he is also a member in that s/he will use the services provided. If s/he sits on a professional body, then s/he may also be an actor who is trying to influence the form of service provision. Further, these multiple hats may not always fit the person neatly. To continue the above analogy, the nurse may, as a provider, wish for particular clinic opening times to meet her individual personal responsibilities but as a member may wish for more flexible times. Table 2.5 gives examples of the three overlapping groups.

Table 2.5
Examples of members, stakeholders and actors

Category	Definition	Examples
Health system members	Those whom the health system is set up to serve	All resident individuals in the country
Stakeholders	Those with an interest in the health system	All health system members Health care providers Health care funders Advocacy organisations Academic organisations Commercial ventures providing inputs to the health system Commercial ventures concerned about health promoting restrictions

Table 2.5 continued

Table 2.5 continued

Category	Definition	Examples
Actors	Those attempting to influence decision-making in the health system	Active health system members who are actively attempting to influence the health system design or operation
		Health care providers who are actively attempting to influence the health system design or operation
		Health care funders who are actively attempting to influence the health system design or operation
		Academics actively attempting to influence the health system design or operation
		Advocacy organisations
		Commercial ventures providing inputs to the health system who are actively attempting to influence the health system design or operation
		Commercial ventures concerned about health promoting restrictions and who are actively attempting to influence the health system design or operation

Any analysis of the health system needs to understand these groups and their interest and activities in the system. Examples of these stakeholders include:

- *The users and non-users of the health service*: non-users may have no current needs, have constraints hindering usage or they may be future users
- *Providers of health care*: see below for some of the key groupings in this category
- *Suppliers of resources*: these include both commercial companies providing hardware and medical supplies and training bodies responsible for 'providing' health professionals
- *Advocacy organisations* with a particular interest in a specific health issue or a professional group (such as a medical association)
- *Academic researchers* interested in understanding how elements of the health system operate
- *Professional policymakers, planners and managers*
- *State bureaucrats, staff of social security agencies and local government*
- *Politicians* whose interest in the health system may reflect an interest in social justice and health promotion, or may be more related to general power or self-advancement.

In order to analyse the function of any particular health system, it is necessary to identify the key stakeholders and actors, their different roles and interactions, their interests and motivations. It is also important to understand how these change over time. Underlying this are their values and motives. A key governance question for any health system relates to the relative rights of any particular group to influence decision-making. This 'political' aspect of the health system is often forgotten, or a naïve assumption made either of shared objectives or of the medical supremacy in health decision-making. However, the reality is that health policy and the resultant use of scarce resources is heavily contested, though not always explicitly.

Health care providers are a key group within the aforementioned list and it is important to recognise the potentially wide range of providers. This includes:

- publicly funded and managed services
- private-for-profit commercial organisations or individual professionals
- non-governmental providers
- occupational health provision
- informal health care providers including pharmaceutical outlets
- traditional providers of health care
- self-care

Various points need to be made at this point, but will be expanded upon in subsequent chapters. First, there is often a tendency within public policy to focus on public sector provision. Yet, there are few countries that do not have significant private health care. Self and family care/ treatment is also widespread and though often unrecognised by health professionals, it is a major response by individuals to many basic illnesses.[65] This may be for good reasons, where effective self-treatment is available but, unfortunately, may also be the result of either financial constraints or ignorance. Self-care also has a major caring role in parallel with medical interventions. Indeed, it has been estimated that between 65 and 85 per cent of all health care is provided by the individual or the family, without professional intervention, using folk, non-allopathic or allopathic technology.[66] Closely related to self-care are 'informal' services provided by street pharmacists and unlicensed practitioners. Within this category, traditional practitioners often belong, though there may be associations of such practitioners which leads to regulation and hence 'formalisation'. Policy needs to respond to this wide range of types of activity.

Second, the boundaries between these providers are increasingly blurred, again raising a challenge for health policy. Two examples illustrate this. There are many health systems where professionals may work in the public sector *and* have a private practice. Furthermore, the growth of publicly financed private provision makes definitions of public and private hard to sustain. Both examples can be illustrated in the UK NHS—the first through hospital consultants with parallel private practice, the second through the primary care general practitioners who, though publicly funded, are effectively 'private' in managerial terms.

Third, it is important in policy terms to consider not only the performance of these providers on their own terms but also the interrelationships between them. Such interrelationships may be at the level of patient referrals or at the level of sharing or taking resources (such as professional staff). They may also be at a more nebulous level in terms of influencing values, culture and attitudes—as we have seen with the permeation, in many health systems, of private sector values into the public sector.

One key role of the central state agency in health is ensuring the regulation of their activities. We explore issues related to regulation in Chapter 3.

5.6 Resources to Provide Services and Advocacy

In order to carry out the two key functions of health service delivery and action for inter-sectoral health, resources are needed. Some of these—such as staff, consumables, buildings and transport—are common to any activity. However, there are various characteristics of the health system that mark it out. First, health service provision is a very labour-intensive activity with a high level of skill required in professional cadres. This high level of 'professionalism' also carries with it particular issues in terms of governance and power structures. Second, it is also reliant on technology, both in the form of specialist equipment and medical supplies. Lastly, its information requirements include both specialist health information and management-related information. The management of such resources is critical both to the achievement of the health system goals and its efficiency.

Underpinning these resources is the need for finance. The level of finance devoted to health care varies between 1 and 18 per cent of Gross National Product (GNP) representing a range of per capita expenditure between low- and high-income countries of between US$ PPP 14–6,000.[67] The way in which finance is raised for health services has been the subject of much policy debate in recent years with the three key national mechanisms being user charges, social insurance and taxation; in low-income countries, this may be significantly supplemented with external funding. Each of these financing mechanisms has major implications both for the equitable distribution and uptake of health care and the signals they send to providers through incentives. We discuss the effect of different financing mechanisms on the health system further in Chapter 4.

5.7 Processes

In order to translate resources into services and advocacy, processes are required. We suggest that there are five essential processes for a health system. First, there is a requirement that the health system is given direction in the form of policies and plans that set objectives and priorities both in terms of programme areas and the system itself. Second, as we have seen in the previous section, resources need to be generated—and in particular, finance needs to be collected to allow these plans to be implemented through the generation of resources such as training and employment of health professionals. Third, there are processes of management whereby the resources are combined to deliver services or to undertake inter-sectoral action for health. Last, there is governance (including regulation) which we interpret as relations of power and authority in the health system. These relations penetrate all the other health systems processes and have a major impact on how they operate.

Within each of these broad areas, there are sub-processes and we explore these in more detail in the rest of the book. Examples include financial management, personnel management, resource allocation and professional regulation. One key issue for any health system is ensuring that such processes and sub-processes act in a consistent and concerted fashion. For example, management processes need to both influence and be tailored to implement set policies and plans. Such processes not only need to be evidence-informed, but also need to respond to the wider values of the health system. Thus, a health system that values participation by communities and other stakeholders needs to develop processes that allow and indeed encourage this.

5.8 Context

The health system operates within a wider context—those aspects of the environment that have a significant impact on health and the health system and are also affected by health and the health system. This context reflects the wider political system and its dominant ideology, the socio-economy and the general social cultural values and mores. It also reflects current policies and practices in other sectors. The particular context facing the health system has a number of features that make its analysis both complex and important. These include the particular issues that health focuses on—including matters of life and death, making its cultural and ethical treatment particularly important, the nature of the provision of health care and in particular the relation-ship between health professionals and the (potential) service user, the fast changing nature of technology and ethical questions relating, for example, to issues such as cloning and transplantation.[68] The wider context also incorporates the regional and international place of the nation and international relations. All these have implications for the current health system. There are three features of the context that we wish to emphasise at this point.

First, we do not see the context as some sort of embroidery to be stitched onto the analysis of the health system at some convenient point. Rather, it needs to permeate the analysis showing why features of a health system are as they are, why contradictions appear, why changes are on the policy agenda and the prospects for producing change. Consideration of this context is critical for the development of the health system and its policies. As we saw earlier in the chapter, one of the failures of the reform movement of the 1990s can be attributed to a failure to consider adequately the wider context of particular health systems, but to assume a single solution irrespective of the wider context. Our framework reminds us of the all-pervading nature of the context that surrounds the health system.

Second, we need to be aware of the different approaches we can adopt in interpreting the context. At the risk of oversimplification, we suggest combining two approaches—synchronic and diachronic. The former shows the context at a particular point of time—a sort of cross section of the health system and its context (for example, the present proportion of the GNP spent on health in a country). The latter looks to explain the historic contradictions and development of the health system (for exam-ple, how the power of the medical profession or the particular mixture of funding emerged over time in a health system).

Third, our approach needs to be ever vigilant in that the context is fluid and changing. We need to be aware of the economic, political and social changes in a society and how these impact the health system. Part of that change can be traced to the health system itself. Those who work in health systems should not view the context as immutable. For ex-ample, where the local context includes communities with low levels of consciousness around health, then work can be done to raise that consciousness. Where powerful capitalist groups seek to impose their interests on the health system by putting profit before the health interests of the citizens, then political coalitions need to be developed to change the political scene. We discuss these issues in Chapter 3 and again in Chapter 8.

5.9 Strengthening Health System Capacity

Health systems throughout the world need strengthening. This is particularly the case for those in low and middle income countries, as a result of the double challenge of low levels of resources and high health needs. Throughout the book we will be both attempting to identify the causes of poor performance and, related to our values, suggest how they can be addressed. Underlying this is the need to strengthen the capacity of the health system and we particularly return to this in Chapter 8. Development strategies have often focused on the issue of capacity, though different eras and different agencies have approached it in a number of different ways—from capacity building, strengthening and 'releasing', each giving a different slant on capacity. One definition of capacity is that of the United Nations Development Programme (UNDP) who see it as 'the ability of individuals, institutions and societies to perform functions, solve problems, and set and achieve objectives in a sustainable manner'.[69] This definition fits the needs of a health system well by both referring to the need to have and pursue clear objectives and to carry out functions. We would add to this, however, the need to recognise and respond to social values.

However, this overarching definition of capacity needs operationalising. There is a general understanding that 'capacity'—in this case of the health system—needs consideration at three interdependent levels: the individual, the organisational and the enabling environment.[70] At the individual level, capacities refer to the skills and knowledge of people. Organisations provide the framework that can bring together individual capacities to deliver collective goals. The capacity of the enabling environment includes the overall policies, rules and values that affect the performance of the health system as a whole. In UNDP's words: 'These factors determine the "rules of the game" for interaction between and among organisations'.[71] Beyond the more immediate enabling environment are global trends and conditions that can affect the capacity of the health system.

A useful hierarchy of capacity needs is set out in Figure 2.8. This, though using different levels to those of the UNDP approach, highlights the interdependence of the different levels. Whilst throughout the book we will be looking implicitly at issues of capacity, we return explicitly to it in Chapter 8.

Figure 2.8
Capacity pyramid

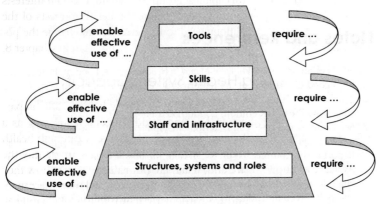

Source: Reproduced with permission from Potter and Brough. 2004.[72]

6 Final Thoughts

Debates on the health system have tended to coalesce around the PHC approach and neo-liberalism. While the former has emphasised equity, action on the social determinants of health and community participation, the latter looked more to limiting the state, expanding the role of the private sector in the financing and provision of health care, a shift to more individual forms of funding and the marketisation of the public sector. These different positions reflect strong differences in values. We argue in this book in favour of values of rights to health, equity, efficiency and effectiveness, participation and empowerment, transparency and accountability, sustainability, minimal negative environmental effects and wider social cohesion. The chapters in this book seek to show how these values can be developed throughout the health system in its aims and objectives together with the processes of governance, resource generation, planning, policymaking, management, inter-sectoral action for health and service delivery. In so doing, we point out the importance, among other things, of developing a proactive public sector, participatory governance, inter-sectoral action for health, transparency and democratising information use, decentralisation, regulating the role of the private sector, funding through collective forms of prepayment, evidence-based policymaking and planning, efficient resource management, management linking and service delivery with a view to improved quality of care, access and equity. This is a tall order and requires a broad process of capacity strengthening, to be discussed in Chapter 8. We turn now to look at governance of the health system, a key process which should permeate the other processes discussed in the book.

Notes and References

1. See Abel-Smith. 1976. *Value for Money in Health Services*. London: Heinemann for a good description of the historical developments of health systems.
2. Turshen, M. 1989. *The Politics of Public Health*. New Brunswick: Rutgers University Press, UK edition, London: Zed Books.
3. See Commission on Social Determinants on Health. 2008. *Closing the Gap in a Generation: Health Equity through Action on the Social Determinants of Health*. Report of the Commission on Social Determinants of Health, WHO, Geneva. Available at: http://whqlibdoc.who.int/publications/2008/9789241563703_ eng.pdf (accessed 12 March 2010) for a comprehensive and recent discussion and policy recommendations on issues of health determinants and inequity.
   The Chair of the Commission also led a review of similar issues in the UK: The Marmot Review (2010) *Fair Society, Healthy Lives*.
   A separate study has looked at the impact of inequalities on a variety of aspects of life in high-income countries and between the states of the United States: Wilkinson, R. and Pickett, K. 2009. *The Spirit Level: Why More Equal Societies Almost Always Do Better*. London: Penguin (see also http://www. equalitytrust.org.uk/).
4. See Gilson, L. 1989. 'What is the Future for Equity within Health Policy?' *Health Policy and Planning*, 4(4): 323–27 for a discussion of equity and Gwatkin, D.R. 2007. '10 Best Resources on Health Equity', *Health Policy and Planning*, 22(5): 348–51 for a list of useful equity articles.
5. Whitehead, M. 1992. 'The Concepts and Principles of Equity and Health', *International Journal of Health Services*, 22(3): 429–45.
6. See Cullis, G.G. and West, P.A. 1979. *The Economics of Health: An Introduction*. Oxford: Martin Robertson for a discussion of this.
7. We will, in the book, often refer to these extreme positions, recognising the existence of these other variations, to illustrate the effect of values. Readers will need to develop their own analysis for the specific political system in which they are interested.
8. A useful reference to equity issues and their measurement can be found in the Equity Gauge website http://www.gega.org.za/
9. Marmot, M. 2010. *'Fair Society, Equal Lives'*, The Marmot Review—*Strategic Review of Health Inequalities in England*. Available at http://www.marmotreview. org/ (accessed 16 November 2010).
   Wilkinson, R. and Pickett, K. 2009. *The Spirit Level: Why More Equal Societies Almost Always Do Better*. London: Penguin (see also http://www.equalitytrust. org.uk/).
10. WHO. 2010. *World Health Statistics*. Available at http://www.who.int/whosis/ whostat/EN_WHS10_Full.pdf (accessed 22 June 2010).
11. We recognise another interpretation of participation, often deployed by neo-liberals, that relates to the provision of finance or time by patients in the delivery of health services. However, we do not see this as participation

in the governance sense that we are concerned with here and as such do not discuss this.

12. http://www.nice.org.uk
13. Lawn, J., Rohde, J., Rifkin, S. et al. 2008. 'Alma-Ata 30 Years On: Revolutionary, Relevant, and Time to Revitalise', *The Lancet*, 372(9642), 917–27.
14. World Bank. 1993. *World Development Report 1993: Investing in Health*. New York: Oxford University Press.
15. Walsh, J.A. and Warren, K.S. 1979. Selective Primary Health Care: An Interim Strategy of Disease Control in Developing Countries, *New England Journal of Medicine*, 301(1 November): 967–94.
16. Lipsky, M. 1980. *Street-level Bureaucracy; Dilemmas of the Individual in Public Services*. New York: Russell Sage Foundation.
17. Labonte, R., Schrecker, T. and Sen Gupta, A. 2005. *Health for Some: Death, Disease and Disparity in a Globalizing World*. Toronto: Centre for Social Justice.
18. Buse, K. and Walt, G. 2000. 'Global Public–Private Partnerships: Part I—A New Development in Health?' *Bulletin of the World Health Organization*, 78(4): 550.
19. Buse, K. and. Harmer, A.M. 2007. 'Seven Habits of Highly Effective Global Public-Private Health Partnerships: Practice and Potential', *Social Science and Medicine*, 64(2): 259–71.
20. See Walker, L. 2009. *Global Health Initiatives (GHIs): Institutional Innovation and the Challenge to Development Evaluation*. Centre for the Study of Globalisation and Regionalisation, Working Paper 263/10. Available at http://www2.warwick.ac.uk/fac/soc/csgr/research/working/2010/26310.pdf (accessed 18 September 2012).
21. The Paris Declaration of 2005 and the subsequent Accra Agenda for Action of 2008 can be found at http://www.oecd.org/dataoecd/11/41/34428351.pdf (accessed 12 March 2010).
22. http://www.phmovement.org/(accessed 12 March 2010).
23. See, for example, the two Global Health Watch reports initiated by a collaboration between activist movements including the People's Health Movement. Available at http://www.ghwatch.org/(accessed 12 March 2010).
24. Labonte, R. and Suhrecker, T. 2007. *Towards Health-equitable Globalisation: Rights, Regulation and Redistribution*. Final Report to the Commission on Social Determinants of Health by Globalisation Knowledge Network. Institute of Population Health, University of Ottawa. Available at http://www.who.int/social_determinants/resources/gkn_report_06_2007.pdf (accessed on 18 August 2012).
25. CMH. 2001. *Macroeconomics and Health: Investing in Health for Economic Development*. Report of the Commission on Macroeconomics and Health. Available at http://whqlibdoc.who.int/publications/2001/924154550x.pdf (accessed 12 March 2001).
26. See UN. 2009. *The Millennium Development Goals Report*. http://www.un.org/millenniumgoals/pdf/MDG_Report_2009_ENG.pdf (accessed on 18 September 2012).
27. UN. 2000. http://mdgs.un.org/unsd/mdg/host.aspx?Content=indicators/official list.htm (accessed 30 April 2013).
28. WHO. 2008. *The World Health Report 2008—Primary Health Care (Now More Than Ever)*, WHO, Geneva. Available at http://www.who.int/whr/2008/en/index.html (accessed 12 March 2010).

See also Rawaf, S., De Maeseneer, J. and Starfield, B. 2008. 'From Alma-Ata to Almaty: A New Start for Primary Health Care', *The Lancet,* 372(9647), 1365–67.

29. WHO. 2008. *The World Health Report 2008: Primary Health Care (Now more than ever).* Geneva: WHO, p. xvi.

30. CSDH. 2008. *Closing the Gap in a Generation Health Equity through Action on the Social Determinants of Health Report of the Commission on Social Determinants of Health,* WHO, Geneva. Available at http://whqlibdoc.who.int/publications/2008/9789241563703_eng.pdf (accessed 12 March 2010).

31. CSDH. 2008. *Closing the Gap in a Generation Health Equity through Actions on the Social Determinants of Health Report of the Commission on Social Determinants of Health,* WHO, Geneva. Available at http://whqlibdoc.who.int/publications/2008/9789241563703_eng.pdf (accessed 12 March 2010).

32. CSDH. 2008. *Closing the Gap in a Generation: Health Equity through Action on the Social Determinants of Health. Final Report of the Commission on Social Determinants of Health.* Geneva: World Health Organization.

33. de Savigny, D. and T. Adam (eds). 2009. *Systems Thinking for Health Systems Strengthening.* Alliance for Health Policy and System Research. Geneva: WHO. Available at http://whqlibdoc.who.int/publications/2009/9789241563895eng.pdf (accessed 18 September 2012).

34. Roemer, M.I. 1991. *National Health Systems of the World,* Vol. 1, *The Countries.* Oxford: Oxford University Press.

35. Mills, A.J. and Ranson, A.K. 2012. The Design of Health Systems in Merson, M.H., Black, R.E. and Mills, A.J. (eds), *Global Public Health: Diseases, Programs, Systems and Policies.* Jones and Bartlett Learning, Third Edition, pp. 615–651. Boston: Jones and Bartlett Learning.

36. Mills, A.J. and Ranson, M.K. 2012. The Design of Health Systems in Merson, M.H., Black, R.E. and Mills, A.J. (eds). *Global Public Health: Diseases, Programs, Systems and Policies.* Jones and Bartlett Learning, Third Edition, p. 619, Figure 12–2.

37. WHO. 2000. *The World Health Report 2000: Health Systems: Improving Performance,* WHO, Geneva, p. 25.

38. WHO. 2000. *The World Health Report 2000: Health Systems: Improving Performance.* Geneva. WHO, p. 25, Figure 2.1.

39. WHO. 2001. *Report of the Scientific Peer Review Group on Health Systems Performance Assessment,* WHO, Geneva. Available at http://www.who.int/health-systems-performance/sprg/report_of_sprg_on_hspa.htm (accessed 16 March 2010).

40. For a full report on the technical aspects of the measurements underlying the WHO 2000 Report, see Murray, C.J.L. and Evans, D. 2003. *Health Systems Performance Assessment Debates, Methods and Empiricism.* WHO, Geneva.

41. WHO. 2001. *Report of the Scientific Peer Review Group on Health Systems Performance Assessment,* WHO, Geneva, p. vii. Available at http://www.who.int/health-systems-performance/sprg/report_of_sprg_on_hspa.htm (accessed 16 March 2010).

42. WHO. 2007. *Everybody's Business: Strengthening Health Systems to Improve Health Outcomes: WHO's Framework for Action.* Geneva: WHO, p. 3, Figure, 'The WHO Health System Framework'.

43. Mtei, G., Mulligan, J., Ally, M., Palmer, N. and Mills, A. (2007). *An Assessment of the Health Financing System in Tanzania* Report on SHIELD Work Package 1, SHIELD, Cape Town: Health Economics Unit, University of Cape Town.

44. Ministry of Labour and Employment, Government of India (n.d.) Rashtriya Swasthya Bima Yojna. Retrieved 4 January 2010 from http://www.rsby.in/

45. Frenk, J., Sepúlveda, J., Gomez-Dantéz, O. and Knaul, F. (2003). Evidence-based health policy: Three generations of reform in Mexico, *The Lancet,* 363(9396): 1667–1671.

46. Towse, A., Mills, A. and Tangcharoensathien, V. (2004). Lessons from the introduction of universal access to subsidised health care in Thailand, *British Medical Journal,* 328: 103–105.

47. Mills, A.J. and Ranson, M.K. 2012. The Design of Health Systems in Merson, M.B., Black, R.E. and Mills, A.J. (eds). *Global Public Health: Diseases, Programs and Policies.* Jones and Bartlett Learning, Third Edition, p. 617, Exhibit 12–1.

48. For a wider discussion of the role of values in development activities, see Crompton, T. 2010. *Common Cause: The Case for Working with our Cultural Values.* Available at http://www.wwf.org.uk/what_we_do/campaigning/strategies_for_change/?uNewsID=4224 (accessed 20 November 2010).

49. See, for example, an example of applying values to delivery aspects of the health system in Unger, J.P., Marchal, B. and Green, A.T. 2003. 'Quality Standards for Health Care Delivery and Management in Publicly Orientated Health Services', *International Journal of Health Planning and Management,* 18 (S 1): 79–88.

50. See J. Goldstein and Koehane, R.O. (eds). *Ideas and Foreign Policy: Beliefs, Institutions, and Political Change.* Ithaca and London: Cornell University Press.

51. WHO Constitution. Available at http://apps.who.int/gb/bd/PDF/bd47/EN/constitution-pdf (accessed 7 July 2012).

52. We return to this in the discussion on planning in Chapter 4.

53 See http://www.gega.org.za/ for more information on the Global Equity Gauge Alliance.

54. See Gwatkin, D.R., Bhuiya, A. and Victoria, C.G. 2004. 'Making Health Systems More Equitable', *The Lancet,* 364(9441): 1273–80 for a discussion of this.

55. We are conscious that for some readers, the term *member* may have connotations of voluntary membership in groups such as mutual societies. We stress that we are using the term to mean that all residents within a country (both citizens and non-citizens) are 'full and equal members' of the health system.

56. Economists recognize this perspective through the concept of social time preference and build it into their tools for assessing different interventions such as the use of discount rates in economic appraisal, usually, though not necessarily, giving greater priority to the present than to the future benefits.

57. Within the research community, there has been a long-standing debate between different researchers as to the worth of different research methods. Quantitative researchers often hold the RCT ups as the gold standard of research; they may disparage qualitative methods as having little scientific value, ignoring both the qualitative and interpretative aspects inherent in quantitative research and the limitations on the questions that quantitative research can answer. In reality, multiple forms of research are necessary and need to find ways of working together to harness their complementary nature.

58. See Green, D. 2008. *From Poverty to Power: How Active Citizens and Effective States can Change the World*. Oxford: Oxfam International. Available online at http://policy-practice.oxfam.org.uk/publications/from-poverty-to-power-how-active-citizens-and-effective-states-can-change-the-w-115393 (accessed 18 September 2012) for a strong justification for this position.
59. See the discussion later in the chapter on the term *member*.
60. Sen, M. 2001. *Development as Freedom*. Oxford: Oxford University Press.
61. This is often reinforced by the biomedical focus of professionals working within such ministries who are less comfortable with a wider social determinants approach to health.
62. CSDH. 2008. *Closing the Gap in a Generation Health Equity through Action on the Social Determinants of Health Report of the Commission on Social Determinants of Health*, WHO, Geneva. Available at http://whqlibdoc.who.int/publications/2008/9789241563703_eng.pdf (accessed 12 March 2010).
63. Walley, J. and Wright, J. 2010. *Public Health: An Action Guide to Improving Health*, Second Edition. Oxford: Oxford University Press.
Adams, L., Amos, M. and Munro, J. (eds). 2002. *Promoting Health: Politics and Practice*. London: SAGE Publications.
Ashton, J. and Seymour, H. 1988. *The New Public Health*. Milton Keynes: Open University Press.
64. For example, preventive services are sometimes divided into primary, secondary and tertiary activities which aim to stop individuals contracting diseases (primary prevention), or if contracted, limiting their effects (secondary and tertiary prevention). Curative activities can fall into the second and third categories.
65. See WHO SEARO. 2009. *Self-care in the Context of Primary Health Care*, Report of the Regional Consultation Bangkok, Thailand, 7–9 January for a useful overview of issues related to self-care.
66. Bhuyan, K.K. 2004. 'Health Promotion through Self-care and Community Participation: Elements of a Proposed Programme in the Developing Countries *BMC Public Health*', 4(16 April): 11.
67. Source: UNDP. 2009. *Human Development Report*. Available at http://hdr.undp.org/en/statistics/data/ (accessed 18 March 2010).
68. See, for example, Gauld, R. 2001. 'Contextual Pressures on Health—Implications for Policymaking and Service Provision', *Policy Studies*, 22(3/4): 167–79.
69. UNDP. 2008. *Capacity Development Practice Note*. New York: UNDP. Available online at http://www.undp.org/content/dam/aplaws/publication/en/publications/capacity-development/capacity-development-practice-note/PN_Capacity_Development.pdf (accessed 18 September 2012).
70. UNDP. 2008. *Capacity Development Practice Note*. New York: UNDP. Available online at http://www.undp.org/content/dam/aplaws/publication/en/publications/capacity-development/capacity-development-practice-note/PN_Capacity_Development.pdf (accessed 18 September 2012).
71. UNDP. 2008. *Capacity Development Practice Note*. New York: UNDP. Available online at http://www.undp.org/content/dam/aplaws/publication/en/publications/capacity-development/capacity-development-practice-note/PN_Capacity_Development.pdf (accessed 18 September 2012), p. 5.
72. Potter, C. and Brough, R. 2004. 'Systematic Capacity Building. A Hierarchy of Needs', *Health Policy Planning*, 19(5): 336–345, Figure 1.

3

Governance

1 Introduction

Governance in the health system refers to the way in which power, authority and responsibilities are exercised. It is particularly concerned with the manner in which decisions are made, the predominant values and ideologies of the health system and its institutional framework. It penetrates and affects all the key processes of the health system—financing, policymaking, planning, management, service delivery and regulation.

To explain the governance of a health system requires an understanding of its context and stakeholders. Social, economic and political power run through the health system and shapes the forms of health system governance. Stakeholders are the individuals and groups with a potential or actual interest in the operation and impact of the health system. They have values and ideologies and act to represent and further these interests. Power and authority in the health system are important for them. They have interests in access to decision-making, who pays for the funding of health care, how resources are used, the types of health care provided and to whom it is provided and the impact of the health system on the health of individuals and groups. The processes and structures of power and authority in the health system are fundamental to the way in which stakeholders are able to realise their interests.

How we interpret good governance depends on the values we hold and the aims and objectives of the health system. We have based this book on our own values of right to health and equity, efficiency, participative and accountable decision-making and long-term perspective. We also see a good health system as one that *has access to a level of resources commensurate with the national level of income and uses these resources in the most efficient way to ensure an equitable and maximised level of health which is sustainable over the long term and which empowers the citizens and other health system members in areas concerning their health.* We interpret good governance therefore as consisting of structures and processes of power, authority and responsibility that lead to the exercise of the above values and the development of this sort of health system.[1]

Good governance manifests itself in many ways. We view the concept of good governance through eight key features: a *proactive state* that takes the strategic lead in developing a good health system; *effective accountability* to ensure that those who are entrusted with responsibilities are answerable for what they do; the *decentralisation* of decision-making to provide a more efficient, needs-based and participative health system; *inter-sectoral action* to support action on the social determinants of health and inequity; a more *inclusive involvement* in decision-making processes and particularly among users, non-users and communities with a view to their empowerment; *ethical conduct* among stakeholders and represented in the correct use of resources to minimise corruption and disreputable behaviour in relation to a range of activities including patient treatment; effective *regulation* of activities in the health system particularly of the private-for-profit sector; and *transparency and democratising information.* In the rest of the chapter, we examine the implications for the health system of each of these in turn.

2 Proactive State

The neo-liberal approach to health reform we described in Chapter 2 has sought to limit the role of the state and widen the role of the private sector in the health system. We argue in what follows that the state needs to be proactive in the sense of having the power, authority and responsibility to take the strategic lead in the development of a good health system.

2.1 Potential of the State

The state has important *potential* strengths. It can have the political and democratic authority to provide the strategic lead in a health system and formulate and implement social goals relating to equity and human rights that go beyond, and indeed potentially limit, individual and group gain. It has the potential to mobilise and allocate significant amounts of resources to areas of health and health care need, organise a political coalition of support to develop progressive health policies, structure service delivery on the basis of universal and equitable access and formulate and implement regulations that control the behaviour of individuals and groups (and the range of service providers including the private sector) for better health and health care. The state can embody the rule of law which means that 'Legal frameworks pertaining to health should be fair and enforced impartially, particularly the laws on human rights related to health'.[2] Lastly, it has the potential to bring the systems of health, education, agriculture, industry and others together to work on the social determinants of health and associated inequality.

We recognise these are only *potential* strengths and that there are hefty constraints on their realisation. We examine these constraints in the next section.

2.2 Problems of the State

There are negative tendencies in the state that can reduce its capacity to achieve the potential outlined above. These may be presented as overlapping and interrelated syndromes of behaviour in the state—the *dormant* state, the *dependent* state, the *politically manipulated* state and the *hollowed out* state.

The *dormant state* shows a tendency towards inactivity in relation to aims of improving health and health care. In many respects, this is due to poor capacity. The dormancy can be manifest in a number of often-related and coexistent characteristics. There may be a lack of sustained growth in public sector expenditure on health, a low generation of resources commensurate with the income status of the country while the health system may be allocated a relatively low proportion of the overall government expenditure. India is a good example of this with only 3.4 per cent compared to 18 per cent in Malawi.[3]

This dormancy is not related solely, however, to a lack of resources. In such states, there may also be little in the way of new meaningful health policy initiatives and the national health plan, if it exists, does not give strategic direction to the health system. Resource allocation is based on last year's allocation rather than on criteria of health and/or health care need. There is little evidence of management objectives and decision-making. Administrative and bureaucratic practice dominates over management; following the rules is more important than setting and achieving objectives. Managers lack delegated authority and interest in taking initiative. Structures and processes of governance are weak. In this type of state, organisations in the health system do not receive the organisational and managerial space and autonomy to formulate and implement plans and programmes for improved health and health care. Health staff lack the skills, knowledge, values and motivation to provide effective health care. There is little interest in regulating the private sector; regulations may exist but they are not implemented. Lastly, the public health sector adopts a narrow and limited perspective to the health system, failing to take the initiative in getting health on the agenda in other sectors.

The *dependent state* is found among low-income countries where international aid takes on a significant role in funding and directing the health system. During the 1990s, this took the form of structural adjustment programmes forced on weak and indebted governments by international organisations such as the World Bank and IMF. These programmes required governments to adopt policies such as user fees, deflationary reductions in the fiscal deficit, limits on the role of the state and incentives for the development of the private sector. The important role played by bilateral and multilateral agencies, including the GHIs, within the decision-making of the health system is another facet of the dependent state. Ministries of Health are populated by short- and medium-term consultants, priorities of disease control are determined by international funding bodies and parallel systems of decision-making and programme implementation are developed. This suggests a measure of 'policy capture' by these international groups. This leads to both duplication and a diversion of resources and energies to internationally funded programmes; resources are sucked out of the general health services which are weakened as a result.

The *politically manipulated state* exists where individual and group political gains strongly influence decision-making in the health system, redirecting it away from the aim of improved and more equitable health. Dominant individuals and groups wielding political power are able to influence decision-making in key areas, such as paying for health services, location of health facilities, co-opting civil society groups for the manipulation of political control, awards of contracts to the private sector, implementation of health and health care regulations and employment of staff. The exercise of this influence can be a source of enrichment to these dominant individuals and groups and also a source of political support through patronage. It may also allow them to accumulate support among clients who gain from favours such as contracts and employment. The politically manipulated state can be another face of the dormant system; objectives of improved health and health care are sacrificed as powerful interests gain from both patronage and corruption.

In the *hollowed out* state the core of its operation adopts more individualistic values and activities. From a distance it looks like a public sector, but closer examination shows that it lacks the substance and values of the public sector. Many of the new set of values draws on the neo-liberal health sector reforms of the past 20 years. Health staff are primarily motivated by additional monetary incentives such as performance-related pay and bonuses and not by the responsibility to improve health and health care. Public sector health facilities are required to fund themselves, mostly through the sale of goods and services to consumers. Provider interests dominate over user interests on the type of health care to be provided. Market competition between service providers, both public and private, operates in health care delivery that is then more influenced by market signals rather than health and health care need. Health system funding is based on individual payments, such as user fees and private health insurance premiums and not collective pre-payment systems, such as progressive taxes and social health insurance. Health care users are treated as consumers who make 'choices' between funding systems and providers for service delivery. A variation of the hollowed out state is where corruption plays a significant part in resource use and we return to this below.

Actual state systems can approximate to one or more of these syndromes of poor performance. There are many reasons for these syndromes and their detailed analysis would constitute a study in itself. Suffice it to note that they raise major issues around the role of the state, its class and political control and international inequality. For example, the public sector can take on an employment role, soaking up increasing numbers of potentially unemployed people to avoid social and political unrest. Political manipulation and patronage are forms of political control. Neither is the health system immune from the international inequality in economic, social and political relations. We recognise that these underlying causes can constrain the development of a proactive state. However, we also recognise that there is potential for moving towards such a state as part of a general shift in international and national power relations.

2.3 Developing the Proactive State

None of the above forms of the state will deliver the sort of health system that is consistent with our values. Instead, we argue for a proactive state that takes action towards the development of the good health system, as outlined in Chapter 2. We indicated above the potential capacities of the proactive state. Table 3.1 provides a guide to the potential strengths and how they are developed and where discussed in this book. They require changes in the relations of power and authority in the health system and redirecting these relations in the direction of good governance.

In order to move towards a proactive state, there needs to be an enabling environment. Particularly important is the existence of

Table 3.1

Characteristics of capacity of the state required to realize its potential strengths

Potential strength	Capacity to…
Strategic lead	…play a lead and mediating role in the formulation of values and goals in the health system; …formulate and implement health policy and a national strategic health plan (see Chapter 5)
Resource generation and allocation capacity	…ensure a significant slice of GNP is used to fund the role of the state health sector that is commensurate with the national income (see Chapter 4); …allocate these resources in such a way as to meet the goals of the health system (see Chapters 4 and 5)
Political capacity	…generate a political coalition of support for the values of a good health system (as signalled in various chapters but particularly Chapter 2 and this one)
Management capacity	…bring together, combine and use resources in such a way as to meet the objectives of the health system (see Chapter 6)
Service capacity	…take the lead in providing services in such a way as to meet the key values, such as improved health and equity (see Chapter 7)
Regulatory capacity	…have the authority to formulate and implement regulations that control action in both the public and private sectors (as discussed in this Chapter)
Inter-sectoral capacity	… ensure that health is high on the policy agenda of other sectors and to develop legislative and regulatory capacity (as discussed in various chapters, but particularly this one and Chapters 5 and 7)

organised social and political groups in agreement with the values discussed in this book and able to support a proactive public sector. Social and economic progress and the opportunity to generate increased resources for the health system are also important, though this is not to suggest that low-income countries cannot develop a good health system. We argue that a good health system generates funds *commensurate with its level of national income*. International funding agencies need to be less directive in how and where funds are used and form part of more collective arrangements, such as SWAps. The legal and democratic legitimacy of government to formulate and implement regulations is also required as is the existence of a supportive public service for government health staff to achieve performance. However, enabling features are often absent. War, famine, economic recession, political repression and upheavals are just some of the problems. We still argue, however, that this should not lead to despair and a feeling of impotence but rather to strategies to develop the features of a health system as outlined in Table 3.1 *to the extent that is feasible within the existing context*. Our analysis recognises that the state is not powerless in modifying the context to make it more amenable to the good health system. For example, a political coalition needs to be developed and maintained that crosses the state–civil society boundaries and provides the political underpinning to a progressive health system. It is important that those in the state system who are responsible for health policymaking, planning and management recognise the political nature of their actions. The term *political* here refers not to the political patronage and manipulation described above. Neither is it limited to the affairs of political parties. Rather, it recognises the division of society into different groups and that effective use of power requires understanding of the relations of power and the process of negotiation, participation and consultation in decision-making. In support of this, we emphasise below the importance of making decision-making more inclusive and transparent as part of good governance.

3 Accountability

Accountability is one of the values we champion for the health system. Our interest in good governance is how we make this a reality. Within the health system, funds are collected and allocated, policies and plans are made and implemented, management and regulation are carried out and services are delivered. These processes involve responsibilities held by an extensive network of actors in the form of organisations, groups and individuals. Accountability is about making these actors answerable for what they do.[4] Quite simply, the effectiveness of accountability in the health system is a major determinant of whether the system works or not.

Accountability is referred to at various points in this book and particularly in Chapter 6. However, we stress five key points in this section.

First, effective accountability requires clarity in where responsibility lies for decision-making in the organisation. This is important as some organisations practice an opaque and informal regime of 'corridor' decision-making; decisions are made away from public scrutiny making the exercise of accountability almost impossible. Transparency requires clarity in where and how decisions are made with a more formal structure indicating the terms of reference, forms of involvement and the rights of decision-making. These structures can be, for example, the formal directorate, department and unit structure of the organisation, recognised committees (or similar groups) and the individual definitions of jobs. The important point is that there is a documented, accessible, common and transparent understanding of why, when and how these different structures operate. Chapter 6 refers to functional reviews of organisational structure and it is important that this whole structure of decision-making responsibility be part of that review. For example, to avoid the multiplication of committees it is also important that an organisation's network of formal group decision-making be regularly reviewed. Decisions need to be made on the functions and terms of reference (including their rights and responsibilities) and membership of committees, the rights of members to information and the role of external, including civil society organisations, to be consulted by committees. Committees do not have to be permanent—their 'permanence' should reflect their function and be fit for purpose. Standing committees, for example, would make sense, in monitoring equity on health policies while the less permanent committees would make sense for formulating a five-year health plan.

Second, accountability needs teeth; it is more than making those entrusted with responsibilities respond to others for information and explanations but must also involve potential sanctions.[5] These sanctions will vary but could range from, for example, community representatives publicly denouncing absentee health staff from the local health centre, to dismissal of staff for poor performance or imprisonment for corruption. Accountability should also involve positive rewards such as community recognition for good staff performance in the local health centre or staff promotion or new training opportunities for achievements in a job.

Third, accountability needs to permeate the health system and therefore should adopt diverse forms. There are many different forms of accountability.[6] For example, in Chapter 6 we refer to managerial, community, professional and political accountability in relation to a district health authority. There are also many different stakeholders in accountability processes. In the same case of the district health authority, we give examples of district level staff (District Health Officer, District Transport Manager), staff in health facilities (village health post), representative bodies (Village Health Committee, District Council), a team (District Health Team) and a professional body (Nursing Council).

Fourth, action to improve accountability must be guided by the key values of the health system. Criteria for assessing what happens through relations of accountability need to express these values and objectives such as equity and participation. At the same time we need to develop mechanisms of accountability that realise these values. Communities and their representatives can make health care providers accountable through the sort of mechanisms for participatory governance identified later in this chapter. Efficiency requires that health workers and managers need to have their responsibilities clearly indicated; this is also essential for the exercise of accountability. Accountability mechanisms need to have a degree of sustainability in that they gain the confidence and recognition of the community. Greater transparency and accessibility to information is also a foundation for accountability, allowing those who exercise it to examine the performance and work of those with responsibility. Developing new mechanisms of accountability underpin any attempt to make the public sector proactive and requires more transparent, open and inclusive policymaking (see Chapter 4), the development of clear sets of responsibilities and organisational structures (see Chapter 6), improved procedures for contracting health services (see Chapter 7), improved procedures for supplies and financial management (see Chapter 6) and participatory governance, control of corruption, regulatory authority and developing a public service ethos (see this chapter).

Last, the way accountability is conducted needs to be periodically updated taking account of the changing context and recognising the major challenges facing changing health systems. A good example is the case of international funding through the global health initiatives referred to in Chapter 4. Research has uncovered the '... *fragmented, complicated, messy and inadequately tracked state of global health finance* ...',[7] which raises critical issues of accountability, particularly concerning those funds that pass through the private sector. Indeed, the rapid growth of the private sector in funding and service provision in some countries raises important questions as to how the private sector is made accountable. To rely on user choice and market solutions suggested by those of a more neo-liberal persuasion reduces accountability to individual recourse of choice and downplays the greater strength users and non-users have in groups and community. In part, the accountability of the private sector is an issue of regulation and greater transparency of information discussed below. Public contracting of private providers also raises crucial issues of the division of responsibilities and accountability between the public and private sectors. Governments need to respond to these challenging, complex and rapidly changing forms in health systems.

4 Decentralisation

The public sector is highly centralised in many countries. Under such models, authority is retained at the centre of the health system (typically in the Ministry of Health) with decision-making in key areas such as policy, staff matters and financial management being in the hands of central bureaucrats. There are, of course, strong arguments for central control over some of these areas. These include the development of national-level policies where national consistency of approach is sought. This may be on the grounds of technical consistency, equity or economies of scale. It may also include control over the allocation of resources such as centrally raised revenue to ensure equity between different parts of the health system. One argument that has been advanced in defence of centralisation of management functions has been that the limited amount of managerial capacity suggests that this should be centralised, with lower levels of the health system having *administrative* rather than managerial functions. However, central bureaucratic controls can stifle innovation, delay decision-making, suppress health worker motivation and sense of ownership over health policy and distance decision-making from community health needs and service delivery. It is difficult to formulate and implement progressive policies for health development through centralised bureaucracies. Furthermore, the arguments that focus on a lack of low-level capacity are often tautological—there is a lack of capacity because capacity has not been nurtured at lower levels as there is no given managerial role. They are also sometimes deployed as a smokescreen to hide reluctance on the part of central managers to give up the benefits of power they enjoy.

Whilst centralisation has been the norm in many low-income countries, it is important to recognise that there are many models that have been in existence, which have given effective power to lower levels. Often these are based on district health systems and indeed in some cases go back to colonial periods where low-level colonial officers were given considerable autonomy, in part due to the poor communications with the central authorities. In this section, we look at the overall process of decentralisation and the different models and the relationships with the health system values.

Decentralisation is a process in governance whereby responsibilities, authority and resources are moved from the centre to the periphery.[8] The term can also be used to describe a situation where the periphery possesses a significant amount of responsibilities, authority and resources. We are using it in both these senses. It can occur in both the public and the private sectors; in what follows, we are referring to the public sector. Decentralisation has also been seen by some to include a shift of resources from the public to the private sector. However, we do not regard the transfer of resources, authority and responsibilities to the private sector as decentralisation but as privatisation.[9] Decentralisation has been a prominent policy for some health systems for some years, although it has not always been successfully formulated and implemented. In order to understand it and how it can be developed effectively, three key issues will be discussed: the diversity of decentralisation, its benefits and problems and a framework for making it effective.

4.1 Diversity and Decentralisation

Policymakers have to choose the type of decentralisation to be pursued in a country; to do this they need to know the available options and how to assess them. Decentralisation varies greatly from one country to another, particularly in the way it fits into different policies of health systems change and thereby the aims we attribute to it. In a PHC approach, decentralisation is seen as bringing decision-making nearer to communities, thus allowing for community participation and a better understanding of community health needs and how to achieve greater equity. It also gives the authority to local managers required for local inter-sectoral collaboration. Alternatively, decentralisation can be seen as an integral part of a more market/neo-liberal approach to reform. The justification for decentralising under such a policy is based on agency self-financing through, for example, user fees and the breaking up of inefficient large-scale bureaucracies into smaller more flexible and adaptable organisations. It is also seen as giving the authority to local managers as part of a managed market and can be seen by some as related to privatisation. Although there is some overlap in these approaches, they do lead to significantly different types of decentralised systems. We see decentralisation as being developed as part of a PHC policy which aligns with our proposed values.

Decentralisation can take on very different organisational forms.[11] The typical and formal categories are deconcentration, devolution and delegation. Deconcentration refers to the transfer of workload in a hierarchy of control whereby the periphery remains under the ultimate line management control of the centre. The former is given some authority, responsibilities and resources to act without having to seek the approval of the centre. A typical form is that of functional deconcentration (see Figure 3.1) wherein the transfers down the hierarchy take place within the line ministries, such as the Ministry of Health. While

Figure 3.1
Decentralisation as functional deconcentration

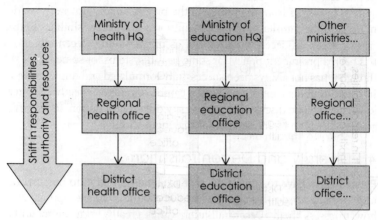

Source: Adapted from Collins. 1994.[10]

this allows for policy cohesion within the hierarchy, it nevertheless is, more often than not, a weak form of decentralisation and does not include clear and formal mechanisms at the district level for linking with either the community or other sectors; district officers tend to look upwards within the hierarchy to the source of authority and account-ability and not outwards. Mechanisms to develop inter-sectoral collaboration and community participation have to be added on to this type of decentralisation.

A variation on this system is that of integrated deconcentration (see Figure 3.2). In this case, the regional and district health officers lie under the authority of both the Ministry of Health and a separate line of control from a central office (such as the president or the Prime Minister) or another line ministry (such as a Ministry of Local Affairs). This is intend-ed to promote a more integrated approach at the decentralised level but raises the issue of how such dual authority will work. Country systems can vary in the nature of the authority held by the downward line within the Ministry of Health and the more diagonal authority of the Regional and District Commissioner.

Devolution refers to the transfer of authority between separate levels of government that possess multifunctional responsibilities, a le-gal identity, sources of income and are not subject to the line manage-ment authority of the higher level of government (see Figure 3.3). We would normally assume that the different levels include some form

Figure 3.2
Decentralisation as integrated deconcentration

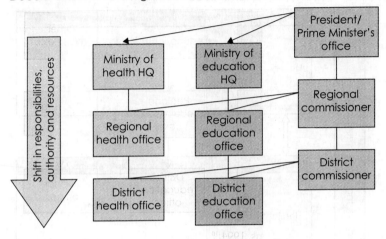

Source: Adapted from Collins. 1994.[12]

of elected authority. This introduces the possibility of greater local accountability and democracy but can raise questions about the level of cohesion within the government system and the capacity at the local level.

Delegation occurs where an agency is attached to, but semi-autonomous from, the parent organisation. Once again, there is no line management authority between the two. Instead, a contract or service-level agreement may be made between the two—as a separate funding organisation and a different provider agency. The latter then has dele-gated responsibilities. This is evident in semi-autonomous hospitals or a research agency with delegated authority but attached to a ministry (see Figure 3.4 for an example of a semi-autonomous hospital and a health research agency). As such, delegation is a form of the purchaser/provider separation and/or policymaking/policy implementation separation.

The forms of decentralisation found in a national health system only approximate to these 'classical' definitions often with elements of different approaches being present in a more hybrid form. Further-more, health systems change their forms of decentralisation over time. This results in a great variety of decentralisation among countries. In South Africa, for example, provincial governments are responsible for primary health care and will provide these services through its decon-centrated district system. Alternatively they can make service-level agree-ments with the devolved system of municipalities. The formal system of

Figure 3.3

Decentralisation as devolution

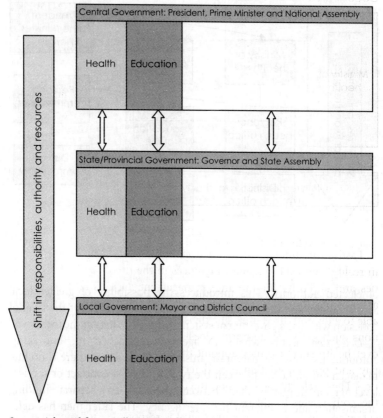

Source: Adapted from Collins. 1994.[13]

decentralisation in Ghana has a policymaking—implementation separation between the Ministry of Health and the delegated system of the Ghana Health Service. The latter operates a deconcentrated system of regions and districts. The District Assemblies have the function of monitoring the districts and also have some functions in relation to the district mutual health insurance scheme. It should also be noted that there can be significant differences between the formal system and the real situation of decentralisation. Local governments may, for example, appear autonomous on paper but financial and planning controls from the centre in practise impose centralisation on the system.

Figure 3.4
Decentralisation as delegation

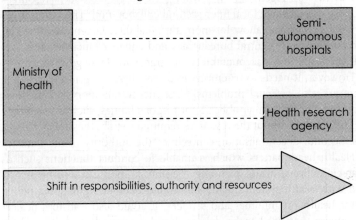

Lastly, the different forms of decentralisation (both on paper and in reality) can lead to major differences in the division of responsibilities and authority for funding, management and planning. Bossert[14] assesses this, for example, in his analysis of the 'decision space' available to a decentralised unit. The division of responsibilities raises questions such as: what authority does the decentralised authority have over health staff? Do they appoint their own staff and decide on staff pay and promotion? Can they determine their own spending priorities? These refer to decisions on the *use* of resources. The other side of the coin relates to the generation of such resources (including the extent to which the decentralised level is responsible for generating its own funding through, for example, user fees, loans and local taxes) and, where resources are allocated centrally, the criteria used for this allocation and the parameters within decisions on how such resources can be used.

4.2 Decentralisation, Benefits and Problems

As we suggest above, decentralisation has a number of potential benefits. Reducing the distance between government and communities offers the potential for community participation and empowerment, a better understanding of community health needs and thereby more appropriate and equitable health care. Moving the focus of government from the centre to the periphery and giving a voice to the periphery has the potential to shift resources to where they are most needed. The transfer of authority and responsibilities allows for greater local and community ownership together with a willingness to generate local resources and also can facilitate local inter-sectoral collaboration. This community ownership may also allow for more sustainability. Decentralisation can also cut out costly central bureaucracy and enhance efficiency and provide more improved accountability and transparency of government.

However, it needs to be emphasised that these are *potential* benefits; there are also *potential* problems. First, decentralisation is sometimes confused with reducing public sector responsibilities, such as when they are transferred without the resources required to fulfil these responsibilities. Second, decentralisation can reduce the authority of the Ministry of Health headquarters which is unable to conduct functions such as strategic national health planning. Decentralisation can also be associated with health system fragmentation and debilitating national public sector health programmes and services. It could also lead to a neglect of services that need to be delivered and organised centrally such as tertiary hospitals, national training programmes or drug quality assurance laboratories. Third, decentralisation can lead to greater inequity, particularly when the decentralised authority has to generate its own income. Forms of income, such as user fees and regressive local taxes, can lead to inequity. Poor areas will not be able to generate the same level of income as richer areas. Decentralisation can also be exercised as a mechanism of political domination through, for example, a divide and rule strategy and to pass power to locally dominant classes. The latter can use this power to further their own interests above those of the poor and vulnerable. Fourth, increased administrative costs can result from decentralisation, particularly when it means nothing more than a move from a single central bureaucracy to many local bureaucracies and where local managerial capacity is not invested in. Last, there may be a reduced emphasis on health care. Given their many responsibilities and potential lack of awareness of technical issues in health, local government may not pay sufficient attention to health care.

Once again we need to recognise that these are *potential* problems of decentralisation. Under appropriate conditions, they can be avoided. Furthermore, decentralisation's success depends on what is being sought by introducing decentralisation. Decentralisation is a chameleon-like process of change; it changes its form to suit the context, and in this case the policy context in which it has been developed. Decentralisation can be part of a strategy (usually not explicit) in one country to weaken the public sector and in another to strengthen the public sector. Whether decentralisation is effective or not depends on two groups of factors. First, the type of decentralisation programme and the values that underpin it—we outline what we believe this should consist of below. Second, the context; we need to recognise that decentralisation is not introduced in a vacuum but in a social, economic and political context. At national, local and community levels, the context can have an important impact on the formulation and implementation of decentralisation. For example, decentralisation will survive and perform better in districts with good political support and acceptance from the community. It will also do better where the economy allows for an expanding flow of both local funds and central allocations.

4.3 Making Decentralisation Effective

Given the potential benefits and pitfalls of decentralisation, how then can an agenda be developed for making decentralisation effective and consistent with the values we have espoused? Table 3.2 suggests a set of issues that such an agenda should include. Any programme for achieving decentralisation is not without its dilemmas. On the one hand we want to extend authority to those closest to the community and their health needs. On the other, we have no guarantee that local politicians and staff are interested in understanding and taking action on these needs. Dealing with dilemmas such as these requires a balance between central authority and local autonomy, promoting capacity strengthening at the local level and the development of local democracy and accountability. There are also paradoxes in decentralisation; while it is about improving local autonomy and strengthening the district, it nevertheless requires an effective central authority to give strategic guidance, provide support

Table 3.2
An agenda for effective health system decentralisation

Agenda item	Commentary
1. Formulating, implementing, monitoring and evaluating the decentralisation	This should be done in a manner consistent with policy-making as we set out in Chapter 5. Attention should be paid to defining the values upon which decentralisation is based, its aims and ensuring a good monitoring system to check on progress towards those aims. Phasing the implementation and learning from experiences are recommended. Good consultation with stakeholders and conducting in-depth analysis of how the different parts of the health system fit into the decentralisation is important to ensure that decentralisation is not seen as imposed from 'outside' onto the health system.

Table 3.2 continued

Table 3.2 continued

Agenda item	Commentary
2. Organising decentralisation	This requires determining the forms of decentralisation to be introduced and clarifying key issues, such as how the national health programmes fit into the decentralised system and the extent to which service delivery shifts from a top-down vertical form to a more integrated one (see Chapter 7). The organisational systems and authority at the different levels need to be determined. Priority needs to given to the district[15] level (or the sub-district level depending on the size of the district) as the principal level for the development of primary health care services.
3. Determining the responsibilities, authority and resources at the different levels	Resources, responsibilities and authority go together – all must be present and interrelated. Responsibilities at the district level will include: formulating and implementing a district health plan, undertaking resource management (financial, staff, information and logistics); conducting community health programmes; directing government health units such as the district hospital, health centres and health posts; regulation, support and collaboration with the private-for-profit and NGO sector; ensuring links with other sectors in support of the health agenda; developing community participation. In turn the centre has to change by becoming a more strategic, supportive, and regulatory level. Most, but not all, of its more operational responsibilities will be transferred.
4. Determining resource generation and allocation	The level of resources to be generated locally compared to those allocated from the central level need to be decided. Criteria for central resource allocation need to be determined which are consistent with the values particularly of equity and efficiency. Particular attention needs to be paid to developing equity between districts.
5. Decentralising national health planning	Decentralised agencies need to be incorporated into the planning system. They need to assess their community health needs and priorities through local planning and these should be transmitted to the central planning process. The latter should, in turn, clarify national values, objectives, systems and priorities to the local level and couple this to the

Table 3.2 continued

Table 3.2 continued

Agenda item	Commentary
	resources to be allocated. Key aspects of the national planning process are this exchange and negotiation between centre and periphery and therefore the development of an appropriate balance between national targets and local needs.
6. Strengthening the decentralised health system	The capacity of the centre and the districts plus delegated agencies (such as hospitals) need to be strengthened for their new roles and new aims; systems, organisational structures, and staff skills need to be developed. For example, it may be necessary to develop the importance of investing in health and health care among local politicians and staff.
7. Clarifying accountability and community involvement	Participation and accountability do not develop automatically with decentralisation; they have to be worked at. The mechanism and structures need to emerge as discussed in this chapter and Chapter 6. Clear documentation of these mechanisms and structures need to be developed and made publicly available.
8. Developing inter-sectoral collaboration	Intersectoral collaboration will not happen automatically with decentralisation; mechanisms need to be developed (such as joint budgets and cross-involvement in sectoral plans) to allow its development (see the following text and Chapters 6 and 7).

and monitor change. This is important to avoid fragmentation of the health system and ensure cohesion around key values.

5 Inter-sectoral Action for Health (IAH)

Our definition of the health system recognises that improved and more equitable health depends on more than health services; it is affected by a wide range of economic, social and environmental factors. These include (changing) climate, levels and forms of employment and incomes, housing, transport, access to adequate drinking water and sanitation, nutrition, education and tobacco and alcohol consumption. Intertwined in these social determinants are social and economic inequalities based on social class, gender, ethnic groups and age. These are transferred into and become an integral part of the inequity within the health system. The WHO has in recent years raised the profile of the wider determinants of health in two important initiatives; the Framework Convention on Tobacco Control in 2005 (see http://www.who.int/fctc/en/) and the Commission on Social Determinants of Health[16] (CSDH) which drew out the important link between social determinants and equity and proposed an overall strategy of '... *improving daily living conditions ... tackle the inequitable distribution of power, money and resources ... measure and understand the problem and assess the impact of action ...*'[17] Some countries and states have gained a reputation for taking a broad view of health and focusing, alongside health care, on the wider determinants of health. For example, Kerala state in India, Cuba and Sri Lanka are often cited as having an above average (for their income level) set of health indicators which are attributed to wider strategies in areas such as female education. However, for many health systems, crossing the sectoral boundaries remains a significant policy challenge.

Issues related to the social determinants of health and how they are dealt with by the health system are discussed in various parts of this book. In particular, we refer to Inter-sectoral Action for Health (IAH) in Chapter 7. Here we bring together governance issues around IAH. Two such issues will be discussed: instilling IAH into the health system and the politics of IAH.

5.1 Instilling IAH into the Health System

Whilst we may presume that the Ministry of Health is the natural leader of IAH, in practice it has, in most countries, failed to live up to this, restricting its focus largely to medical practice, and within this on curative and, to some degree, personal preventive action. The attempt to cross-sectoral boundaries in pursuit of a broad health agenda is a long-standing challenge to policymakers, and there is no single clear solution. The PHC strategy of Alma Ata referred to multi-sectoral collaboration and in the 1980s there were attempts to develop coordinated cross-sectoral policies particularly through the mechanism of national coordinating committees. Such committees had little power however and were often reducing to a role of 'talking-shops'. The challenge of HIV/AIDS and the recognised need for cross-sectoral strategies led to the development of specific institutions in some countries such as National AIDS Commissions organisationally housed at high levels of government such as the President's office. However, most aspects of life have a health dimension; this solution of involving high-level political leverage cannot be available for *all* these health issues and such an approach would lead to a proliferation of unmanageable cross-sectoral agencies. Governments continue to struggle with seeking ways to discourage excessive division of organisational labour and what has been called 'silo' mentalities between the different sectoral boundaries. Given this, one can see the need for two clear organisational strategies in government. First, a department that has an organisational remit, to which it is held to account, to point out the inter-sectorality of health issues, to advocate for health-promoting activities and indicate the health-constraining nature of specific sectoral policies. Whether this is the Health Ministry or another department will depend largely on whether the Health Ministry is able to overcome the vested medical interests and perspectives referred to above. Second, the supreme organisational organs of government (which may be the President's office or the Cabinet) together with the legislative bodies, need to recognise, and be held to account for, their responsibilities to impose inter-sectoral action. This organisational authority needs to be backed up by values and politics and it is the consideration of these that we now turn to.

An important theme in this book is how IAH needs to permeate health system processes of financing, policymaking planning, management, regulation and service delivery. Developing values supportive of IAH play a key role in this. The broad and underlying values of the health system need to focus attention on the health system and not just the health *care* system. The values of equity and empowerment are also bound up with our understanding and action upon the social determinants. The right to participation by health system members, as discussed in Chapter 2 and this chapter, rejects the ideas and practices behind the near exclusive domination in most countries of a restricted medical approach. Challenging the medical dominance in the health system, and more specifically in an organisation like a Ministry of Health, requires many changes. These include the opening up of opportunities for employment and promotion of other health professionals and non-health professional people, changing the medical bias in health information systems to capture the social determinants and changing the perspective of health policymaking, planning and budgeting to focus on health and not just health care. In Chapter 7 we present a simple framework for IAH consisting of health needs assessment, three basic strategies of joint programmes between sectors, advocacy for health and legislation and regulation. This is followed by monitoring of IAH which feeds into the health needs assessment. To back this framework up, we recognise that IAH also requires a more inclusive strategy of relations with stakeholders. Communities can possess a less institutionally focused and hence a much more open perspective on the determinants of health and the type of inter-sectoral action required. Furthermore, the idea of 'working to-gether' is based on the notion that no single organisation or intervention has the whole solution; there are networks of organisations that need to work together and that policies to improve health need to approach the problem from many different angles. As Chapter 6 indicates, the development of outward-looking management and a culture of trust are important in securing better inter-organisational links.

5.2 IAH and Politics

We need to recognise that politics is an important feature of IAH. The nature and immensity of the changes required to respond to the so-cial determinants of health and the related inequality together with the mechanisms of change affect and stir dominant interests in society. For example, to advocate for a living wage affects the rate of profit of the owners of capital; to provide good water, sanitation, housing and edu-cation requires dedicating increased amounts of GNP to these areas; to develop an inter-sectoral focus in the health system affects dominant medical approaches and interests; to improve environmental conditions in areas of industrial pollution involves regulating the activities of pow-erful industrial interests.

Any IAH therefore requires us to understand the groups involved in the process and how they could fit into the policy process. This can be facilitated through a stakeholder analysis[18] for a particular area of IAH by asking about the stakeholders, their interests, their interactions and their power in the decision-making process. As an example, Box 3.1 lists possible stakeholders for improving road safety.

In Chapter 5 (Box 3.5), we look at the roles assumed by actors in the policymaking process. We use these groups below to illustrate how groups could be involved in a process of inter-sectoral policymaking (see Box 3.2).

There is a need in IAH to balance collaborative action with the use of political authority. This book argues strongly in favour of collabora-tion in health systems processes; every attempt should be made to work together, bridging the differences between various sectors and tackling inequality and the social determinants of health. There is, however, a limit to voluntary collaboration. Entrenched and privileged interests do not necessarily give up their power through simple collaboration. Agreements may be reached only as a result of social, political and eco-nomic pressure and conflict. At the same time, IAH can be the imposition of change, not as the result of agreement but as the result of political and social movements and political coalitions for better health and equity.

Box 3.1 Potential stakeholders for road safety

Public sector

- Central government – executive: Ministries of Transport, Industry, Health, Justice
- Special national agency for road safety
- Central government – legislature: Parliamentary committees and councils such as the Parliamentary Advisory Council for Transport Safety in the UK
- Sub-national governments: Provincial and local governments concerned with local safety and passenger transport by roads
- Police: Particularly for the regulation and control functions

Private-for-profit sector

- Manufacturers of vehicles
- Insurance companies
- Vehicle maintenance and repair organisations
- Transport companies (haulage)
- Passenger transport
- Companies with vehicle fleets

Civil society

- Pressure groups, such as Mothers Against Drunk Driving in USA and Drive Alive in South Africa, car driver groups (such as Automobile Association)
- Professional groups (for example, health professions)
- Citizens (for example, neighbourhood associations)
- Media

Sources: Various including Peden et al. 2004.[19]

Box 3.2 Involvement of groups and actors in policy-making for inter-sectoral links and involvement

Policy makers: They possess the final power to *make* policy. Decisions to ban smoking in public places will be made at the highest political level while more operational joint programmes to improve road safety in a town may be made at the municipal level.

Policy leaders: Controversial policies, for example, to control alcohol abuse and restrict gun control may need an individual or group to champion and *lead* the process of setting a policy. They are the figureheads of the process.

Policy facilitators: Evidence of the health problem needs to be gathered and presented, different groups consulted, coalitions of support to be developed,

Box 3.2 continued

Box 3.2 continued

and continuity given to the policy-making process. These need to be people capable of maintaining and working with issue networks and policy communities.

Policy analysts: The links between social determinants and health status are not always clear. Specialised people and groups able to analyse the evidence in different contexts are important in doing this, in addition to systematically setting out the possible options and criteria for decision-making. A good example of this is the summary of research presented by Global Health Watch[20] showing the strong link between women's education and women's health, health-seeking practices and use of health care.

Policy advocates: These could be civil society organisations advocating for measures on, for example, rural land reform to allocate land to the rural landless and poor as a means of improving health and welfare, as in the case of the Movement of Rural Landless Workers.[21]

Evidence providers: The link between the social determinants and health is often complex and disputed. Interests will dispute the links and put pressure on decisions on interventions. Coalitions to improve health need people to gather, analyse and present robust evidence to the policy process.

Policy implementers: Joint programmes linking organisations are particularly complex in their funding flows, organisational structures, management systems and monitoring processes. Those responsible for regulation need to breach the implementation gap often found in countries. Action to improve water supply, sanitation, roads and housing in shanty towns involves working with a wide range of agencies attached to municipal governments and civil society, in addition to state and national level agencies.

Policy evaluators: This role may be taken by the policy advocates and/or the evidence providers. Given the controversial and complex nature of interventions to affect the social determinants of health, the political neutrality of the evaluators and the difficulty of signalling attribution are problems in the evaluation.

Box 3.3 illustrates this with the case of the movement to protect breastfeeding against the profit interests of multinational corporations. Regulations to limit the use of powdered milk have an important impact on child health.

Box 3.3 The movement to protect breastfeeding

Poor breastfeeding practices lead to health problems for infants and this has been associated with the marketing of powdered substitutes for breast-milk by companies such as Nestlé. The latter have engaged in intensive advertising, giving out free samples and associating powdered milk with visions of good

Box 3.3 continued

Box 3.3 continued

health and good motherhood. Research has shown a significant impact of the use of powdered substitutes on higher child morbidity and mortality. There is an International Code of Marketing Breastmilk Substitute (approved by the World Health Assembly) and the International Baby Food Action Network has played an international role in promoting the Code. There has also been an international campaign to pressure Nestlé to stop its marketing of substitutes.

In the Philippines, high-level legal conflicts have surrounded government attempts to ban the advertising; the result determined by the Supreme Court in the Philippines has been restrictions on the advertising. During the conflict, baby food companies were able to mobilise large resources to campaign for their interests.

Legal battles against the multinationals in India have also been prominent as civil society groups such as the Breastfeeding Promotion Network of India and the Association of Community Action on Safety and Health sought to counter the resources mobilised by baby food companies. *'The Indian experience demonstrates how the sustained advocacy and action by civil society groups can influence public opinion and decision makers'.*[22] It also showed the importance of constantly monitoring the action of the companies, media support, developing links with political party representatives and updating the legal regulations.

Source: Global Health Watch. 2008.[23]

6 Participatory Governance

6.1 Values and Participation

We see participative decision-making as a value in itself to underpin the health system. In this section we look at the means to develop this through participatory governance. We have argued in favour of a more inclusive involvement of stakeholders and health system members (individuals, groups and organisations with actual and/or potential interests in the health system) from two perspectives—that of rights and of pragmatism. It is important to see participation both as an end in itself and as a pragmatic means to improving the capacity of the health system to meet health needs and improving efficiency and effectiveness of the health system.[24] Greater involvement is also a key feature of the other values we have espoused, as explained in Table 3.3.

6.2 Shifting Participation

Changing the forms of governance to allow greater participation is a challenge fraught with tensions and contradictions. First, the social,

Table 3.3

Relevance of participation to the health system values

Values	Relevance to participation
Right to health and equity	Opening up the health system to diverse and popular interests can break narrow medical control over policy-making and provide a broader perspective on health and its social determinants. Greater openness in participation can lead to a voice in decision-making to those social groups underserved by the current system.
Efficiency	The representation of local community groups can lead to less costly and more local management processes that take into account local knowledge. More open participation provides decision-making with better understanding of community health needs and provides a basis for policy to be more informed to take the appropriate action
Transparency and accountability	Local community groups can play an important part in monitoring service delivery and holding providers to account for their performance. In so doing these groups can demand and use health and health care information that is openly available.
Longer term perspective	Participation can lead to a greater sense of ownership in that health interventions are not viewed as imposed from outside but generated locally. This acceptance and agreement can improve both effectiveness and sustainability.

economic and political contexts provide different opportunities and problems for the exercise of a more inclusive health system. For example, war, poverty, famine, fragile states and political repression limit opportunities for the exercise of a more inclusive decision-making process. Second, the exercise of power in society points to the fact that the stakeholders do not operate as equals. Some have more resources and power than others. Related to this, the structure and processes of the health system are not politically neutral. They give preferential access to some stakeholders over others. There is a strong history of research and analysis that has shown the way in which more powerful groups can control the decision-making processes, keep issues off the agenda and dominate the ideology and consciousness of powerless groups.[25] Redirecting a health system according to new values will require a shift in the access of stakeholders within the health system. We do not underestimate the difficulties represented in such changes that go far beyond the boundaries of the health system and are rooted in the overall polity of a country. Yet, neither do we accept the inevitability and immobility of popular exclusion nor the unchallenged domination of the powerful.

The changes in a health system for more inclusive participation are many and interdependent. These changes are not context-free; they are facilitated and often come on the wave of social, economic and political change. Their contextual character means that they cannot be easily transplanted from one country to another. There is no universal blueprint of how we can introduce a new participatory system. At the risk of oversimplification, we suggest that the changes need to involve three processes: reducing, restructuring and opening access to different groups. In other words, the change in governance is not about removing the bias built into the health system and its decision-making but shifting its partiality and bias. That is, the predisposition of the health system to favour the access of certain groups over others needs to be restructured. Which groups are involved in this restructuring will vary from one society to another, although certain tendencies may be identified in LMICs.

6.2.1 Reducing Participation of Over-represented Groups

Some groups have excessive influence and control in the health system. Their privileged position contradicts the values and overall goals of the system. As such, control needs to be exercised over the access to power and authority by such sectional interests, removing their control over the processes and structures of decision-making.

Sectional interests have been criticised for their excessive exercise of control over health systems in low-income countries. An oft-criticised group is the multinational pharmaceutical companies viewed in terms of 'the corrupting influence of profit-driven pharmaceutical companies on health professionals, academics and regulatory bodies'[26] Within health systems, similar profit motives can lead to behaviour by a variety of organisations from building firms through to tobacco companies, concerned that health policies may affect their interests. However, profit is not the only driver of sectional interests. International agencies may seek to influence health systems to enhance their more general regional political influence or to protect home populations against the spread of infection. This can often be significant and distorting of national policy processes. It can also absorb significant energies from the policy processes where external funders have different and potentially conflicting interests.

Within countries, urban upper- and middle-class groups may lobby to ensure privileged access to hospital care despite the detrimental effects this may have on rural poor populations.

Reducing the control and influence of these traditionally dominant interests would be a significant step in the direction of a more
democratic and participatory health system. For example, the strong financial and political pressures exerted by multilateral and bilateral international agencies over decision-making in low-income health systems
(particularly during the 1990s with structural adjustment programmes)
have been partially replaced by debt reduction, general and sectoral budget support and sector-wide approaches (see Chapter 4). These set up
new requirements linked to, for example, agreements around Poverty
Reduction Strategy Papers. Nevertheless, the influence of the bilateral
and multilateral agencies may at least be reduced by less emphasis on
separate project funding, greater use of general and sectoral budget
support, clearer definition of strategic national health system goals, more
transparent and open policy consultation between governments and
international agencies and greater emphasis on general health systems
support and the general health services by the Global Health Initiatives.

6.2.2 Modifying Participation

In other cases, the form of participation exercised by certain groups can
be modified by reshaping *who* participates and *how*. Health providers
are a case in point. Nobody would deny that health providers should
have an important role to play in decision-making in the health system.
However, this group can be divided into three—health professionals,
managers and other staff. The first group has often claimed the right to
involvement on the grounds of the professionals' expertise, and clearly
their involvement in policy processes can be productive. The medical
profession has a major role to play in decision-making in health systems. However, within this medical group there are likely to be significant imbalances between the participation of different subgroups, levels
and specialities. The profession often controls the upper echelons of
the ministry of health, health facilities and health programmes leading
to a medical hegemony in the health system and limiting the development of a PHC approach. In order to develop values consistent with
those advocated in this book, this power of the medical profession needs
to be changed—with less reliance on incorporating doctors from the
upper echelons of the profession and opening up participation and
consultation with those involved in primary care services and public
health. Greater community involvement opens up the possibility of
comparison between the perceived needs of the community and the
health professionals. While there may be overlap between the two, there
may also be important differences.[27] More pluralism is also required in
the ministry of health, allowing stronger participation for public health

specialists (whether medically trained or not), other health professionals such as nurses, and other non-health professionals, such as economists, statisticians, sociologists, anthropologists, managers and planners. Nurses, for example, the largest professional group, often are given less opportunity to participate than their medical colleagues. In countries where there is a strong professional body such as medical or nursing colleges, this may provide the mechanism for engaging with such professions, but where these are non-existent or weak, it may be harder to find appropriate professional representation. The second key group consists of managers who are likely to lead the process of planning and policy at their level and could be expected to have expertise in this field. Other staff, including support and ancillary staff, who are rarely provided with opportunities to engage in policy processes, may have an important perspective to offer, particularly concerning the feasibility of different strategies. Private manufacturing companies outside the health system may feel that they can contribute to the policy processes or that they need to ensure that it is not against their interests. Media and religious bodies may also be interested in particular policies and even run campaigns. Religious bodies may be concerned about policies related to sensitive areas such as sexual and reproductive health. The organisations interested in health, or likely to affect it, include other sectors within the public sector, such as education, transport and water agencies. We have seen that they can have a major effect on the promotion (or diminution) of health. Whether their involvement is encouraged or not depends on their current power and values and those of the policymakers. This will shape the extent to which such groups are represented in decision-making bodies, their views are sought by policymakers, information is shared with them and their collaboration sought in the implementation of policies.

6.2.3 Opening Participation

The public sector provides services (health care and health related) on behalf of the citizens of the country—the health system members. As such, these members can claim a right to involvement in decisions about the policies, priorities and ways in which such services are to be delivered on their behalf. This argument holds for all public services. In practice, of course, there are limits to the desires, abilities and possibilities of citizens to become involved and to the feasibility of such involvement. The shift to a more equity-based system requires governance relations that are politically backed by those previously excluded from, or poorly served by, health services. There are various possible ways of doing this, as set out in Table 3.4.

In developing these forms of participation, four points need to be emphasised.

First, communities differ widely in their economic, social and political history and relations and therefore the options and potential for participation. Box 3.4 refers to participatory governance in Brazil and suggests the importance of both the institutional mechanisms for participation and the historical context of participation. There is no universal pattern of participatory governance across countries. The political context will

---

Box 3.4 Participatory governance in Brazil

The emergence of the Unified Health System in Brazil during the 1980s and 1990s marked an important shift in principles towards universality, public funding, participation, equity, decentralisation and integrated care. Participatory governance was marked by several key mechanisms that channel the involvement of large numbers of citizens. These mechanisms have gained international recognition.

Participatory budgets (for part of the investment budget) at the municipal level of government mean successive cycles of community meetings and discussion, priority-setting, and resource allocation. Health Councils also exist at the national, state and municipal levels of government, and have responsibilities in relation to planning, expenditure and service provision. Health Conferences also take place at the different levels of government and are held every four years to deliberate on the strategic direction of the health system and health policy.

An appreciation of the importance of the Conferences and Councils is given in the following:

> What makes the Conferencias especially interesting from a future health systems perspective is the place they occupy within a more complex architecture of public engagement. This architecture couples open-ended deliberation across large numbers of people - the estimated 300,000 people, for example, who participated in municipal and state-level conferences leading up to the National Conferencia - with more than 5000 regularised, smaller-scale conselhos that bring over 100,000 citizens together with state officials every month to hold the state to account for their commitments and monitor health spending.[33]

It would be wrong to suggest however that these spaces of democratic governance have not been without contradictions and criticisms. The effectiveness of these mechanisms varies in the country. It is also important to note the historical context of these mechanisms of participatory governance and how they form part of the transition of Brazil.

Sources: Collins et al. 2000; Cornwall et al. 2008; Cornwall and Shankland. 2008.[34]

Table 3.4
Forms of popular participation in the health system

Form	Commentary
Electoral and political	There is a wide array of different political processes with variations in terms of the nature and frequency of the election of representatives, the mechanisms of accountability back to the electorate and the degree of delegated power (with, for example, the potential in some systems for referenda involving all or some of the electorate in key decisions). Within any country, there are also likely to be interlocking political processes between different administrative and political levels.
	Electoral representation is a recognised form of participation and the devolution of power provides an opportunity for improved participatory governance. There are questions about the nature of political representation, both generally and in the health system. The mechanisms for accountability vary between countries and their effectiveness depends on the availability of public information and scrutiny and the confidence of the electorate to hold them to account. Representation through politicians faces the problem of whose interests are being represented and the exercise of patronage as a form of local and national political domination. Yet politicians can be a heterogeneous group; they are important in the decision-making process and it is difficult to see how many actions (such as developing the health agenda) could be taken forward without having them on board. Efforts should be made to inform them better on health and the health system through, for example, policy briefing papers and policy fora.
	There are issues as to whether politicians *should* always reflect and follow the desires of their electorate or whether they should, once elected, feel free to lead through making decisions which may not always have popular support. Within the health system, the prioritising process inherent in planning will inevitably lead to some policies which do not have the support of all groups. Furthermore, the very nature of health and health care means that decisions will be made which can be seen as very value-laden—for example, in areas such as abortion in reproductive health.
	Finally, political processes may be able to deal with broad policies but are less amenable to detailed planning and implementation suggesting that other representative mechanisms may be desirable to ensure accountability on levels of detail.

Table 3.4 continued

Table 3.4 continued

Form	Commentary
Representative councils and committees	Community and provider interests can be represented on health councils which may oversee the broad policy direction of the district health system, approve certain key decisions and monitor service provision. Health facility committees and boards can vary from provider and community representation on health centres to community representatives sitting on the governing boards of semi-autonomous tertiary hospitals. The importance of these will depend on their terms of reference and the decision-making authority invested in them. The nature of community representation on such bodies is also an issue and, in particular, the extent to which groups suffering from the inequity of the health system and the social determinants of health are represented on these.
Community meetings	Open community meetings can play a role in priority-setting through, for example, a participatory budget processes. As with representative bodies, issues relating to the role of such meetings in decision-making and which groups have a voice in such meetings are important.
Health needs consultations	Consultation about what are seen as health needs could be through more formal one-off processes such as Participatory Rapid Appraisal where research is conducted to seek the views of participants about health needs.
Social movements	Community protest about the inadequacy of health care provision or against a danger to health (such as pollution) is a form of popular participation in the health system. It is an expression of need that the planning process should understand while governance needs to become more inclusive of such movements. In Chapter 6, we point to the management process and its capacity to link with such movements, although this raises political issues and the extent to which managers feel this is politically feasible. These can take on an international dimension, as in the People's Health Movement.[28]
Advocacy groups	These overlap and are related to social movements. Some health systems appear to be witnessing a growing role for advocacy organisations to speak on behalf of communities or sections of communities. Such organisations (a subset of a wider group of organisations, NGOs and may be known as Civil Society Organisations) may be set up deliberately to represent particular interests; these may reflect particular health conditions or age or gender groups. Within the health care field, there is a growing tradition of advocacy in areas such as HIV/AIDS and disability. A good example of such

organisations includes the Treatment Action Campaign,[29] which has campaigned on behalf of people living with AIDS in South Africa. For policymakers, these may bring particular expertise on a condition into the policy process; there may however also be a resultant imbalance between priorities given to different conditions, where there is imbalanced advocacy. Box 5.2 in Chapter 5 illustrates this within the field of reproductive health where strong advocacy from groups with political leverage effectively altered the priority given to different forms of female cancer. At a wider level, mental health is often viewed as an inadequately represented health condition. Policy processes need to have mechanisms that consider, amongst other issues, the legitimacy of such organisations including the accountability to the constituents they represent.

Community role in provision

Communities may volunteer or be asked to be involved in the provision of services. This may range from community contributions of land, labour and materials to build health centres through to community volunteers following up TB 'defaulters'. The importance of Community Directed Interventions[30] has also been documented. Critical issues to consider are inequity and the extent to which some poorer communities are asked to be involved where less poor communities are not.

User choice

At the individual level, the relationship between a patient and health care professional ideally involves participation by the former in any resultant decision. This relationship is seen by proponents of a market approach to health care as being enhanced by a direct financial relationship as we see in Chapter 7. Users are allowed to choose their public and/or private health care provider. The latter compete for the custom of the users who can 'participate' by 'voting with their feet'. Voucher schemes of service provision can operate as a form of this participation.[31] These are seen as the 'short' routes to provider accountability by the World Bank.[32] We raise critical issues around user choice in Chapter 7. For example, the users need to be able to assess the quality of care despite the asymmetry of knowledge between the user and the provider.

particularly shape the form of participation and determine the extent to which participation is politically managed by those in power. The historical experience of communities will determine their consciousness of their own interests and their political capacity to organise themselves around their health interests.

Second, developing a more participatory process is not straightforward; social and political contradictions are channelled through the mechanisms and structures of participation. There are important considerations about the type of decisions and the means of selecting (including electing) such representatives. The latter is particularly complex given the heterogeneity of communities and the power structures that are likely to exist; such structures often favour adult men but may have also class and race dimensions. Groups participating through the mechanisms outlined in Table 3.4 and Box 3.4 have differing interests and perspectives on health and health care and these can also differ from those of service providers and managers. Previously excluded or underserved groups can also have their own perspectives on the appropriate forms of participation that might differ from those planned by others in the health system. Resolution of such differences is not easy. Mediation is needed but not simple; even those involved in mediation are not neutral and will have their own personal views which make such mediation difficult. Nevertheless, a clear grounding in the values and in particular the transparency and equity argued for in this book can provide the basis for resolution and mediation.

Third, governance changes for greater participation should not be seen as simple add-ons to the health system. The other chapters of this book highlight how participation needs to permeate the health system, changing its innermost structures and processes. For example, Chapter 6 suggests a number of ways in which management needs to change. Neither should participation be seen as short-term measures limited to specific projects. This process has to be about long-term sustainable change and be embedded as part of a more general development of empowerment, moving beyond the pragmatic concerns of this or that service.

Fourth, we need to differentiate between community involvement in policy, planning and management and involvement at the individual level in relationship between a patient and health care professional. The reality of patient participation in clinical decisions will vary significantly depending on the context, the access to, and ability to use, information by the patient and the attitude and skills of the professional and time available for the consultation. Such participation is likely to focus on the specific condition and its treatment and not on wider policy and delivery issues. It is also restricted to patients who are seeking treatment.

Patients unable or unwilling to seek treatment and members of the community without current health needs will not engage in such dialogue, by definition.

7 Ethical Conduct and Corruption

We view corruption as the unethical and illegal use of authority in pursuit of gain which may be personal or on behalf of an institution. It can occur in the public and/or the private sector. Such gain is often seen as material but may also be leading to status or enhancement of power. Kickbacks, bribes, embezzlement, production and sale of counterfeit drugs, supplier-induced demand, informal (under the counter) payments to health providers and payment to 'ghost' health workers are just some of the forms of material corruption. Box 3.5 gives examples of forms of corruption in the field of HIV/AIDS.

It is not, however, the only form of unethical conduct to be found in the health system; there is also bullying of staff by managers and senior health professionals, selection of patients by providers (often referred to as 'cream skimming'), neglect of duty, patronage, racism, and gender and age discrimination. The line between corruption and some of these practices is not that clear. Yet, a common theme in all these cases is the manipulation of power and authority to serve the interests of a few. It could be argued that all health systems favour, in some way or another, the few over the many in terms of inequity. However, the relations of power and authority referred to here are particular cases of unethical conduct within this overall state of affairs.

Health systems are particularly susceptible to corruption. Throughout the world, approximately US$3 trillion is spent annually on health care with losses from corruption in some countries of up to 10 per cent.[35] This is due to various reasons including the asymmetry of knowledge between provider and user, the large sums involved, the dispersal of actors within the health system, the levels of trust required to run a health system and low salaries paid to many health workers.[36]

Corruption can make health care unaffordable, particularly for the poor. The 2006 Global Corruption Report cites a man from Morocco: *'When my wife went to the hospital they examined her and prescribed some pills. They said that none were available there, but if we paid 20 or 30 dirhams, someone could provide the "free medication". The problem is we can't afford the drugs'.*[37] Corruption diverts scarce resources from promoting health and health care to the pockets and bank accounts of the rich or

---

Box 3.5 Corruption and HIV/AIDS

Corruption can occur in both the prevention and treatment of HIV/AIDS. In the case of the latter, the scaling up of international funding and treatment programmes has increased the potential for corruption through, for example, embezzlement in the medicine supply chain, drug counterfeiting, bribes, and illegal fees. According to one man from Nigeria:

> The ARVs that come to the centre are not given to those of us who have come out to declare our status, but to those "big men" who bribe their way through, and we are left to suffer and scout round for the drug.[38]

Another source[39] in Kenya stated the following about medicines

> In Tsavo Road, Nairobi, huge quantities are traded every day. (...) Some come from patients, others leak out of the health system, and a large proportion is counterfeit.

This type of distribution can lower treatment effectiveness.

Attempts to restrict corruption through international funding being channelled through separate government management systems can ultimately weaken health systems as resources are diverted from them. Hence the interest in moving towards budget support mechanisms for the dispersing of international funding. Action can be taken to prevent corruption by more transparency, mechanisms to protect those who inform on corruption, action to prevent the re-importing of medicines from low to higher income countries, and regional pressures on national governments to prevent corruption.

Source: Tayler and Dickinson. 2006.[40]

---

powerful. It has a corrosive impact on the quality of care, the ethos of public service and the motivation of health staff. It also sends inappropriate signals to providers affecting their responses.

Under such circumstances it is hardly surprising and indeed appropriate that corruption should engender strong emotions. However, this needs to be accompanied by a sense of perspective about where it is found and who is involved. Although corruption is a big problem in LMICs, we should not see it as a problem *specific* to these countries. Szeftel[41] comments that '... *those looting the African State can only envy the size of the 'pot' available to those in other countries'.* Savedoff and Hussmann[42] also write that:

> Corruption in the health sector is not exclusive to any particular kind of health system. It occurs in systems whether they are predominantly public

*or private, well funded or poorly funded, and technically simple or sophisti-
cated. The extent of corruption is, in part, a reflection of the society in which
it operates. Health system corruption is less likely in societies where there is
broad adherence to the rule of law, transparency and trust, and where the
public sector is ruled by effective civil service codes and strong accountability
mechanisms.*

As the last quote suggests, there is no simple or single solution to
corruption. Solutions have their roots in the underlying values and
relations in society as a whole, and the health system in particular, together
with the nature of the broad political coalition supporting these values.
Box 3.6, for example, exemplifies attempts to reinvigorate anti-corruption
processes and the constraints they face.

The spread and penetration of values based on improved and more
equitable health, empowerment, transparency, accountability and social
cohesion is a medium to long-term antidote to the spread of corruption
and unethical conduct in the health system. These principles should not

---

Box 3.6 Anti-corruption case study: Karnataka state, India

Within India, attempts to reduce corruption in the public sector have included the introduction of State level public complaints agencies. These
'Lokayuktas' (ombudsmen) have had variable success. The Karnataka Lokayukta (KLA), was set up in 1986 but had limited success until the appointment of a new Lokayukta in 2001 following an election which had included
anti-corruption as a key plank. This person, a retired and well respected former judge, appointed a similarly well respected Vigilance Director for Health
(VDH) who had previously formed part of a commission that had reviewed
the Karnataka health system and concluded that corruption was one of the
major threats to the system.

Prior to their appointment the KLA itself was perceived to be corrupt
and ineffective in challenging corruption. The Lokayukta and his VDH were
seen to bring a combination of high moral standards and technical expertise.
They were effective in mobilizing the media and the public about governance
issues. Their investigations revealed corruption within the public health sector at all levels as well as in public/private collaborations and in the political
and justice systems.

Contextual issues limited their effectiveness however and in particular
a lack of continued and high level political support for the activities of the
agency. The departure of the Lokayukta, upon completing his term, was due
to lack of continued political support for controlling corruption.

Source: Huss et al. 2010.[43]

just be figurehead statements but should permeate the processes in the health system. They should be implemented through a strengthening of regulation, transparency, democratising of information, participatory governance and effective accountability mechanisms, all of which are discussed in this chapter. Improved management systems, improved remuneration of health staff and clarity in the definition of responsibilities are referred to in Chapter 6. The Global Corruption Report also refers to 'codes of conduct', rules governing the 'conflict of interests' and 'integrity pacts' to reduce corruption. Whilst there are particular instruments, such as these, there is also the need to develop a leadership style in the health system which leads by example and refuses to condone or turn a blind eye to unethical conduct. Within the public sector, there is the need to strengthen the public service ethos where commitment to the wider social good, rather than personal advancement and gain, is seen as paramount. The importation of some private sector management styles into the public sector may however work against this. For example, reforms may see staff rewards as primarily monetary rather than emphasising staff development and work performance and its contribution to the wider good.

8 Regulation

The process of regulation refers to the mechanisms by which the state (and the delegated body) ensures that its policies are followed by agencies within the health system and, in some cases, beyond it. It is a key process in the health system. It involves the setting of standard requirements which are then monitored and assessed with a set of penalties and incentives (including both financial and non-financial ones) to ensure compliance.[44] For regulation to be effective, it requires regulatory bodies that set the standards, monitor their compliance and apply penalties and incentives. A study of four countries (Zambia, India, Mexico and Thailand)[45] identified 19 mechanisms of regulation within health systems, including licensing (of providers, facilities), controls (for example, on the number and sizes of medical schools and the introduction of expensive technology), incentives to cover underserved areas and quality assurance mechanisms.

In this section, we focus on the importance, problems and underlying issues in the development of an effective regulatory process. Issues of governance form a crucial part in the analysis.

8.1 Importance of Regulation

Regulation assumes greater importance in a context of increasing dispersion and possible fragmentation in the health system. This is certainly the case of the increased role of the private sector in the funding and delivery of health care in many countries. Traditionally, regulatory processes have been seen to refer primarily to bodies outside the direct control of the public sector with internal managerial and supervisory processes performing the same role within the public sector. However, the current situation for many health systems is less clearly demarcated. This is partly the result of the blurred boundaries of what constitutes the public sector following forms of public–private integration. Also, processes such as decentralisation, semi-autonomy and contracting within the public sector have led to new types of relations within the public sector which are different to typical line management. Common standards may be seen as applicable in both public and private sectors, requiring the application of regulations to both, though the mechanisms for regulation might have to be different in recognition of the different characteristics of the two sectors. In what follows, we will seek to treat regulation as covering all agencies; however, we recognise that the particular nature of the private sector requires specific tools and processes.

Regulation can be a vital means for the realisation of key values and objectives such as improved equity, participation and quality of care. Table 3.5 provides examples in the exercise of the regulatory function and how regulation permeates the other health system processes that we explore in this book.

The lack of an effective regulatory function in the health system can have important implications for health system objectives. This is apparent in the case study of Lebanon set out in Box 3.7.

8.2 Problems in Regulation

The record of regulation in the health system in LMICs is not good. This is hardly surprising considering the social, political and economic context in which they operate and the fragility and weaknesses of state systems in some of these countries. Specific problems of regulation may be grouped into two broad and interrelated categories.

First, it is commonly accepted that regulatory agencies require a strong measure of autonomy to be able to exercise their authority 'independent' of outside influences. However, this may be lacking; one possibility is that the group affected by the regulation is so strong that they are too politically powerful to regulate. In extreme cases, the regulatory

Table 3.5
Health system processes and examples of regulations

Health system process	Examples of regulation
Governance	• Requirements and procedures for the existence of community representation on district health committees • Requirements for private firms to provide regular information on their internal governance and activities
Financing	• Coverage of health problems (such as HIV/AIDS) by private health insurance companies • Amount charged and groups of users required to pay user fees in government health facilities
Policy-making and planning	• Requirements on the provision and use of health information • Requirements to be fulfilled in the location of future health facilities
IAH and health service delivery	• Ensuring IAH through environmental health and food standards • Ensuring common standards of quality in the provision of care in district health facilities • Setting standards for the use of medicines and technology in health care • Setting standards for training (both pre and in-service) and conduct of professionals • Providing mechanisms to redress grievances
Management	• Determining the qualifications and experience required of an officer in charge of health centres in a district • Determining how transport is to be programmed and used by public sector health facilities • Setting out the manner of provider payment

authority ends up being controlled by those it is supposed to regulate. This can be a problem in situations where self-regulation by industrial and professional groups is perceived as the only means of regulation. It can also be the case in attempting to regulate international and national companies with an interest in and impact on health and health care. For example, the regulation of tobacco consumption can come up against the formidable resources and political power of the international and national tobacco industry plus additional industries related to entertainment and alcohol. Tactics employed by the tobacco industry include conducting public relations, funding politicians, funding research and

---

Box 3.7 Health system regulation in Lebanon during the 1990s

Following the 1975–1990 civil war, the health care system of Lebanon consisted of a predominantly private sector. This was made up of private-for-profit practitioners offering ambulatory care, a smaller NGO group of health centres and a growing number of private hospitals using high technology. The private sector was funded through out-of-pocket expenditure, private health insurance and payments from government expenditure and public insurance. There was a general lack of government regulation and control by the government over the private sector. In particular, the Ministry of Health lacked information and qualified staff to carry this out. This led to increasing hospital costs, irrational and fragmented health care, a short term perspective and lack of sustainability and an emphasis on high technology and secondary care to the detriment of primary care.

Source: Van Lerberghe et al. 1997.[46]

---

consultancy, sponsoring in the areas of sport and entertainment, corruption and legal conflict through challenges to laws and regulations.[47]

Second, there can be a lack of resources allocated to and used in the regulatory authority. Finance and means of transport for the regulators may be deficient. Staff may be poorly qualified and have little information about who, what and how they should be regulating.

8.3 Developing Regulatory Capacity

Studies into the regulatory capacity of country health systems have developed various frameworks, key questions and sets of recommendations;[48] these can be useful for conducting country reviews of regulation. A starting point for strengthening regulatory capacity has to be a common and shared recognition amongst policymakers and managers about the rationale for regulation and that it forms a focal part of government health policy. It is often easy for politicians and those of a free market persuasion to see regulation as petty interference and look for a 'bonfire of regulations' to free up individuals from the excesses of 'political correctness'. The paradox of such instances is that it becomes 'politically correct to be politically incorrect'. There is also a paradox around the need for, and political interest in, regulating the health system; those governments politically interested in developing the private sector are hardly those governments most willing to possess a positive ideological view about regulation. Effective regulation for better and more equitable health and health care needs political advocacy that shows how it can be a positive force. Consistent with our analysis of governance in the health system, the political character of regulation also needs to be recognised. The values of the health system therefore need to be instilled in the regulations. For example, regional equity can inform regulations on the location of health facilities, sustainability can inform regulations on licensing the private sector and inclusiveness can inform regulations on user representation on bodies such as health facility committees.

It is also important that regulatory capacity keeps ahead of the need for regulation in a rapidly changing health system. In particular, the growth of the private sector means that it can gain political strength and make the introduction of regulatory capacity more difficult.[49] It is important to build up government regulation of the private sector before the latter becomes too strong.

The organisational and staff capacity of the regulator needs to be developed for effective regulation. The regulators of the private sector need to have information on what the private sector is, what it does and what impact it has. Information systems and technology, qualified staff and good means of transport are all required. In addition, it is important that opportunities and motivation for corruption within such agencies are minimised by ensuring adequate remuneration, ethical codes and clear and transparent procedures that can be monitored. A balance also needs to be struck between ensuring that the regulatory body has the authority and independence to act but at the same time is not above the law and clear accountability.

Standards and rules to regulate with need to be developed. As Box 3.8 on regulation in Thailand indicates, it is important to identify possible gaps in the set of regulations that exist. Regulatory capacity needs to be supported through a series of complementary measures. This is well brought out in Box 3.8 through, for example, the education of health professionals. Self-regulation may also be considered, though the problem of this (as mentioned above) needs to be considered.

Attention also needs to be paid to international regulation, such as regulating the international mobility of the health workforce given the problems in retention identified in Chapters 4 and 6. With the growth in international markets, both in traditional areas such as pharmaceuticals and technology, and in emerging areas such as health staff there is a need to develop international mechanisms for regulation in these areas. Currently there is no obvious international governance body taking an authoritative lead in this area and this is a challenge facing national health systems with little sovereignty in these areas.

Box 3.8 Regulation and the health system in Thailand

Work in Thailand[50] found a comprehensive set of rules and functions covering medicines (for example, quality, price control, and advertising), health care facilities (for example, licensing of private facilities) and professionals (for example, compulsory period of service in rural areas). The regulatory functions are carried out by the Food and Drug Administration, Medical Registration Division, professional organisations, and health care purchasers while the roles of the media and 'consumers' were also noted. Deficiencies in this formal framework were identified, such as concerning the setting up of new private health care facilities. The study recommended changes such as to rules to fill the 'gaps' in the regulations, additional resources for developing regulatory capacity, and developing the roles of Professional Councils and health care purchasers. To complement these measures, suggestions also included improving continuing education and ethical behaviour of health professionals. Stronger roles for 'consumers' were also recommended by allowing them to be represented on professional organisations and strengthening consumer organisations.

---

9 Transparency and Accessibility of Information

In order for the above governance processes to be effective, information is required that is accessible and accurate. In the absence of such information, accountability is difficult, corruption is hard to detect and regulation is impossible. A key process in governance therefore relates to ensuring the appropriateness of the information systems. In Chapter 5, we discuss the importance of information within the policy and planning processes. Here we refer to key characteristics of information systems that relate to ensuring that governance supports our chosen values for a health system.

First, it is important that the information available covers the issues we are concerned with. In particular, given the importance in our values of both efficiency and equity, our information systems need to reflect these. However, many information systems provide few insights into the distributional issues that underpin an equitable perspective. Though information may be available by gender, there is less routine coverage of characteristics such as income or ethnicity, restricting the ability to monitor the health system's response to such aspects of equity. Similarly, information systems often are closely linked to the delivery of health care and as such reflect the current preoccupations of the health system with such activities. As a result, there is often little coverage of the wider social determinants of health and the potential for inter-sectoral action for health. Information on the costs of health activities is also rarely captured, restricting the ability of decision-makers to identify and pursue the most efficient routes to equitable health gain.

Second, it is important that information is accessible to the appropriate stakeholders. The confidential nature of much 'medical' information rightly means that management of clinical information has to be carefully managed. However, wider access to aggregated information about health, service performance and governance mechanisms themselves are key to developing accountability of the health system. Freedom of Information Acts, such as that in operation in India, provide opportunities for laying down responsibilities for organisations to provide information either routinely or on request. However, mechanisms such as this can contain the seeds themselves of inequity if the processes of accessibility themselves do not take this into account.[51] Accessibility refers however not only to the ability to obtain information but also the form of that information. For civil society groups to be able to use technical information productively, it needs to be presented in an accessible fashion.

The development of information technology brings opportunities for access to information but also challenges. Information is much more widely available from a range of national and international sources, but the lack of regulatory processes on the internet itself means that the quality of such information is not always assessable, and given the huge amount of information available, the ability to choose the appropriate information is critical. Access to the technology itself is skewed both in terms of the cost and also in terms of the information literacy required.

10 Final Thoughts

This chapter has sought to develop a value-based interpretation of good governance in the health system. Our interpretation of governance rests on our understanding of the relations of power, authority and responsibility consonant with the values and aims of what we interpret as a good health system. The analysis has led us to some key points around a proactive public sector, effective accountability, decentralisation, inter-sectoral action, participatory governance, ethical conduct, regulation and transparency and accessibility of information.

We recognise that these issues are politically contested and controversial. We interpret the development of participatory governance as requiring a shift in the bias in decision-making that involves reducing, modifying and opening up the avenues of participation to different groups. While collaboration between interests is an essential practice of governance, there are limits to the practice of collaboration. The politically contested nature of action for health requires regulatory authority and action with a view to better and more equitable health.

Although we have treated the aspects of good governance as separate themes, it should be clear that they rest on each other. For example, professional accountability must surely include the ethics of conduct, community accountability rests on transparency and democratising information and participatory governance democratises decentralisation and allows for community forms of accountability.

Underlying this chapter is an economic, social and political reality. The extent to which improved governance can be achieved is constrained by the context; fragile states, extreme poverty and economic recession are not a productive environment for good governance to emerge. Decisions have to be taken about the political feasibility of change and how far governance can be developed in country contexts. Yet, the context is not immutable. Part of good governance is the development of international, national and more local political coalitions for better and more equitable health that includes progressive groups within public sectors, NGOs, faith-based organisations, community groups, social movements, academia, trade unions, political parties and cooperatives. The movement for better and more equitable health and health care forms part of a broader movement to change the context.

Notes and References

1. Compare with Siddiqi, S., Masud, T.I., Nishtar, S., Peters, D.H., Sabri, B., Bile, K.M. and Jama, M.A. 2009. 'Framework for Assessing Governance of the Health System in Developing Countries: Gateway to Good Governance', *Health Policy*, 90(1): 13–25—which develops a framework for assessing good governance based on a number of key principles.
2. Siddiqi, S., Masud, T.I., Nishtar, S., Peters, D.H., Sabri, B., Bile, K.M. and Jama, M.A. 2009. 'Framework for Assessing Governance of the Health System in Developing Countries: Gateway to Good Governance', *Health Policy*, 90: 18.
3. UNDP. 2009. Human Development Report 2009, *Overcoming Barriers: Human Mobility and Development*, Table N, UNDP, New York. Available at http://hdr.undp.org/en/reports/global/hdr2009/ Data refer to 2006 (accessed on 29 December 2009).

4. Brinkerhoff, D. 2003. *Accountability and Health Systems: Overview, Framework, and Strategies,* Technical Report No. 018. Bethesda, MD: The Partners for Health Reform*plus* Project, Abt Associates Inc.

5. Brinkerhoff, D. 2003. *Accountability and Health Systems: Overview, Framework, and Strategies,* Technical Report No. 018. Bethesda, MD: The Partners for Health Reform*plus* Project, Abt Associates Inc.

6. Brinkerhoff, D. 2003. *Accountability and Health Systems: Overview, Framework, and Strategies,* Technical Report No. 018. Bethesda, MD: The Partners for Health Reform*plus* Project, Abt Associates Inc.; Lindberg, S. 2009. *Accountability: The Core Concepts and Subtypes, Africa Power and Politics Programme,* Working Paper No. 1, April.

7. McCoy, D., Chand, S. and Sridhar, D. 2009. 'Global Health Funding: How Much, Where It Comes From And Where It Goes', *Health Policy and Planning,* 24(6): 407.

8. C.f. Rondinelli, D.A. 1980. 'Government Decentralization in Comparative Perspective: Theory and Practice in Developing Countries', *International Review of Administrative Sciences,* 47(2): 133–45.

9. See Collins, C.D. and Green, A., 1994. 'Decentralisation and PHC: Some Negative Implications in Developing Countries', *International Journal of Health Services,* 24(3): 459–75.

10. Collins, C.D. 1994. *Management and Organisation of Developing Health Systems,* Oxford: Oxford University Press, p. 70, Figure 3.1.

11. Cheema, G.S. and Rondinelli,D.A. (eds). 1983. *Decentralisation and Development.* Beverly Hills: SAGE Publications; Collins, C.D. 1994. *Management and Organisation of Developing Health Systems.* Oxford: Oxford University Press.

12. Collins, C.D. 1994. *Management and Organisation of Developing Health Systems,* Oxford: Oxford University Press, p. 71, Figure 3.2.

13. Collins, C.D. 1994. *Management and Organisation of Developing Health Systems,* Oxford: Oxford University Press, p. 74, Figure 3.4.

14. Bossert, T. 1998. 'Analysing the Decentralisation of Health Systems in Developing Countries: Decision Space, Innovation and Performance, *Social Science and Medicine,* 47(10): 1513–27; Bossert, T. and Beauvais, J.C. 2002. 'Decentralization of Health Systems in Ghana, Zambia, Uganda and the Philippines: A Comparative Analysis of Decision Space', *Health Policy and Planning,* 17(1): 14–31.

15. The generic term *district* is used here, although countries may adopt other terminology such as municipality.

16. Commission on Social Determinants (CSDH). 2008. *Closing the Gap in a Generation: Health Equity through Action on the Social Determinants of Health.* Final Report of the Commission on Social Determinants of Health. World Health Organization, Geneva.

17. Commission on Social Determinants (CSDH). 2008. *Closing the Gap in a Generation: Health Equity through Action on the Social Determinants of Health.* Final Report of the Commission on Social Determinants of Health. World Health Organization, Geneva, p. 2.

18. See, for example, Varvasovszky, Z. and Brugha, R. 2000. 'How To Do, Or Not To Do, a Stakeholder Analysis', *Health Policy and Planning*, 15(3): 338–45.
19. Peden, M., Scurfield, R., Sleet, D., Mohan, D., Hyder, A.A., Jarawar, E. and Mathers, C. 2004. *World Report on Road Traffic Injury Prevention: Summary*. World Health Organization, Geneva. http://www.paho.org/ English/DD/PUB/Summary_World_report_Road_safety.pdf (accessed 27 March 2008).
20. Global Health Watch. 2005. *Global Health Watch, 2005–2006. An Alternative World Health Report*. London: Zed Books.
21. Commission on Social Determinants (CSDH). 2008. *Closing the Gap in a Generation: Health Equity through Action on the Social Determinants of Health*. Final Report of the Commission on Social Determinants of Health. World Health Organization, Geneva, p. 77.
22. Global Health Watch. 2008. *Global Health Watch 2: An Alternative World Health Report*. London: Zed Books, pp. 350–51.
23. Global Health Watch. 2008. *Global Health Watch 2: An Alternative World Health Report*. London: Zed Books.
24. See the discussion in Rifkin, S.B. 1996. 'Paradigms Lost: Toward a New Understanding of Community Participation in Health Programmes', *Acta Tropica*, 61(2): 79–92; and Morgan, L.M. 2001. 'Community Participation in Health: Perpetual Allure, Persistent Challenge', *Health Policy and Planning*, 16(3): 221–30.
25. Lukes, S. 1974. *Power: A Radical View*. London: Macmillan; Gaventa, J. 1980. *Power and Powerlessness, Quiescence and Rebellion in an Appalachian Valley*. Oxford: Clarendon Press.
26. Global Health Watch. 2005. *Global Health Watch, 2005-6. An Alternative World Health Report*. London: Zed Books, p. 103.
27. Green, A. 2007. *An Introduction to Health Planning for Developing Health Systems*, 3rd edition. Oxford: Oxford University Press.
28. http://www.phmovement.org/en
29. See TAC website for further details: http://www.tac.org.za/community/
30. http://apps.who.int/tdr/
31. World Bank. 2004. *World Development Report 2004. Making Services Work for People,* The International Bank for Reconstruction and Development/The World Bank. Oxford, UK: Oxford University Press.
32. World Bank. 2004. *World Development Report 2004. Making Services Work for People,* The International Bank for Reconstruction and Development/The World Bank. Oxford, UK: Oxford University Press.
33. Cornwall, A. and Shankland, A. 2008. 'Engaging Citizens: Lessons from Building Brazil's National Health System', *Social Science & Medicine*, 66(10): 2181.
34. Collins, C.D., Araujo, J. and Barbosa, J. 2000. 'Decentralizing the Health Sector: Issues in Brazil', *Health Policy*, 52(2): 113–27.
   Cornwall, A. and Shankland, A. 2008. 'Engaging Citizens: Lessons from Building Brazil's National Health System', *Social Science & Medicine*, 66(10): 2173–2184.

Cornwall, A., Romano, J. and Shankland, A. 2008. *Brazilian Experiences of Participation and Citizenship: A Critical Look*, IDS Discussion Paper 389, Institute of Development Studies, University of Sussex, UK.

35. Quoted by Tayler, L. and Dickinson, C., 2006. 'The Link between Corruption and HIV/AIDS', in Kotalik, Jana and Rodriguez, Diana (Eds), *Transparency International*, Global Corruption Report, 2006, Germany: Pluto Press, p. 105. Original source: Statement by CSO at the fourth ordinary African Union Summit of Heads of States, January 2005, Nigeria.

36. Quoted by Tayler, L. and Dickinson, C. 2006. 'The Link between Corruption and HIV/AIDS', in *Transparency International*, Global Corruption Report, 2006, Germany: Pluto Press, p. 105. Originally from *The Nation* (Kenya), 22 January 2004.

37. Tayler, L. and Dickinson, C. 2006. 'The Link between Corruption and HIV/AIDS', in Kotalik, Jana and Rodriguez, Diana (eds), *Transparency International Global Corruption Report 2006* (pp. 104–111). Germany: Pluto Press.

38. Transparency International. 2006. *Global Corruption Report, 2006*. Germany: Pluto Press.

39. Vian, T. 2008. 'Review of Corruption in the Health Sector: Theory, Methods and Interventions', *Health Policy*, 23: 83–94; Savedoff, W.D. and Hussman, K. 2006. 'Why are Health Systems Prone to Corruption?', in *Transparency International*, Global Corruption Report, 2006, Germany: Pluto Press, pp. 4–16.

40. Transparency International. 2006. *Global Corruption Report, 2006*, Germany: Pluto Press, pp. xii.

41. Szeftel, M. 1998. 'Misunderstanding African Politics: Corruption and the Governance Agenda', *Review of African Political Economy*, 25(76): 221–40.

42. Savedoff, W.D. and Hussman, K. 2006. 'Why are Health Systems Prone to Corruption?', in *Transparency International*, Global Corruption Report, 2006, Germany: Pluto Press, p. 4.

43. Huss, R., Green, A., Sudarshan, H., Karpagam, S.S., Ramani, K.V., Tomson G. and Gerein, N. 2010. 'Good Governance and Corruption in the Health Sector—Lessons from the Karnataka Experience', *Health Policy and Planning*, 26(6): 471–484.

44. See, for example, Mills, A. and Ranson, K. 2006. 'The Design of Health Systems', in Merson, M.H., Black, R.E. and Mills, A.J. (eds), *International Public Health*, 2nd ed., p. 523. Sudbury, Massachusetts: Jones and Bartlett; See, for example, Kumaranayake, Lilani, Lake, S., Mujina, P., Hongoro, C. and Mpembeni, R. 2000. 'How Do Countries Regulate the Health Sector? Evidence from Tanzania and Zimbabwe', *Health Policy and Planning*, 15(4): 357–67.

45. See Mills, A. and Ranson, K. 2006. 'The Design of Health Systems', in Merson, M.H., Black, R.E. and Mills, A.J. (eds), *International Public Health*, 2nd ed., p. 525. Boston: Jones and Bartlett, for original sources.

46. Van Lerberghe, W., Ammar, W., El Rashidi, R., Sales, A., Mechbal, A. 1997. 'Reform Follow Failure: 1 Unregulated Private Care in Lebanon', *Health Policy and Planning*, 12(4): 296–311.

47. Global Health Watch. 2008. *Global Health Watch 2: An Alternative World Health Report*. London: Zed Books, p. 353.
48. See, for example, Kumaranayake, Lilani, Lake, S.,Mujinja, P., Hongoro, C., Mpembeni, R. 2000. 'How Do Countries Regulate the Health Sector? Evidence from Tanzania and Zimbabwe', *Health Policy and Planning*, 15(4): 357–67; Teerawattananon, Y., Tangcharoensathien, V., Tantivess, S. and Mills, A. 2003. 'Health Sector Regulation in Thailand: Recent Progress and the Future Agenda', *Health Policy*, 63(3): 323–38.
49. Kumaranayake, Lilani, Lake, S.,Mujinja, P., Hongoro, C. and Mpembeni, R. 2000. 'How Do Countries Regulate the Health Sector? Evidence from Tanzania and Zimbabwe', *Health Policy and Planning*, 15(4): 357–67.
50. Teerawattananon, Y., Tangcharoensathien, V., Tantivess, S. and Mills, A. 2003. 'Health Sector Regulation in Thailand: Recent Progress and the Future Agenda', *Health Policy*, 63: 323–38.
51. See, for example, http://www.trust.org/trustlaw/good-governance/news-and-analysis/detail.dot?id=bb274ba1-92f8-4658-8289-03fc7f022a73 (accessed 12 July 2010), which argues that the Indian Freedom of Information Act provides few opportunities for the rural poor.

4
Financing

Health systems require resources to function. In particular, they require staff (both professional and non-professional), supplies of materials (particularly medicines alongside a variety of other consumables), buildings and equipment. Underpinning all these are financial resources, which are, of course, only important as a means to acquire the above real resources. Health systems (or more precisely key decision-makers, both within and outwith health systems) make choices as to both the level of financial resources available to the health system and, closely related to this, how such resources are to be obtained. Both decisions reflect the underlying values of the health system and its performance. Given the critical nature of financing, this chapter will focus on how finance for the health system and its two key sets of health system activities—inter-sectoral action for health and health services—is raised, the values underlying these decisions and the resultant effects of these decisions on the objectives of different (value-based) health systems.

The chapter starts with an overview of health financing levels and then turns to an explanation of the in-country sources of funding. This is followed by a discussion of how these funding sources relate to the values of a health system outlined in Chapter 2. The chapter then looks at international funding and discusses this in relation to the values.

1 Overview of Health Financing Levels and Sources[1]

There is considerable variation in the levels of spending on health between different national health systems. For example, in 2007, spending in the Democratic Republic of the Congo (DRC) was around $ppp22[2] per person, compared with the USA at a level of over US$4,703—a ratio of 1:213.[3] This massive disparity immediately raises major questions of international equity. Such expenditure differences clearly do not relate to differences in need. The USA life expectancy from birth (for 2008) is 78 years; in the DRC it is 54.[4] What is being demonstrated here is an international version of what has been called the inverse care law[5]—that the level of resources provided is *inversely related* to the needs. Indeed, there is a point at which continued increases in expenditure on health has little effect on health status as measured for example by mortality rates. This is demonstrated in Figure 4.1.

Figure 4.1
Life expectancy versus health expenditure

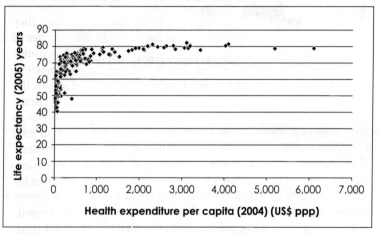

Source: Derived from UN. 2008. Tables 1 and 6.[6]

Most of the difference in the levels of expenditure by different countries appears to be related to the level of income of a country—the richer a country, the more it spends both in absolute and in relative terms on health care. This can be seen in Figure 4.2, which shows the level of expenditure on health by selected countries against their level of national per capita income.

However, closer examination of the data also shows variations in the levels of expenditure between countries at the same level of income. For example, the USA and Norway have similar income levels but significant differences in their expenditure on health. This suggests that health systems are either given different priorities within different countries or operate at different levels of efficiency. This, in turn, raises questions as to *how* a country makes such decisions. In practice, of course, there is no single decision made by a single set of actors as to the levels of

Figure 4.2
Levels of expenditure on health by per capita income

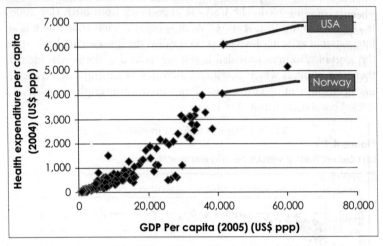

Source: Derived from UN. 2008. Tables 1 and 6.[7]

expenditure on health. Health finance for such expenditure comes from a complex variety of different sources and each of these has different sets of decision-makers—including a vast array of users of health services. Nevertheless, there *are* some macro-level decisions that can be seen to reflect a national and explicit set of priorities. In particular, decisions on the level of public expenditure on health reflect, among other issues, the way a society or its ruling political power views both health and the role of collective or public responses to it.

Neo-liberal ideology aims to minimise the role of the state particularly within the area of social welfare where it sees individuals as having greater responsibility for their own health and health expenditure. It sees the market as a more appropriate mechanism for both expressing individuals' own priorities regarding health expenditure (the demand side of the market relationship) and for responding efficiently to this through private structures (the supply side). In contrast, socialist ideologies see health as a collective endeavour with the state having a responsibility to provide services for, and on behalf of, its citizens. Between these two positions, there is a variety of alternative positions reflecting both different views on the responsibility of the state in terms of responses to need and views as to the efficiency of the market as an approach to prioritising and providing health care. Indeed, most market-based health systems include a significant role for the public sector both in the areas of public health and as a 'safety-net' for those who are not covered under market provision. Since the health reforms of the 1990s, there have also been a significant number of countries that have maintained a collective responsibility for health but adopted various forms of internal market or contracting with the private sector, seeing this as a driver for efficiency. This has often diverted debate about the wider role of the state into discussion in technical economic terms related to the failure of the market in the health field (see Box 4.1).

Box 4.1 Market failures in health care[8]

Classical and neoclassical economics see the market mechanism as the most appropriate means of making decisions about both the level of production of goods and services and their distribution within society. The market mechanism is seen as optimizing such decisions through perfect competition. This position can itself be generally challenged (including as to whether the conditions for perfect competition ever exist). However whether their position is generally accepted or not, there are specific widely accepted reasons for market failure in the health sector. These include:

- Information asymmetry between providers of health care and users of health care (exacerbated by the fact that health care is not homogenous) and the agency role of professionals who make decisions on behalf of patients, leading to the potential for supplier-induced demand and unnecessary care.
- The difficulty of producing 'free entry into the market' and of ensuring the availability of sufficient providers to ensure competition or at least contestability.
- The existence of externalities, whereby the consumption of some health care or other products affects a third party as is the case in immunization (positive), or passive smoking (negative). This can lead to individual decisions being sub-optimal for the wider society. The related free rider effect refers to a situation in which an individual may decide not to pay for an activity on the grounds that others will, and that the resultant good will still be available (free) to him/her. For example, if immunization was charged for, some individuals may decide not to 'buy' it on the grounds that they would benefit from herd immunity caused by others buying it.
- The existence of public goods (whose consumption by one person does not lead to a reduction in its availability for another) such as availability of a clean environment. Such goods are likely to be under-produced in terms of social benefit if left solely to the market.

Beyond these market failures, a further powerful argument relates to the nature of health care as a fundamental service whose distribution should be dependent on need rather than ability to pay—the equity argument.

However, underlying this, there is a broader division of view as to values related to the role of the state in the lives of individuals, and in particular in relation to social welfare. This was clear, for example, in the debate in the USA during 2009–2010 about proposed health care reforms and the role of government in financing of health care. It should be obvious already, but we reiterate, as authors, our own values as espousing a clear interventionist and collectivist role for the state in the area of health related in part but not solely to our view that this is the only *potential* means of achieving equity.

The level of state (public) expenditure on health reflects in part, then, the wider prevailing ideology, and we can see this in Figure 4.3 with variations in the level of public expenditure between countries from 1 to 10 per cent of Gross Domestic Product (GDP). The graph demonstrates some relationship between the wealth of a country and its public expenditure on health suggesting that, as countries grow economically, they prioritise their response to different types of social goods (such as defence, law and order, economic structures and social welfare). However, it is also interesting to note that, at all levels of income, there is a considerable range of public sector expenditure illustrating the range of ideologies and views about the role of the state in health care existing in different contexts. The figure shows some outliers as examples of this diversity.

Figure 4.3
Public expenditure on health as percentage of GDP by per GDP per capita ($ ppp) for selected countries

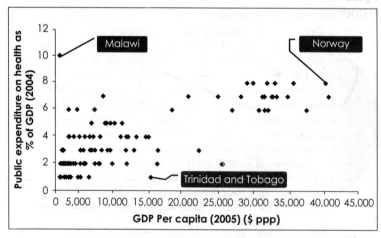

Source: Derived from UN. 2008. Tables 1 and 6.[9]

One cautionary note needs to be sounded at this point. Public expenditure cannot be equated directly with collective mechanisms of collection. It is possible for state health expenditure to be financed by non-collectivist mechanisms. Under the reforms of the 1990s, there was encouragement to, and in some cases pressure on, low-income countries to increase the amount of funding derived through user charges within public facilities. However, the proportion of state funding derived in this way is still relatively small, with the bulk being linked to more collectivist systems of financing such as taxation and social insurance. Nevertheless, even here it is important to recognise that even such mechanisms can be regressive. Taxes, for example, can be highly regressive, with a disproportionate amount being raised from poorer groups in society—such as sales tax on basic necessities.

2 Sources of Finance

We turn now to examine the different sources of finance potentially available for the health system. We start by looking at in-country mechanisms. However, for many low-income countries, external finance is a major source of funding and we also briefly examine this before then looking at the implications for our values of different financing mechanisms.

Figure 4.4 sets out a framework showing the main approaches to financing health and the flows of finance and services between the key

Figure 4.4
In-country sources of finance

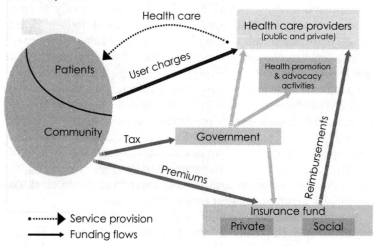

actors. The figure makes an important distinction between patients (who receive services and pay user charges) and the wider community (which comprise the patients and non-patients); as a group in addition to the user charges, they may also pay insurance premiums and pay taxes.

Health care is provided by a variety of different agencies (both private and public) to *patients*. Patients may pay directly for health care through *user fees* or *charges* paid at the time of receiving the service—the market approach to health care which sees it as a commodity for purchase. Such an approach is easily understood by patients in market economies as it mirrors the way in which *most* goods and services are provided and exchanged in the economy. Such charges may be a simple fee that is fixed irrespective of the activities carried out or resources devoted to the visit; such an approach is administratively simple. The alternative is to assign a charge to each aspect of diagnosis and treatment. This clearly can lead to a heavy burden in complex or chronic conditions. User charges have equity implications in that those less able or indeed less willing to pay for health care may not receive the care that their needs warrant.[10] They are particularly inequitable to the poor and the ill and can lead to catastrophic expenditure, pushing individuals and families into poverty and further ill-health. It has been estimated that 100 million people are forced into poverty each year through such catastrophic expenditure, of whom over 90 per cent are from low-income countries.[11]

The public sector in many countries traditionally avoided user charges, but two policies in the 1990s encouraged the adoption of such charges under certain circumstances. Most importantly, the health sector reform movement led by the World Bank promoted their use, for certain health services;[12] public health activities are generally accepted as being unsuited for direct payment. The second endorsement of user charges is associated with what is now known as the Bamako Initiative,[13] which sought to encourage community-based financing schemes. The best known of these is the Revolving Drug Fund that involves a user charge to contribute to a fund to replace medicines prescribed.

The WHO has had a rather ambivalent attitude to user charges. For example, their endorsement of the Bamako Initiative suggested support for their use; however, their report on maternal health made a clear statement opposing the use of charges for such services[14] and their report on PHC[15] advocated shifts towards universal coverage pointing out the dangers of user charges in terms of both lower levels of utilisation and catastrophic health expenditure.

Insurance mechanisms share (or 'pool') the risk of falling ill by collecting regular prepaid premiums from the community (potential patients) and then using the fund generated to pay (either directly or in the form of reimbursement) for subsequent health care needed. Such insurance can be operated as a private voluntary system or as a social compulsory mechanism (social or national insurance) through a public institution. The former is a market response to user charges and operates on market principles. As such (primarily) profit-focused schemes seek ways of maximising income and minimising costs. There is a variety of different potential policies with variations dependant on the level of cover sought/offered. Cost minimisation strategies include policies with co-payment (or deductible) elements, where patients agree to pay part of any treatment bill; this is seen both to 'share' costs between the insuree and the insurance company, and to dissuade insurees from seeking 'unnecessary' treatment. Liability ceilings are another cost minimisation strategy. Insurance companies may also attempt to bar individuals from certain cover (or charge very high premiums) where the risk is seen to be particularly high (or where the applicant has an existing health condition). Such cherry-picking may be the subject of government regulation. Workplace schemes may also be set up, which cover staff either through internal private insurance mechanisms or through direct funding from the company's revenue. In some countries, government may encourage private insurance contributions though tax exemption schemes; such approaches are inherently inequitable given the skewed coverage of private insurance.

Social insurance schemes share a number of features of private insurance. They pool risk and may develop similar cost minimisation strategies. However, as we will see, there are some striking differences with voluntary private schemes.

Social insurance schemes are linked to employment and compulsory for defined groups of the population. They are closely related to 19th century concepts of mutuality. They originated in Germany under the German Chancellor Bismarck and have been widely adopted initially in Europe and then in a diverse set of countries including Latin America, India and parts of South East Asia. They are less common in Africa. Social insurance schemes charge their members and their employers a premium that is proportionately related to their income (this may be supplemented by a contribution by government) and hold these contributions in a social fund that is expected to meet the needs of members (and usually their dependants). The process may be linked to other benefits such as maternity leave or pensions. Countries show a great deal of diversity in their systems of social health insurance in, for example, level of compulsion, form of premiums paid, terms and conditions of services covered, coverage of dependants, extent of market competition within the system, forms of cost containment and mechanisms of payment. There may be a number of schemes within a single country—each covering a different defined employment group (such as car workers or civil servants) or there may be a single unified scheme—known as a national insurance scheme. A key aspect of social insurance is their compulsory nature that enforces risk-pooling across groups with different income levels and needs. By being compulsory for a defined group, it overcomes an inequity that exists within private schemes where premiums are unrelated to ability to pay and indeed may, as we have seen, be related to need with those with existing conditions being charged higher premiums or refused cover.

Health care may be provided directly or indirectly under both social and private insurance. In the former case, the insurance companies own health facilities (under private insurance this may be known as Health Maintenance Organisations) whilst the indirect model involves a process of reimbursement or direct payment to third-party providers contracted to provide services.

The final broad approach is to raise finance for the health system through *taxation* levied at either (or both) the national and local levels and then distributed to health care providers (either public or private). As we have seen, the effects of a tax-based approach depend to a large degree on the profile of taxation within a country and the degree to which it is progressive. In a number of low-income countries, taxes are levied on goods such as agricultural crops or essential commodities, with only a small percentage of the tax revenue coming from income tax or luxury goods. This can lead to regressive and inequitable taxation. Taxes are seen by many as the only feasible way to raise funds for public health activities which individuals would not pay for either through lack of recognition of the importance of these activities or their externality nature (see Box 4.1). Whilst taxation provides a mechanism for universal coverage for a national population, it can also suffer in situations when priorities change in government, or when total government revenue is reduced such as during a macroeconomic downturn. At such times, the allocation to the health system may suffer.

The above has introduced the main forms of in-country financing. However, in recent years the term *community financing* has emerged and is often linked to the Bamako Declaration referred to earlier. This umbrella term covers a variety of different means of raising finance which have two key characteristics. First, funds are generated and retained within a defined local area; and second, there is a mechanism for linking the management of the funds to the local community in some form. The precise funding mechanisms can vary but the two most well known are Revolving Drug Funds and community insurance. The former has often been supported by external agencies and involves the setting up of a locally controlled fund usually at the primary care level, which is initially used to buy a stock of medicines. The fund is then topped up (hence the term *revolving*) by funds generated through a charge levied on patients at the facility. The management of the Fund involves the setting up of a committee that oversees its use and may have wider governance responsibilities. Community insurance has been promoted by the International Labour Organisation (ILO)[16] and can take various forms. Generally, however, they are fairly simple arrangements including a fixed annual fee with limited cover. They may be linked to existing social mechanisms (such as, in Uganda, a 'funeral society'). One of the downsides of such localised funding mechanisms is the potential for the development of inequity between different areas depending on their relative economic status and ability to set up such mechanisms.

A number of comments need to be made about the above and the overview of different financing mechanisms. First, we have at this stage restricted ourselves to *internal* sources of finance within a country. Shortly we will look at external sources such as support to general budgets and to programmes or projects. Second, Figure 4.4 does not refer to community-based financing, as this is seen as a variation on one or other of the main methods. Third, the figure refers to *formal* mechanisms of payment and service delivery. As such, it does not include informal or under-the-table payments (though, to the user, these may be seen as a form of unofficial user charge) which can, in some systems, be significant. It also does not refer to costs of accessing care, such as transport or lost earnings. Nor does it explicitly include services provided by informal providers including traditional practitioners and street pharmacies, both of whom may be significant. Again, however, the forms of payment used in these situations are predominantly user charges. One important form of informal service provision is, however, the family in which there are no formal financial charges, but where there are likely to be opportunity costs in terms of foregone income due to any caring role (see Chapter 2, page 62).

Lastly, Figure 4.4, almost inevitably, may suggest the existence of a *single* mechanism in any particular health system. This, of course, is clearly not the case. All health systems have a mix of different ways in which finance is raised, though there is considerable variety in the particular mix between health systems. Such a mix brings both difficulties in analysing the precise effects of each mechanism on the health system and, closely related to this, the effects of the dynamic interaction between different methods, to which we return later in the chapter. Table 4.1 illustrates this mix for a selection of countries. Note in particular how even a country, with a socialist ideology, Vietnam, raises over 50 per cent of its health care finance from 'private', that is, individual sources. At the other end of the spectrum, the US health system

Table 4.1
Sources of finance for selected countries, 2008

	Total expenditure on health (as percentage of GDP)	General government expenditure on health (as percentage of total health expenditure)	External resources for health (as percentage of total health expenditure)	Per capita total expenditure on health ($PPP)	Per capita government expenditure on health ($PPP)	Out-of-pocket expenditure (as percentage of private & public expenditure on health)	Social security expenditure on health (as percentage of private & public expenditure on health)	Private prepaid plans (as percentage of private & public expenditure on health)
Argentina	10.0	50.8	0.1	1 322	671	21.1	29.9	25.4
Bangladesh	3.4	33.6	7.7	42	14	64.7	0.0	0.0
China	4.3	44.7	0.2	233	104	50.9	24.7	3.9
Cuba	10.4	95.5	0.1	917	875	4.1	0.0	0.0
Ethiopia	3.8	58.1	43.9	30	17	33.8	0.0	1.3
France	11.0	79.0	0	3 709	2 930	6.8	73.8	13.4
India	4.1	26.2	1.4	109	29	66.3	4.5	1.5
Kyrgyzstan	6.5	54.0	11.3	130	70	42.3	32.3	0.0
Malawi	9.9	59.7	59.9	50	30	11.4	0.0	6.3
Nigeria	6.6	25.3	2.2	131	33	71.6	0.0	2.3
South Africa	8.6	41.4	0.8	819	340	17.4	1.2	38.8
Sweden	9.1	81.7	0	3 323	2 716	15.9	0.0	0.2

Tajikistan	5.3	21.5	7.8	93	20	74.1	0.0	0.0
Thailand	3.7	73.2	0.3	286	209	19.2	7.1	5.2
Uganda	6.3	26.2	31.6	74	20	37.6	0.0	0.1
United Republic of Tanzania	5.3	65.8	49.9	63	41	25.7	2.2	3.6
United States of America	15.7	45.5	0	7 285	3 317	12.3	12.7	34.6
Viet Nam	7.1	39.3	1.6	183	72	54.8	12.7	1.6
Low income	5.3	41.9	17.5	67	28	48.3	4.6	2.1
Lower middle income	4.3	42.4	1.0	181	76	52.1	15.8	3.1
Upper middle income	6.4	55.2	0.2	757	419	30.9	21.0	11.8
High income	11.2	61.3	0	4 145	2 492	14.0	25.6	19.9
Global	9.7	59.6	0.2	863	493	17.7	24.6	18.2

Source: Devrived from WHO. 2010.[17]

with its dominant neo-liberal ideology still collects over 40 per cent of its finance through government in part to pay for its safety net mechanisms of Medicare and Medicaid. It is also significant that as a group, the low- and low-middle–income countries raise a far higher proportion (around 50 per cent) of expenditure through regressive user charges than the high-income countries where it is as low as 14 per cent.

This difference in mix reflects a number of influences that are important to note, as they explain, in part, the difficulties involved in attempting to change current financing methods. First among these are historical influences. Health systems are notoriously difficult to modify, and financing mechanisms are no exception. The current mix of financing mechanisms is heavily influenced by those of yesterday. Thus, the importance of tax-based systems in Anglophone Africa reflects the early development of the formal health system in British colonial times. The next influence is related to ideology to which we have already referred. A good example of shifts related to ideology occurred in Chile in the 1970s where the wider political shifts in the country between Allende and Pinochet led to shifts towards and away from a public sector role and changes in associated private spending through user charges[18] which, as we have seen, are closely related to a neo-liberal ideological position. Box 4.2 summarises key changes in China in recent years with financing.

Box 4.2 Principal forms of health insurance financing in China

China has undergone major social and economic changes in recent decades particularly associated with the shift from a state-dominated economy to a market-based one, and industrialisation. Associated with these changes has been a transformation in the funding of health care in the country.

A particular feature of China is the existence of different funding and health care arrangements for the rural and urban areas. During the pre-market period health care was organised through the Cooperative Medical Scheme (CMS) in rural areas. Historical changes in the rural areas and the demise of the commune during the 1980s were accompanied by the eventual decline of the CMS and increasing inequity among rural inhabitants. The development of the New Cooperative Medical Scheme (NCMS) since 2002-3 has been rapid with coverage of over 90% of the rural population. The system is controlled nationally by the Ministry of Health although county governments are responsible for managing it and have some authority in setting the regulations. It is based on local government and beneficiary contributions plus central government subsidies in poorer areas and covers mostly inpatient services. The urban areas are covered by the Basic Health Insurance Scheme (and other smaller schemes from the pre 1997 period), created in

Box 4.2 continued

Box 4.2 continued

> 1997 to increase coverage, control costs and develop a more cohesive frame-work. National control is exercised through the Ministry of Labour and Social Security although there is also a fair degree of decentralisation in its manage-ment. Contributions are made by the employers and employees and applies to both the public and private sectors. Although there are important differ-ences between the rural and urban schemes they also have similarities: insur-ance funds pay for care to separate health facilities and members normally operate two levels of funds – an individual one which saves money to pay for the individual's care and a social fund which is a pooled fund and used when the individual one runs out. Strict forms of cost containment exist in the form of deductibles, co-payments and ceilings on the use of the funds.
>
> There has been considerable research on the impact of the rural and urban health insurance on the utilisation of, and access to, health care. For example, research[19] in two provinces found an increase in utilisation of inpatient ser-vice in general under NCMS; however, people with high income tended to benefit more than those with low income Particular issues facing these insur-ance systems include the impact of cost containment measures on access to health care, the problems faced by those not covered in the urban areas (such as rural migrants), the limited services covered by the schemes (such as the lack of outpatient care in the NCMS) and the impact of decentralisation on inequity between different locations.

In the 1990s we also witnessed attempts by dominant neo-liberal ideolo-gies often led by the World Bank to 'encourage' African health systems to impose user charges for health services. In Uganda, for example, user fees were introduced in 1993 as a condition of getting a World Bank loan[20]—their subsequent removal in 2001 led to an increase in utilisa-tion in health care by 77 per cent.[21]

The next broad factor relates to the wider economic context. Some forms of health financing lend themselves to particular economic struc-tures; most obviously social insurance systems which are funded by a levy on employment income require a well-structured formal sector with adequate means of obtaining information about employment and payrolls. Countries with largely informal economies or inadequate in-formation systems, as is the case in many LICs, struggle to set up such a mechanism. Last, though different funding mechanisms are not *neces-sarily* linked to any particular type of health provider (and, in particular, public or private ownership), there are historical links. Private provi-sion has been historically funded by user charges and private insurance and public provision by taxation and social insurance. This association reflects and expresses the nature of the market and the values underly-ing collectivist (state) and individualist (market) approaches. However, this pattern, and its historical association, is changing. The use of contracting within the public sector means that private providers may, through contracts, be funded by collective mechanisms; furthermore, the public sector has, as we have seen, adopted, in some countries, user charge mechanisms usually associated with the private market. Under-pinning this is a theme of the book—the need to revisit the tradition-al catagorisations of 'public' and 'private' as the characteristics of, and boundaries between, these catagories become more blurred.

We end this section with two comments on the implications of the complexity of financing mechanisms. First, the mix of financing mecha-nisms within any country reflects the complexity and degree of fragmen-tation of the health system. However, this is not neutral. All financing mechanisms bring with them a set of incentives for provider and user be-haviour. For example, the direct relationship between user charges and service provision may lead to provider behaviour designed to maximise their income; this could include, for example, overzealous diagnostic services. The complexity for policymakers is how to predict the specific responses and behaviour of those providers to changes in provider pay-ment mechanisms.

Second, the political difficulties of shifting a financing mechanism that results from the complexity outlined above should not be taken to imply that health systems should not review and, where appropriate, change their financing mechanisms. Indeed, we would argue that financ-ing is an area in particular need of scrutiny in terms of its effects on the values of a health system; reference to this has already been made and later in the chapter we look more explicitly at this aspect of financing.

2.1 International Funding Architecture

The previous sections have looked at issues related to mechanisms for financing health care that are drawn from internal country sources, and health system design needs to take account of these issues. The current reality for many health systems in low-income countries however is that significant amounts of resources are provided through external sources. Figure 4.5 showed, for example, that approximately 60 per cent of fund-ing in Malawi in 2008 was from external sources. The WHO estimates that for low-income countries, there has been an increase in the propor-tion of health expenditure that is from external sources from 12 per cent in 2000 to 17 per cent in 2006.[22] However, the exact amount of funding that comes from external sources is not well documented, and recent research has suggested that the amount of official development assistance (including through a gap between commitments and disbursement) may be less than often suggested.[23]

It has been argued that the addition of external funding can itself lead to a decline in domestic public finance[24]—a form of substitution effect. Indeed, there are wider macroeconomic arguments that aid itself can be dangerous.[25] However, here we are more concerned about the way in which such funding is provided can have significant effects on the health system.

External funding can occur in a variety of forms, and the complexity of this is in itself a major challenge for any health system. Figure 4.5 provides a simplified overview of the main categories of flows.[26]

Figure 4.5
International donor support flows

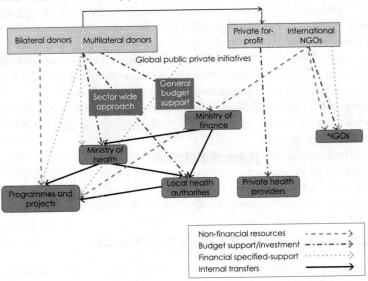

The different variables for such support include the source of support, the recipient of the support and the means of support. Each is discussed briefly below followed by some comments about the implications for a value-driven health system.

2.1.1 The Source of Support

Funding may be provided by governments through bilateral donors. In some donor countries, these are single agencies (such as Department for International Development [DfID] for the UK) or various (such as United States Agency for International Development [USAID] and President's Emergency Plan for AIDS Relief [PEPFAR] in the USA).

It may also be provided by multilateral funders such as the WHO, the Asian Development Bank, the European Community or the World Bank. In 2006, funding for health and population activities was estimated by the Development Assistance Committee of the Organisation for Economic Co-operation and Development [OECD] as totalling around $9.577 6 billion of which $7.173 2 billion was from bilateral sources.[27] As the countries' economic positions change, both the targets of such support change, and the composition of the donor countries themselves. The recent economic global recession has also affected the ability and commitment of some countries to maintain external support programmes. Furthermore, both China and India have recently become significant donors (despite still being recipients of external support).[28] The objectives of funders vary but include, alongside genuine concern for humanitarian issues, historical links (and perhaps guilt for former colonial practice), political manoeuvring and concern over global public health.

Some of these agencies have specialist divisions focusing on support to the health sector, whilst others may be more generic. They may also have different levels of engagement in the country ranging from international offices with limited visits to countries, to regional offices and in some cases in-country offices, some of which may even be 'embedded' in the health ministry.

There may also be private sources of support. This may, for example, occur as an investment in the private health sector, or through international NGOs to national NGOs. In recent years, a set of new international actors has emerged—what are now often called GHPPs or GHIs. There are over 100 of these,[29] but the best known are the Global Fund to Fight AIDS, TB and Malaria and the GAVI. The Global Fund was responsible for channelling $2.56 billion in 2006.[30] As we saw in Chapter 2, these have been set up as an international response to an apparent failure to provide adequate activities in specified areas. They are seen as ways of raising the profile of particular health issues or diseases, of attracting multiple (and new) financial support including through the private sector with major foundation donors such as The Bill and Melinda Gates Foundation[31] and of channelling this support in a targeted fashion.

2.1.2 The Recipient of the Support

External support to the health sector may be aimed at a variety of different agencies. The health ministry is the most obvious target, though in practice funding is likely to be channelled through, and require the approval of, the finance ministry. Such support may be aimed at particular programmes and projects or may be through general budgetary support mechanisms or through sectoral support as in the SWAp mechanisms (discussed below). The private health system may benefit in some countries from external investment in private hospitals; this may increase in the future with greater globalisation of health care. Occupational health provision tied to private companies may also benefit from external investment. Country-based NGOs, including faith-based organisations, may also receive support from external donors or NGOs including international religious organisations or donors.

2.1.3 The Means and Terms of the Support

Support for the health system can occur in various ways. It may be provided in the form of real resources (such as technical assistance or equipment) where there are no financial transactions. It may also be provided through finance. This may be closely tied to specific activities (such as specific programmes or projects) or may be more general budgetary support within a broad agreed framework. Such support may be provided as a grant, or as a soft or hard loan (depending on the terms of repayment and interest payable). It may have clear strings attached in terms not only of the legitimate activities to be supported by such finance, but also in terms of the way the finance is spent (for example, purchasing policies) and accounted for in terms of reporting; alternatively, there may be a degree of flexibility in its use, as in SWAp arrangements.

Within each of the categories above, we can see a number of different variations possible; this leads to a large number of potential permutations of international funding and resource flows. This complexity, which is impossible to capture fully appears to have been increasing in recent years and has led to various concerns over the negative effects such funding mechanisms can have on national health systems.

These effects firstly relate to the inefficiencies associated with such funding streams linked to the public sector part of the health system. There can be transactions costs related to accessing and then accounting for external funding. Such costs can be considerable and are multiplied where there are several funders of the same activity. Examples of the levels and effects of such monitoring is given in an OECD report,[32] which reports on 14,000 separate donor missions having been conducted in 54 recipient countries in one year; Vietnam had an average of three a day. They can also lead to the need to negotiate between different funders, each with slightly different sets of objectives for similar activities. For public sector officials, considerable resources, and particularly scarce skilled central planning resources, may be devoted to 'servicing' the needs of such external funding bodies. International programmes and projects may also prefer to set up their own management systems such as supplies and information leading to duplication, confusion and inefficiency.

Second, external funders in any sector are likely to seek clear linkages between their funding or investment and resultant outputs. Such linkages are easiest to see where there is either visible hardware, such as buildings or equipment, involved or where particular services can be associated with the funding. The latter occurs most obviously in projects and vertical programmes; as such, international funding has been criticised as reinforcing such verticalism. This criticism has heightened with the growing role of GHIs, which focus on specific programme areas (see Chapters 2 and 7 for further discussion on this). As part of this, the focus on specific programmes can be seen as being at the expense of the needs of the wider health system and its strengthening, despite the fact that this health system provides the platform for such programmes to work from.

Last, and perhaps most importantly, external funding can lead to a loss of national determination of priorities and accountability. Perhaps inevitably, the provision of funding carries with it a perceived right to determine how such funding is used; given the significant levels of external funding in some health systems (and particularly in weak health systems where policy and planning capability may be low), this can lead to a loss of national health sovereignty. An example of this can be seen in the notorious Global GAG rule set in 1984 which stopped any use of US external federal funding for abortion-related activities and which, in different forms, has been in place till January 2009 when it was repealed by President Obama. This rule effectively laid down the terms of US funding for family planning support.[33]

Related to this is the danger that the availability of external funding for particular activities (such as HIV/AIDS) can lead to a shift in domestic real resources (such as health professionals) to respond to this funding, again distorting national priorities. Priority-setting within the country may end up being set by the availability of foreign funding and the identification of needs set by the foreign funders. This may not necessarily accord with the needs of the population and as such may run counter to the objective of equity. This provides a strong argument for pooling of such external resources alongside domestic resources to allow a single nationally determined set of priorities.

Concerns over the negative side effects of the international funding mechanisms led to the Paris Declaration on Aid Effectiveness in 2005[34]

and attempts for grand redesigns of international aid architecture in the
health sector. The most important of these have been given the name
SWAps, which comprise a broad family of initiatives in specific countries
to coordinate aid.[35] Key components of this include common agreement
on a sector-wide strategy led by the national government but approved
by donors as a broad approach to the development of the health system, commitment to broad budgetary support to this strategy through a
common fund, rather than specific earmarked projectised funding and a
common accounting and reporting mechanism.

Given the need for donors to be accountable to their own funding
constituencies, this loosening of the accountability link can be difficult and requires a degree of political bravery and trust on behalf of the
leadership of donor organisations. Some bilateral funders, such as
USAID, have found such generalised accountability difficult and continue to work largely bilaterally. Indeed, there are no examples of national
health systems where *all* external support comes through a single SWAp
mechanism.

3 Assessing Financing Mechanisms

In Chapter 2, we introduced a number of values that we argued should
underpin health systems. We now examine the effect on these values of
the different forms of in-country health financing.

3.1 Equity and the Right to Health

The method(s) of financing chosen within a health system can have
significant effects on equity and the right to health. Two particular
aspects are important—the differential effects on both patients' health
and 'wealth'. We have seen that considerations of equity relate closely
to ensuring that health systems are sensitive to the *needs* of particular
groups or individuals rather than to other factors such as wealth. To
respond to this criterion, we need financing mechanism(s) that not only
do not discriminate against those with greater needs but also enhance
their opportunities of access and utilisation over those with fewer or
lesser needs.

User fees are inequitable, as individual decisions as to the uptake of
care are likely to be affected by the level of personal income and resources,
rather than solely health need. As such, two individuals with the same
health needs but different economic circumstances are likely, through

differing levels of utilisation of health care, to have different health responses. This is the 'health' effect. However, in addition, where services *are* utilised, there is a differential and inequitable effect between different income groups arising from user charges. This is the 'wealth' effect, and it relates to what the WHO calls the 'fair contribution'. Furthermore, under user charges, the burden of paying for health care obviously falls on those who are ill; those fortunate enough to remain healthy benefit doubly—in terms of their health *and their wealth*. Indeed, such a burden can be *catastrophic* where poor patients have to use savings or sell assets such as land essential for their future livelihood and health. Box 4.3 illustrates the difficult economic situation for rickshaw pullers suffering illness and user fees in the private sector in Dhaka city.

Box 4.3 Illness and economic problems of rickshaw pullers in Dhaka city

There is information, albeit partial, that portrays the impact of ill-health on rickshaw pullers in Bangladesh. Once ill, they have to put a halt to working for an average of 4 and 44 days for episodes of acute and major illnesses respectively. This means that they would lose about Taka (Tk) 863 and about Tk 12,000 for each episode of acute and major illnesses respectively. On average, the cost of treatment for acute illnesses is about Tk 263 and Tk 5,453 for major illnesses. Savings, if that is possible, can easily be exhausted following illnesses. Yet half have no assets or savings.

Source: Derived from Begun and Sen. 2005.[36]

Insurance systems appear, at first sight, to address inequity, with all those enrolled having apparently equal access to services for similar needs, and effects on income. However, the prepayment costs of enrolment in a private scheme can themselves be inequitable. The cost of enrolling in *private* insurance with flat rates clearly affects different income groups differently. This may be exacerbated by insurance schemes that demand higher premiums for those with existing conditions or perceived higher risk levels. *Social* insurance can overcome this income inequity by setting premiums proportional to the income of the member. The situation with private insurance, and some social insurance, is further complicated where *co-payments* are introduced. Co-payments represent a contribution by insurees to the cost of any particular treatment and are introduced by insurance companies to reduce the demand for, and costs to them of, treatment. They are, however, effectively a form of user charge and introduce back into the insurance system the equity concerns raised above about user charges—which paradoxically insurance was developed, through its risk-sharing principles, to overcome. Private insurance schemes may also lead to 'cherry-picking' of membership—attempts to encourage low-risk groups for membership (through, for example, lower premiums) leading to another manifestation of inequity.

Tax systems generally are equitable in terms of their effects on utilisation of health care (the health effect); the disconnection between health care needs and payment ensures this (though there may be issues in such systems related to the distribution of the services themselves). However, tax systems can still be inequitable in terms of the contributions by different income groups to health care finance where it is raised through regressive taxes. As we have seen, for some low-income countries, the tax base may be regressive with significant tax being raised through levies on goods or services including basic consumption goods and agricultural exports. Furthermore, taxation may be used as a significant source of funding by local authorities in devolved models. In such cases, irrespective of the equity implications of the particular fiscal approach, there is an additional potential source of intercommunity inequity with areas of low economic capacity less able to raise funds.

This particular aspect of inequity between different geographical communities that arises where funding is generated at local levels can occur in a variety of funding mechanisms. Different communities may have different abilities to fund health care (whichever mechanism), and local generation of funds can therefore lead to different health system capacities between, for example, the wealthier capital city and remote and poorer rural areas. Differences in the insurance conditions of membership between areas in China are referred to in Box 4.2.

The implications on equity of finance flowing from international sources will depend largely on the target institution through which the finance flows. Funding coming direct to government, through a SWAp, will have an equity effect which mirrors the use of the SWAp fund. Funding that flows to a private provider will similarly mirror their equity provision profile. The use of Poverty Reduction Strategies by multi- and bilateral funders may make them more conscious of the equity implications of their support.

The particular system of health finance, and governance, can have significant effects on equity. This is increasingly recognised by organisations such as the WHO, which have shifted their position to stronger opposition to user charges and greater espousal of collectivist approaches on these grounds.

A final point on financing and inequity is the concern that the multiplication of forms of health care funding can be a further mechanism for the fragmentation of the health system. Health systems fragmentation can be a mechanism leading to institutionalised inequity. Thus, different and unequal social groups can use different forms of health care funding that lead to different forms of access to different channels of health care with different levels of quality. The forms of funding open up and close down access to health care. Private health insurance is for those who can afford to pay while user fees sift out those who can afford to pay from those who cannot afford to pay but do pay (leading possibly to poverty and ill-health) or do not pay (and are denied access to good health care). A lack of cohesion between forms of social insurance, community-based financing and decentralised taxes can add to this fragmentation. In particular, the divisions in some health systems between those covered by social insurance and those reliant on tax-based provision of care through government health services is also inequitable. Where social insurance is not universal in a country, then it can lead to inequity as members may gain a better quality of care compared to non-members who may have to rely on an inferior tax-funded health care provided by the Ministry of Health or resort to the informal health care sector, such as street sellers of medicines. Those excluded from social health insurance due to their unemployed or informally employed status tend to be poorer than those enrolled in fixed employment and eligible for social health insurance. There may also be several forms of social insurance in a health system, each one with its own conditions of membership and access to health care. Family members of the insured may not be covered at all or receive a lower level of coverage.

Taking steps to deal with inequitable funding is essential for our overall aim of the health system—improved and more equitable health. Box 4.4 shows how Mexico has taken positive action through the introduction of *Seguro Popular*. While the new system added yet another form of health system funding to an already fragmented system, it was specifically targeted at widening coverage and access among the uninsured poor.

3.2 Efficiency

There are various ways in which the financing of a health system may affect the latter's efficiency. The first key aspect of a health system related

---

Box 4.4 Mexico and the introduction of Seguro Popular

In Mexico two main organisations of social health insurance (*Instituto Mexicana de Seguro Social* and *Instituto de Seguridad y Servicios Sociales de los Trabajadores del Estado*) have financed health care for those working in the formal economy – both public and private – since 1943 and 1959 respectively. As is typical of social health insurance, the system has been based on both employer and employee contributions; the federal government has also provided subsidies. In 2002, 47% of the population were covered by these two systems. In a socially stratified system, the richer social groups have been able to benefit from the social insurance model and/or private facilities based on mostly private health insurance. In 2002, this covered about 3% of the population. In contrast, and prior to *Seguro Popular*, the un-insured (the remaining 50% of the population) used government health services. These could involve a user fee and could mean lower quality of care. Another option for the poor has been to rely on an unregulated and sometimes informal private system of care.

Seguro Popular was introduced from January, 2004 and was designed to reduce catastrophic expenditure and provide the means to improve access to health care for the uninsured and poor. Although using member contributions, the system is funded out of tax income and designed so that the poorest are exempt from contributions. The system also forms part of a broader change in federal expenditure on public health. Members, whose affiliation is voluntary, are entitled to an essential package of services free at the point of delivery. There is also a discrete fund to avoid catastrophic expenditure in certain types of illness. An interesting point of the change is that the federal allocations to the State level Ministries of Health increase according to the State level affiliations to the new system.

Following on from the reform, utilisation of health care services by affiliated persons is higher and catastrophic expenditure is lower than those not insured. Also, inequalities based on State areas and wealth have fallen.[37] The reform and its evaluation are not without critics.[38] The challenges for the future are great and include not only consolidating any advances made but also developing the means by which universal and equitable coverage can be achieved in one system.

---

to efficiency in meeting objectives relates to its ability to raise finance. As we have seen, different societies devote different levels of their national wealth to their health systems and though additional funding does not necessarily lead to better health, in general terms it will particularly at lower levels of expenditure. However, the different contexts faced by different health systems suggest different feasibilities in terms of the various potential health financing systems. User charges have often been seen as relatively easy to implement, in their crudest forms, as they are understandable to the user, requiring little justification and with minimal information requirements. It is also important to remember the administrative costs associated with collecting user fees that reduces the net finance available for health activities. Furthermore, sophisticated systems for user charges require complex information systems and billing processes requiring significant resources. Health insurance systems, however, require complex information systems both to assess risk (in the case of private insurance) and overall costs to the systems in order to calculate feasible premiums. They also require monitoring systems to ensure compliance with the rules. For countries with poor health information systems, the development of such mechanisms may be difficult. Social insurance further requires the existence of information about formal wage levels that may not exist in fragmented and largely informal economies.

At the other extreme, tax-based systems are generally already in place (though we have noted caveats about their potential inequities which might suggest the need to develop new, or shift the balance between existing, approaches). All this suggests that the context of a country is critical to the design of an optimal and feasible in-country financing system. External financing can generate significant inefficiencies in terms of the mechanisms for raising, distributing and monitoring funds. As we have seen, these negative efficiency implications of multiple donor streams that are often project rather than system targeted were a key driver in the move towards more harmonised aid systems.

However, the specific method of raising finance (over and beyond its ability to raise finance) also may affect the type of, and manner in which, services are provided, that is, for every unit of resource raised, how its eventual impact is affected by the *mechanism* by which it was raised. This efficiency relates to the effects of financing methods on the behaviour of both potential patients and providers.

The first effect relates back to the discussion of equity in the previous section and how differing utilisation may result from different financing mechanisms. Clearly, if the concept of equity is built into our definition of the efficiency of a health system, then an inequitably financed health system, tautologically, is inefficient in terms of its response to the equity objective. However, even without that equity dimension, a health system that has lower utilisation by those with greatest needs is using its resources inefficiently by failing to address the greatest needs. As such, the criticisms that we have seen with user fees can also be levied here. The obverse to the effects of utilisation can be seen where patients demand 'unnecessary' (and hence inefficient) investigations or forms of treatment. Where a patient perceives that they have 'paid' for the particular service directly, there may be a desire to maximise the 'return' for this payment. This may occur, for example, where there is a fixed (rather than itemised) user charge system, or in prepayment insurance systems. Indeed, a cycle of inefficiency may be set up, where providers are happy to respond to such demands as it may increase their income levels.

The second effect relates to the behaviour of providers (an aspect of which we have just touched on). This relates to the incentives and disincentives on providers that different financing approaches produce. The way in which health care finance is raised can affect the behaviour of providers in various ways. First, where finance is generated directly and retained by a particular provider (for example, user charges) or has direct links with such a provider (for example, a local insurance scheme being set up by a hospital), there may be an incentive to maximize this income. Such a motivation of maximising income is not confined to private providers whose prime motive is *profit* maximisation. Public sector providers may also, where fiscal responsibility is decentralised, see this as a mechanism for covering their costs; indeed, in some health systems such as China, there may be bonus systems related to the income received or amount of treatment provided. Or they may see this as an opportunity to expand, for entirely laudable reasons, their service provision. However, the income maximisation motive may lead to tension between equity (responding to the greatest needs of the vulnerable), effectiveness (responding to those needs which are most amenable to treatment) and efficiency (the most health gain for the resources available, without sacrificing equity objectives).

Different forms of financing may lead to different behaviours. For example, user charges which itemise each aspect of treatment may lead to unnecessary diagnostic tests, or prescriptions; or, where they are linked to units of activity (such as charges per outpatient attendance), to maximisation of activity levels, irrespective of need or quality of care. Insurance systems in which payment to providers is linked to the numbers of members 'covered' by a scheme may seek ways to attract such patients. Famously, Bangkok has a higher number of Computerized Tomography (CT) scanners than many high-income cities;[39] this is attributed to a desire by private hospitals to attract patients and social insurance members with a belief that ownership of a CT scanner will be perceived as a measure of quality. External donors may also insist on sourcing materials from their home country, which may not be the most efficient in terms of either value for money or long-term maintenance costs.

Systems of health financing that are *not* directly related to the activities of a provider may also affect behaviour. Centralised allocative systems based on tax or social insurance may be criticised for leading to a provider culture that believes funds will be provided irrespective of performance. However, the response to this may be through appropriate management systems rather than changing the financial mechanisms.

Finally, the above has focused on the efficiency aspects of service provision. However, given the wider determinants of health and the role we see in a health service for advocacy towards other sectors, it is also important that the financing mechanism does not militate against such advocacy action. However, where there is a direct relationship between the collection of finance and resultant activities, as, for example, with decentralized systems where providers depend on locally generated funds, then there will be strong pressure to use such resources for service provision rather than advocacy. Hospitals and patients are unlikely to support the use of user charges collected by them for non-hospital–related activities including advocacy towards other sectors. Tax-based systems, where there is distance between the collection of funds and their usage, are the most likely sources of funding both for public health and for such advocacy activities.

3.3 Participative and Accountable Decision-making

As we have seen, participation in decision-making may occur at various levels in the health system and includes involvement in decisions about personal treatment, in decisions about wider service delivery and in setting priorities for services. It may also involve different groups including individual patients or wider social or interest groups. Different financing mechanisms may encourage different forms of participation by different groups in the above decision-making.

User fees have often been argued for as a way of empowering patients in discussions with health professionals about responses to their own needs at the clinical level. This lies at the heart of market thinking—the belief that payment for a good, and the ability to withdraw by the consumer from a transaction, leads to greater consumer power in the transaction. However, health care 'transactions' have very different characteristics from other market exchanges in that there is what is called 'asymmetry of information'; health professionals, by virtue of their training and professional expertise, are in a commanding position. Patients, who have less technical understanding of the needs, are likely to be psychologically, if not physically, vulnerable as a result of their health needs and may find the health care environment intimidating, irrespective of the financial aspect of a consultation. Other forms of health care financing also can affect the patient–professional relationship. Prepaid mechanisms carry with them the potential for patients who perceive that they have already paid for their health care, to demand services which may be seen by professionals as unnecessary.

At a second level, financing mechanisms may affect the opportunities and form of participation by citizens in wider decisions about health care systems. In Chapter 2, we argued that communities have a right to involvement in decisions as to the nature of the system. This could be at the level of decisions as to how services are provided (for example, the opening hours of clinics) or at the management level (for example, involvement in hiring staff and monitoring their performance) or the wider level of planning (for example, setting priorities within a district health service through involvement in the development of a plan). This has often been described as *community* participation (as opposed to *patient* participation), though the form in which such participation is managed affects the groups who are able to participate effectively. In general, as we have seen, there is little tradition in most health systems of seeking participation by community groups, though Alma Ata saw this as a cornerstone of the PHC strategy. One way, however, where a specific link has been made between financing mechanisms and community participation is through the community financing initiatives that were encouraged under the Bamako Initiative. In particular, Revolving Drug Fund initiatives generally include within them processes to include community representatives in the management of the local level Drug Fund. How this management is operationalised in practice varies significantly. However, it is an interesting example of how a financing mechanism sought to develop a link between the generation of finance and its use. Community insurance schemes also have the potential to develop similar linkages.

National collective financing schemes—social insurance and taxation—also incorporate the potential for public participation through their own governance mechanisms. Tax-funded health systems provide the legitimacy and opportunity for elected representatives to interrogate the health system, particularly at the time of setting annual budgets. Social insurance schemes may include within their boards representatives of the members covered by the scheme. Furthermore, the financing in both cases sets up legitimacy for wider accountability within the governance mechanisms, which were discussed in Chapter 3.

The degree to which international financial flows encourage or inhibit participative decision-making will depend on both the mechanism and the institution through which the funding flows. Where funding is targeted at a specific project, then participation, at best it will be within the overall remit of the services covered by that project. Within this, there may be different degrees of community involvement in decision-making. Where funding is directed through a SWAp, then the participation related to the funding will depend on the democratic processes set up by government and the accountwability mechanisms more generally.

In each of these cases, however, different groups have different power over the decisions of the health system. Decisions therefore on the development of financing mechanisms need to take this differential participation into account. This relates to the wider issues of governance and is discussed in Chapter 3.

3.4 Long-term Perspective

Planning for the future development of a health system to meet the future needs of both, the current population and future populations, we have seen, is important given, in particular, the lengthy time required to shift the strategic emphasis of a health system. The different forms of financing may have an effect on the ability of planners and managers to take such a long-term perspective, confident in the future sources of finance under different conditions. We include within this discussion the closely related criterion of effects on the wider environment.

First, the form of finance may affect views on the strategic aims of the health system. Where funding is directly related to specific service delivery, then this is likely to influence the strategic direction of a service. Where income is largely related, for example, to user charges, then health system objectives linked to wider health determinants (either directly through public health or through advocacy to other sectors) or concern over environmental issues may receive lower priority. Collectivist mechanisms that allow greater distance between specific services and the source of income may provide greater opportunity to respond to these broader objectives.

Tax-based mechanisms can be criticised for political vulnerability. Where the health budget is funded from general tax revenues, shifts in public sector priorities away from the health system may result in lower allocations to the health system. In some cases, such shifts may, of course, lead to health improvements, if they have an impact on the wider determinants of health. However, for health policymakers and planners there may be a degree of uncertainty as to the future funding levels for the health system. In some public sector plans, this is recognised and projected envelopes of spending are set, typically for a three-year period. However, firm longer term commitments are rare. Hypothecated taxes (which are related directly to health) may provide one means of ring-fencing future budgets for health, but central finance ministries are generally (and understandably) reluctant to see this as anything other than raising a small proportion of the overall budget requirements. There may, however, be politically feasible ways of linking funding to particular aspects of health; taxes on cigarettes may, for example, be linked to health promotion programmes.

Social insurance funds do, however, provide a means of dedicating income to health activities. In this sense they may provide greater stability for planning. There are, however, still opportunities, depending on the scope of the social fund, for transfer of health targeted funding to other areas covered by a social fund, such as pensions.

External funding is often tied to, and influenced by, political cycles. As such it may provide little long-term security and, as such, reinforce short-term perspectives. However, it can also be used to provide leverage for consideration of issues such as long term environmental sustainability, which short-term political considerations may ignore.

All the financing mechanisms are also vulnerable to changes in the economy. The global recession of 2009/2010, for example, hit individual patients who have less disposable income to spend on health care; it has also hit governments whose tax revenues depend on the wider economy and social funds, whose income depends on the employment market. Funding flows from external funders have also been hit by global recession. There may, however, be a lag between macroeconomic changes and their results on the health system depending on the financing mechanism. For example, budgets set on the basis of income generated by tax may not change until the following tax year, whereas individual responses through user charges may be more immediate.

Lastly, we turn from the specific values to reminding ourselves of our second objective for the health system. This relates to the enhancement of wider social cohesion that we suggested could be an important function of a health system. On the one hand, those financing mechanisms that emphasise the individual nature of ill-health and personal responsibility for responding to this, such as user charges, are limited in their contribution to wider solidarity or social cohesion. On the other hand, those mechanisms that emphasise individual responsibility to contribute to a wider financial pool to be drawn on according to needs— insurance (and particularly social insurance) and taxation—provide a firmer underpinning for social cohesion and action. The collective responsibility that emanates from collective funding mechanisms may be seen as being more likely to result in social cohesion than individual financing approaches, though, for this to be the case, there is a requirement that such mechanisms are seen as inherently *fair*.

Our conclusions from the above must be that a good health system should be developing and using methods of health finance that are based on prepayment and collective rather than focused on the individual. We see progressive taxation as the best form of such finance, particularly given the practical difficulties in many countries of developing a close alternative—social insurance.[40] Where external finance is significant, it is important that both the funders and the national decision-makers attempt to design such flows in ways consistent with the values.

4 Final Thoughts

We have focused in this chapter on the resource that underpins other resources—finance. Finance needs to be generated to pay for staff, medicines, buildings, equipment and the other running costs associated both with health services and with inter-sectoral action for health. However, there is cause for much concern in the in LICs and LMICs around financing. The low levels of funding contrast strongly with the high levels of need. This is in part a reflection of the tendency for poor countries to spend a lower percentage of their (already low) GDP on health than richer ones. Poor countries also show lower collective funding of the health system than richer ones, while LICs and LMICs raise more of their funds through 'out of pocket' expenditure than upper middle (UMICs) and higher income countries (HICs). We have however argued that differences in values in the health system play a part in explaining the level and type of funding in the health system.

We have argued in this chapter in favour of placing the onus of funding on forms of collective prepayment—taxes and social health insurance. These forms of funding have the potential to promote equity. They can be progressive forms of funding and favour the poor and ill. Once funds are collected, they can be allocated in such a way as to support a pattern of health services based on equity. User fees and private health insurance tend to directly fund the immediate provider and/or private insurance company. Collective prepayment mechanisms can bring the funds together in a governmental authority based on the principle of social mutuality and allow for cross subsidies with a view to equity. Particularly in the case of taxes, they fund an authority that can allocate funds for public health and inter-sectoral action for health.

In making this argument in favour of collective prepayment mechanisms, we recognise that strong progressive measures have to be built into taxes and social health insurance. It is not sufficient to simply argue in favour of collective prepayment. Rather, they need to be infused with the values underlined in this chapter.

We turn next to examine the processes by which policy and plans—the mechanism for setting the direction and nature of the health system and for utilising the financial resources discussed in this chapter—are made.

Notes and References

1. Some of the data in this section is taken from the UN Human Development Index website (http://hdr.undp.org/en/statistics/), where there is easy access to a variety of data including financial. The usual caveats about accuracy of data in this field (including how health expenditure is defined) apply; however, the broad levels of data are generally accepted. Readers may wish to access this data for themselves to see data on their own health system.
2. PPP refers to purchasing power parity, a measure that allows international comparison of expenditure which is not affected by fluctuations in exchange rates.
3. WHO. 2010. *World Health Statistics 2010*. Geneva: WHO, Table 7.
4. WHO. 2010. *World Health Statistics 2010*. Geneva: WHO, Table 1.
5. Hart, J.T. 1971. 'The Inverse Care Law', *The Lancet*, February 27, 1(7696): 405–12.
6. UN. 2008. Human Development Report 2007/8. Available at http://hdr.undp.org/en/reports/global/hdr2007–2008/
7. UN. 2008. Human Development Report 2007/8. Available at http://hdr.undp.org/en/reports/global/hdr2007–2008/
8. For a more detailed discussion of the issues related to market failure, see Witter, S., Ensor, T., Jowett, M., Thompson, R. 2000. *Health Economics for Developing Countries: A Practical Guide*. London: MacMillan.
9. UN. 2008. Human Development Report 2007/8. Available at http://hdr.undp.org/en/reports/global/hdr2007–2008/
10. See, for example, Save the Children. 2005. *An Unnecessary Evil? User Fees for Healthcare in Low-income Countries*. London: SCF. Available at http://www.savethechildren.org.uk/sites/default/files/docs/An_Unnecessary_Evil_1.pdf (accessed 18 September 2012); McIntyre, D. 2007. *Health Financing: Learning from Experience: Health Care Financing in Low- and Middle-income Countries*. Global Forum for Health Research. Available online at http://whqlibdoc.who.int/publications/2007/2940286531_eng.pdf (accessed 18 September 2012).
Meessen, B., et al. 2006. 'Poverty and User Fees from Public Health Care in Low-income Countries: Lessons from Uganda and Cambodia', *The Lancet*, 368(9554): 2253–57.
11. Xu, K., Evans, D.B., Carrin, G., Mylena, A-R, Musgrove, P. and Evans, T. 2007. 'Protecting Households From Catastrophic Health Spending Moving

Away from Out-of-pocket Health Care Payments to Prepayment Mechanisms is the Key to Reducing Financial Catastrophe', *Health Affairs*, 26(4): 972–83.

12. World Bank. 1987. *Financing Health Services in Developing Countries: An Agenda for Reform*. Washington DC: World Bank.
    World Bank. 1993. *World Development Report: Investing in Health*. Oxford: OUP.

13. UNICEF. 1995. *The Bamako Initiative: Rebuilding Health Systems*. New York: UNICEF.

14. WHO. 2005. *The World Health Report 2005—Make Every Mother and Child Count*. Geneva: WHO.

15. WHO. 2009. *The World Health Report 2009 Primary Health Care Now More than Ever*. Geneva: WHO.

16. See the ILO website for resources and publications relating to their Strategies and Tools against Social Exclusion and Poverty (STEP), available at http://www.ilo.org/public/english/protection/secsoc/step/index.htm (accessed 10 August 2010).

17. WHO. 2010. *World Health Statistics 2010*. Geneva: WHO.

18. Viveros-Long, A. 1986. 'Changes in Health Financing: The Chilean Experience', *Social Science and Medicine*, 22(3): 379–85.

19. Yu, B., Meng, Q., Collins, C., Tolhurst, R., Tang, S., Yan, F., Bogg, L., Liu, X. 2010. 'How Does the New Cooperative Medical Scheme Influence Health Service Utilization? A Study in Two Provinces in Rural China', *BMC Health Services Research*, 10: 116. Available at http://www.biomedcentral.com/1472-6963/10/116 (accessed on 18 September 2012).

20. Okuonzi, S. 2004. 'Learning from Failed Health Reform in Uganda', *BMJ*, 11 November, 329: 1173–75.

21. McIntyre, D. 2007. *Learning from Experience: Health Care Financing in Low- and Middle-income Countries*. Geneva: Global Forum for Health Research, p. 12.

22. WHO. 2009. *World Health Statistics*. Geneva: WHO, p. 107.

23. See McCoy, D., Chand S. and Devi, S. 2009. 'Global Health Funding: How Much, Where It Comes From and Where It Goes', *Health Policy and Planning*, 24(6): 407–17 for a discussion of both this specific issue and an analysis of wider external financing flows.

24. Chunling, L., Schneider, M., Gubbins, P., Leach-Kemon, K., Jamison, D., Murray, C. 2010. 'Public Financing of Health in Developing Countries: A Cross-national Systematic Analysis', *The Lancet*, 375(9723): 1375–87.
    See also Piva, P. and Dodd, R. 2009. 'Where Did All the Aid Go? An In-depth Analysis of Increased Health Aid Flows over the Past 10 Years', *Bulletin of the World Health Organization*, 87(12): 930–39.

25. Moyo, D. 2010. *Dead Aid* Allen Lane. London: Penguin.

26. For a more complex depiction of the aid flows, see McCoy, et al. 2009. and Ravishankar, N., Gubbins, P., Cooley, R.J., Leach-Kemon, K., Michaud, C.M., Jamison, D.T., et al. 2009. Financing of Global Health: Tracking Development Assistance for Health from 1990 to 2007', *The Lancet*, 373(9681): 2113–24.

27. OECD. 2008a. *OECD Stat Extracts.* Creditor Reporting System. Available at http://stats.oecd.org/WBOS/Index.aspx?DatasetCode•••CRSNEW quoted by McCoy et al. (2009).

28. See, for example, Young, M. 2008. '"New" Donors: A New Resource Family Planning and Reproductive Health Financing?' *Research Commentary*, 3(2): 1–19. Available online at http://populationaction.org/wp-content/uploads/2012/01/EmergingDonors.pdf (accessed on 18 September 2012). Population Action International suggests that new donors may not follow the Paris Declaration on Aid Effectiveness.

29. World Health Organization Maximising Positive Synergies Collaborative Group. 2009. 'An Assessment of Interactions between Global Health Initiatives and Country Health Systems', *The Lancet*, 373(9681): 2137–69.

30. Global Fund. 2007a. *Global Fund Annual Report 2007.* Geneva: Global Fund. The Global Fund to Fight AIDS, Tuberculosis and Malaria. Available at http://www.theglobalfund.org/documents/publications/annualreports/2007/AnnualReport2007.pdf (accessed 18 August 2008). Quoted in McCoy et al. (2009).

31. See Brown, H. 2007. 'Great Expectations', *BMJ*, 28 April, 334: 874–76 and McCoy, D., Kembhavi, G., Patel, J. and Luintel, A. 2009. 'The Bill & Melinda Gates Foundation's Grant-making Programme for Global Health', *The Lancet*, 373(9675): 1645–53, 9 May 2009, for a critical discussion of the role of Gates.

32. OECD. 2008. *2008 Survey on Monitoring the Paris Declaration: Making Aid More Effective by 2010.* Paris: OECD. Available online at http://www.keepeek.com/Digital-Asset-Management/oecd/development/2008-survey-on-monitoring-the-paris-declaration_9789264050839-en (accessed on 18 September 2012).

33. See http://www.populationaction.org/data=and=maps/global=gag=rule=timeline for a timeline of the GAG rule (accessed on 18 September 2012).

34. http://www.oecd.org/dataoecd/11/41/34428351.pdf (accessed on 18 September 2012).

35. Even broader than sectoral support is General Budget Support provided to the government as a whole usually through the Ministry of Finance.

36. Begun, S. and Sen, B. 2005. 'Pulling Rickshaws in the City of Dhaka: A Way Out of Poverty?' *Environment and Urbanisation*, 17(2): 22–23.

37. Gakidou, E, Lozano, R., González-Pier, E., et al. 2006. 'Assessing the Effect of the 2001–06 Mexican Health Reform: An Interim Report Card', *The Lancet*, 368 (9550): 1920–35; Hernandez-Torres, J., Avila-Burgos, L., Valencia-Mendoza, A. and Poblano-Verástegui, O. 2008. 'Evaluación Inicial del Seguro Popular sobre el Gasto Catastrófico en Salud en México', *Revista de Salud Pública*, 10(1): 18–32.

38. Laurell, A.C. 2007. 'Health System Reform in Mexico: A Critical Review', *International Journal of Health Services*, 37(3): 515–35.

39. Bennett, S. and Tangcharoensathien, V. 1994. 'A Shrinking State? Politics, Economics and Private Healthcare in Thailand', *Public Administration and Development*, 14(1): 1–17.
40. We recognise that the process of moving towards this and away from user fees needs to be treated carefully. See, for example, Gilson, L. and McIntyre, D. 2005. 'Removing User Fees for Primary Care in Africa: The Need for Careful Action', *BMJ*, 331: 762.

5
Health Policymaking and Planning

This chapter explores how health policies and plans are made and translated into action. Policies and plans are only useful if implemented, and there are various means to promote such implementation including through management, evaluation and regulatory processes which we examine in subsequent chapters.

We begin the chapter by discussing the importance of policymaking and planning and the links between the two. Although these are critical functions in the overall health system, there are significant difficulties with them in many LMICs. The analysis develops a framework for understanding how they work in health systems by looking at values, context, stakeholders, process and content of policymaking and planning. Particular attention is then paid to decision-making and its rationality, how issues get on the policy agenda, setting priorities, assessing strategies, stakeholder involvement and the role of evidence. The chapter ends by discussing the problems in planning, whether the market is an alternative and what makes good policymaking and planning. Throughout the chapter, the issues of values in policymaking and planning are emphasised.

1 Importance of Policymaking and Planning

The terms *policy* and *planning* are both often used loosely. However, fundamentally they both refer to, and express, the *intentions* of a particular institutional actor(s) and the subsequent use of resources to achieve set planned objectives. We are particularly interested here in the policies of government, but it is important to recognise that all institutions have policies and that all actors have opinions about existing and potential policies of other organisations. As such the making and implementation of policies and plans is an extremely contested aspect of the health system processes.

In what follows, we define policies as *expressions of intent of a particular actor*. They set out the desired position concerning an issue. Plans specify *the set of time-bound activities and associated resources* that will achieve, or move towards, the achievement of these policies.

Policies may be set concerning a variety of aspects of the health system. For example, there may be detailed *clinical* policies about how treatment should be provided for a particular health problem. At a more managerial level, *operational* policies set out the way in which a service or process will be conducted; there may, for example, be an operational policy regarding how an outpatient department functions, which specifies issues such as the opening hours, staff responsibilities and patient flows. Wider policies may be set concerning particular health problems; for example, there may be policies on adolescent reproductive health, TB or cancer. There may also be policies about health system processes themselves such as service delivery (for example, how referral is to be carried out or the role of PHC) or financing (how health care is to be funded). There may even be policies about how policies should be set—covering, for example, levels of authority to make different types of policies, and who should be consulted.

Policies, as expressions of intent, may be articulated in various ways. The most obvious are those that are labelled as policies. Laws may also express aspects of formal policy, though policies may also lead to the development of laws as a means of implementing policy. Within an organisation, there may be various internal statements of policy (for example, expressed through circulars). These are examples of formal, explicit written statements of policy, albeit with different levels of authority. However, policy may also evolve and emerge in a more implicit form. The most obvious example of this is a budget which reflects the importance placed on an activity, thus reflecting wider policy positions. Policies may also be a reflection of evolved institutional practices and attitudes; when analysed, no formal point may exist at which a decision was made to set the policy, though staff may be convinced that 'the policy exists'. Implicit policies are less transparent and less easy to respond to. Later in this chapter we argue that, given the critical role of policies in setting the direction of the health sector, it is important that they *are* explicit to allow stakeholders to support or challenge them and to allow clear responsibilities to be set and accountability exercised.

Policies, if they are to be *effective* expressions of intent, need to be turned into action—put into operation. This can occur in a variety of ways including legal and regulatory action, contracts with providers and direct management processes. In this chapter we focus on the role of resourced plans, which of course are expected to lead to some of the above. Subsequent chapters deal with other implementation processes.

If a policy expresses the desired end point, then a plan[1] shows how to get there. The first is primarily an end, the second a means (though of course there may also be policies about how to implement!). As with policies, there are various types of plans and uses of the term. Thus, within a health system there may be strategic and perspective plans, operational plans, five year plans and, more recently, rolling plans. Each reflects a different time period and degree of specificity (though, unfortunately, the terms are also used differently in different contexts and by different users). In general terms, however, strategic plans set out the broad intent of an organisation over a long-term period (typically ten years), whilst operational plans refer to the more immediate time period (such as the following year). At the broad end of the spectrum, policies may shade into strategic plans; the key difference is that the latter should include statements about overall expected resources.

Figure 5.1 sets out diagrammatically the relationship showing the different types of policies and plans. Not all health systems will have each of these types of policy or plan. However, the diagram illustrates the complementary cascading relationship between the different forms of plan and policy.

The figure also raises the issue of the relationship between policy, plans and management. This is presented in a linear fashion suggesting that management is the end point of the policy and planning process. However, the relationship between management and planning is again rarely clear both in terms of the process and the actors. In a linear 'rational' world, operational plans should be closely accompanied by budgets and provide the link to management through workplans that show the responsibilities of key actors in the implementation of plans. However, for various reasons related to both the process and the key actors involved, it is rarely that simple. Plans can never be specified so tightly that there is no room for manoeuvre; indeed, given the changing context it is entirely appropriate that managers have the opportunity to work flexibly within plans. The process of managing will itself inevitably throw up information and discover unexpected challenges and opportunities that we would expect managers to respond to. Lastly, the roles of managers and planners are rarely watertight. Managers are often responsible

Figure 5.1
Policy and planning relationships

Strategic direction

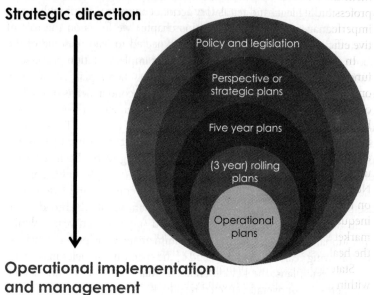

Operational implementation and management

for developing policies and plans as well as implementing them and view this as an integral part of the management process.

The alternative to making and implementing decisions about future directions of the health system through a collective planning approach is the use of the market. The neo-liberal ideology believes that the market both reflects the desires of the population (through what is known as consumer sovereignty) and promotes the efficient use of resources through competitive practice. The failures of planning can often be used as an argument against such a collective approach and for the alternative market approach. However, both the above market arguments can be challenged. Their applicability depend: on a number of assumptions. First, as we have seen in Box 4.1 in Chapter 4, it assumes that consumers (in this case patients) have adequate knowledge about their health needs; the lack of such knowledge may lead to expressions of need, which may not be in the patient or society's interest (for example, low interest in public health by consumers). Linked to this, the lack of technical knowledge about health issues leads to what is known as information asymmetry between the health professional and the 'client'.

This imbalance of knowledge results in a power imbalance between them during their transactions, and in the provider of the service, the professional, having to act as the agent of the user. These, and other, imperfections in the market conditions imply that the theory of competitive efficiency and consumer sovereignty is flawed in the case of health.[2]

In addition to these economic arguments, there is however a more fundamental one which is that the market, in making decisions based on supply of, and demand for, health care will ignore the equity impact of such decisions. Those with fewer resources will be less able to utilise health services; this runs directly counter to the value of equity which we argue should be at the heart of health systems. Whilst there are safety-net arrangements that can, and often are, put in place to overcome these failures, their very nature is inconsistent with the principles of the market. Neither can we expect the market to take decisive and collective action on the social determinants of health which are largely based on the very inequality generated by the market. This leads us to a position that the market is not an acceptable mechanism for allocating scarce resources in the health system, given our equity value.

State-led policy and planning, we argue, therefore are key processes within a socially oriented health system espousing the values we have set out. If conducted well, they set out the desired destination of the health system and the map to arrive at it including decisions on the use of scarce resources. However, frequently planning and policymaking is less robust than this[3] and we turn now to a framework to conduct an analysis of policymaking and planning.

2 A Framework for Policymaking and Planning

Consistent with the framework of a health system presented in Chapter 2 and building on the policy triangle developed by Walt and Gilson,[4] we analyse six closely interconnected aspects of policymaking and planning (as indicated in Figure 5.2)—values, context, stakeholders, processes, evidence and content in order to understand the causes of weak policy processes and strengthen them.

We do not attempt to show all the relationships within this framework (for example, that different stakeholders will favour particular forms of evidence) but focus on the key ones. The framework is that for state policy processes which are usually led by the Ministry of Health.

Figure 5.2
A framework for policy-making and planning

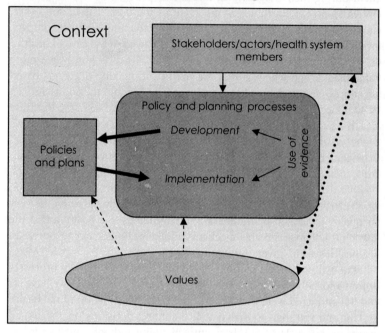

The *values* underpinning all health system processes are a theme throughout this book. In the analysis to follow, we explore the values in policymaking and planning not as a separate item but in the analysis of the other elements of the framework. We argue for a strong value base in policymaking and planning and again refer to our own stated values, though recognise these may not be shared by all readers. Plans and policies often explicitly refer to core values such as equity; indeed, this may be one of the few places in which the government formally states its values. In practice, of course, it is entirely possible, and not uncommon, that policies and plans do *not* reflect the stated values or that plans are inconsistent in their stated values. It is also possible that the values themselves expressed formally do *not* reflect the underlying and actual values of the health system and of the dominant stakeholders. In such cases, governments may adopt tokenistic and/or illusionary positions, proclaiming lofty values that bear little resemblance to reality.

The *context* is crucial to understanding policymaking and planning. Critical *contextual* factors include the health and demographic profile of a country and hence the type of issues to be focused on in the policymaking; the economic situation, both in terms of the level of resources available to underpin policies and the structure of the economy and its effects on health and health strategies; the political system, both concerning the broad approach to the relationship between citizens and the political process (for example, democratic, socialist, centralised or decentralised) and how the various actors or stakeholders interact and the political traditions of policymaking; the social context which affects, for example, the approach to different policy options that are likely to be acceptable. We discuss the context more deeply in the next section.

The *actors* are those institutions, individuals and networks who take an active role in the policy and policy process. These are part of a wider group sometimes known as *stakeholders* who have an interest in the policy but may or may not be involved in the processes. The stakeholders include, but are not restricted to, *health system members* who are the target group of the health system. We discuss their roles later in the chapter, but it is important to recognise at this point that there are significant differences between the power that different stakeholders bring to the policy processes; indeed, as suggested above, some who have an interest may have no place at the policymaking table at all. It is also important to recognise that it is the stakeholders who bring with them, and influence, the values of a health system.

The *policy processes* refer to the way in which the policies are *developed* and *implemented* and includes issues around its degree of rationality, agenda-setting, priority-setting, developing and evaluating policy content, the degree of consultation with stakeholders and the use of *evidence*.

The policy processes result in *policies* and *plans*. As we have seen, the terms *policy* and *plans* are very broad. They can cover a range of situations and issues including specific health challenges (such as a policy on heart disease) through to more systems-focused policies (such as health care financing). They can refer to specific programmes, to geographical areas (such as districts) or to resources (such as staff plans). They may relate to areas over which the health ministry has direct control (such as their own services) or they may relate to other providers. Policies may be very specific (for example, within clinical areas such as the stage of pregnancy at which abortion is no longer allowable) or very broad—such as a statement endorsing a PHC approach. There is a similarly wide range of policy tools which policies and plans may deploy to encourage or ensure compliance with the policy. Such tools include legislative requirements, provision of budgets and incentives, inclusion in codes of practice and training curricula, setting of targets and regulatory mechanisms related to licensing of practitioners and premises. A particular challenge for a health ministry is its relationship with other policies related to health over which it has no direct jurisdiction.

We turn now to examine each of these elements in more detail.

3 Contextual Issues Affecting Policymaking and Planning

We have noted already that the particular context of a health system will affect the policy and planning processes and needs to be considered in the design of the resultant policy content; it is important that policy actors take this into account. In this section we give some examples of the effects of context on both these elements of policy analysis.[5]

First, health policies need to take account of, and respond to, wider contextual issues. These include the demography of the country, the current health needs, the existing infrastructure (both in terms of health care and related services) and the general economy including both levels of income and forms of employment. It will also need to recognise and understand the distribution and causes of inequality in these factors and any changes expected to occur in the future. At a wider level, as we have seen, the particular nature of health will be interpreted differently in different social contexts and cultures resulting both in different views about health determinism and ethical issues related to the choice and management of technology (such as transplantation, genomic interventions or IT) and affecting the cultural determinants of health and health-seeking behaviour.[6] Policymaking and planning for countries in emergency situations or in the transition to development will also need a particular approach.[7]

Second, the development of particular health system policies needs to be considered in the context of wider national policies. Increasingly countries are developing, in part as a result of donor pressure, Poverty Reduction Strategy Papers (PRSPs), which sets out the wider development strategies against which health should be seen.[8] These may affect both the policies related specifically to health care delivery and the interaction between health care and wider social determinants of health. For example, gender policies may have implications for employment policy or services for women within the health care sector. There may also be economic policies, such as encouragement to the private sector, which are expected to be followed within service sectors. Wider educational policies may suggest the need for the health care sector to develop complementary policies or to advocate for health promotional changes within the education sector. An understanding of these broader national policies is therefore an essential component of the policy processes. They may even lead to tensions with the national level policies (such as encouragement to the private sector), which require resolution at a very senior political level.

Third, the wider culture and structures of decision-making will affect the policy and planning processes. The culture will affect the degree to which inclusiveness and openness is expected or resisted. In China, for example, there has been a culture of closed decision-making led by the Communist Party; this however may be changing with a more open process seemingly slowly emerging. The forms of authority both within the health sector and between the health sector and other sectors will influence the policy and planning processes. Decentralised models will have different methods of engagement with national technical leaders to those where policy and planning is centralised. Within these different models, there will be tensions between the desire to have uniform national policy and the desire to have local needs represented in locally adapted policies. Even where national level policies in theory allow policy flexibility at local level, national resource allocation may build in incentives such as targets to encourage compliance with national priorities.

Last, there are likely, in LMICs, to be external regional and international pressures on the policy processes and content. This could include, for example, membership of regional organisations where a regional position may be sought on policy, or where there are attempts to achieve a cross-border agreement on public health issues. It may also be expressed through the actions of powerful international actors such as donors intent on achieving a particular policy content.

Policy processes need to take account of the context both in terms of designing policies and plans that meet the current and future needs arising from this context, but also that are feasible to implement within that context both in terms of overall resources and in terms of the sociopolitical situation. We turn now to look more closely at these policy processes.

4 Processes for Developing Policies and Plans

Analysis and evaluation of the *content* of policies is not uncommon within health systems. Indeed, within LMICs, this is often part of the process of developing new projects and plans. However, there is less research on the *processes* of developing policies and setting plans. In this section, we look at key themes in understanding policymaking. Decision-making runs through these processes and we look at four key elements of this: its degree of rationality, how issues get onto the policy and planning agenda, the process of setting priorities and generating and assessing strategies and policy options.

4.1 Policy, Planning and Rationality

The first issue concerns the apparent 'rationality' of policymaking and planning. At one extreme of this debate lie those who believe that policymaking is, or should be, 'rational'. By this, they mean that it should be based on a defined and logical process of steps or stages which assess the options to meet identified needs and result in subsequent implementation and evaluation. Different commentators have described these stages differently and with different levels of detail. Figure 5.3 sets out a broad set of key stages. The first step is the setting of the policy agenda—the identification of the key issues that a policy should address. Getting issues on such an agenda can be difficult and may take time, particularly where the issue is contentious or politically sensitive. There may also be a limited group of actors with the power or ability to do this (we return to this later). The next step is developing the policy response to the issue, through assessing and deciding on different alternative policy options both in terms of policy aims and policy strategies. Next is the implementation of policies, which involves planning and management processes including the allocation of resources; it also involves monitoring of progress against the set policy and plan targets. The final 'step' is the evaluation of both the implementation progress but

Figure 5.3
Stages of policy processes

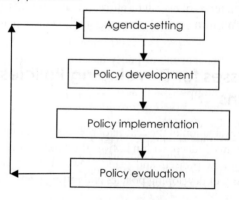

also the policy itself and its appropriateness against the issues originally identified.

At the other extreme are those who see policymaking as inherently 'messy' and responding to political influences. This can lead to what has been called 'disjointed incrementalism' whereby policymaking emerges from, or is continuously adapted through marginal changes, with different interests expressing and pushing their preferences.

There are elements of truth in both positions; furthermore, one's position may depend in part on whether one is looking at what happens in practice or what one might strive towards. The 'stages heuristic' approach should not be seen as a direct reflection of actual practice that divides policy processes into a number of conceptual steps but as helpful in analysing the characteristics and strengths and weaknesses of a particular policy process.[9]

Our interpretation of the health policymaking process draws on both these approaches and seeks to bring out the need for balance and blending. On the one hand, there is a need to move towards a rational approach, in that there are immense challenges to be met and fundamental values to be developed through policies; being rational is a way of developing these health policies, working through their implementation and measuring achievement. On the other, whilst greater 'rationality' may be seen as a means of improving policymaking, it is also important to recognise that policymaking is inherently and inevitably political. Ultimately, and appropriately, the policy processes used will reflect and act as a conduit for the different interest groups in a health system and we have argued in favour of a more open and democratic process of policymaking. In Chapter 3, we argue that this needs to be based on more equal access of interests, particularly of the poor, to policymaking processes. Blending the more top-down rational approach with the more 'bottom-up' process of participatory governance is one of the fundamental challenges of a progressive health system.

The planning process should connect, as we have argued above, closely with the policy processes. Planning should provide the linkage between general statements of policy and their realisation through resourced activities. As with Walt's 'stages heuristic' conceptualisation of policy, the planning process is also often portrayed as a set of logical steps. One portrayal of these is provided by Green (2007)[10] which we outline briefly below.

The planning spiral (Figure 5.4) has six steps. The first step, the situational analysis, is the starting point during which a scan of the health environment is performed to provide the background information against which, and drawing upon, subsequent decisions will be made. The next

Figure 5.4
Planning spiral

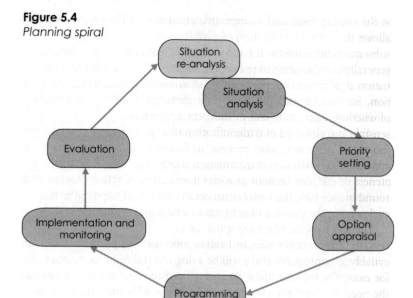

Source: Green, A. 2007. *An Introduction to Health Planning in Developing Health Systems*. Oxford: OUP, Third Edition, p. 36, Figure 2.5. By permission of Oxford University Press.

step is the hardest and involves the setting of priorities for the plan. This stage links closely to the policy-setting process, which incorporates already an expression of priorities. Once priorities are set and expressed in the form of aims and objectives, the various potential strategies for achieving these aims need to be identified and appraised. For each priority area, this will result in a bundle of strategies which have been tested against various criteria including feasibility and cost-effectiveness. These are then consolidated into a single set of actions—the plan—which should set out an overview of the resources, strategies and managerial responsibilities over a defined period.

Such a plan also provides the (planning) link between policies and management through the setting of budgets, which give managers the authority to use resources for specified purposes. The links between management and planning are clear at this point, with the implementation of the plan becoming largely a managerial function, though planners may remain with responsibilities for specific project activities and for monitoring the progress of the plan against set targets. The final step in the planning spiral is that of evaluation. Evaluation may occur during the process of plan implementation (known as formative evaluation) or at the end of an activity (summative evaluation). Formative evaluation allows the early identification of problems during implementation and subsequent adjustment. It has many similarities with monitoring but is generally seen as a discrete specific activity (such as a mid-term evaluation of a project or plan) rather than an ongoing managerial function. Summative evaluation allows a more comprehensive assessment of whether the plan objectives had been appropriate, the strategies were sensible and achieved and identification of any factors that may have affected the implementation process, including any changes in the wider context. This collection of information about the progress and appropriateness of the plan content provides important information for the next round of analysing the wider situational context—hence the concept of a cycle or, to give the idea of progress to a new plane, a spiral.

The stages of the planning spiral are (as with those of the policy process) in practice never neat, ordered or indeed linearly chronological. Inevitably, and properly, there will be a degree of iteration between stages; for example, the identification and assessment of options may lead to the need to revisit the objectives set during the priority-setting stage as the resource implications become clearer. Further information may be sought at various points, requiring a revisiting of the situation analysis, and clearly implementation and monitoring are continuous processes. However, the breaking down of planning into conceptual stages helps to identify the necessary functions, actors and indeed the points at which values may become an important influence.

In developing a plan incorporating the various steps set out in Figure 5.4, the process is likely to be facilitated or led by a professional planner, whose role is to ensure that the process is appropriate and timely. S/he will need to ensure that the process is consistent with the requirements of the public sector in terms of the type of *output* (the nature of the plan document), any set *timetable* and any formal *decision points* (such as consultation or parliamentary approval) have to be built in. S/he will also need to respect the prevailing organisational culture, though where this is inconsistent with the underlying values to be promoted in the plan, there may be a need to attempt to change these; for example, a medically dominant culture of decision-making may be seen as inappropriate.

Processes for making decisions may involve existing mechanisms, such as a standing or ad hoc planning committee or a political group which requires involvement.

We turn now to discuss key elements of the processes and attendant structures: how issues get on to the policy and planning agenda, the process of setting priorities and generating and assessing strategies and policy options.

4.2 How Do Issues Get on the Policy Agenda?

We saw earlier that the entry point for the development of a policy is its recognition as a key issue worthy of policy attention. Without this recognition, a policy issue can remain hidden and not responded to. For example, health issues such as mental health or disability have received relatively meagre policy attention and it is important to understand why this is, and what are the drivers that initiate a policy process. The range of sources for this includes championing by a political leader, the emergence of new evidence, media or activist campaigns or from international agencies with their own policy agenda.[11]

Kingdon[12] suggests that there are three key *streams* which need to converge for policy to get on the agenda. These are the problem stream, the policy stream and the political stream. The first of these refers to the underlying issue—such as high maternal mortality. The policy stream comprises the responses to the problems that different groups may see as appropriate and wish to get embedded in policy and subsequent plans. For example, this may be the development of emergency obstetric care to respond to maternal mortality. The final stream relates to the support for a policy initiative in this area; without this, there is little chance of movement on the policy. Kingdon suggests that the convergence of these streams provides a window of opportunity for a 'policy entrepreneur' to seize.

Other research, focusing on how issues get onto international agendas, has suggested that there are four key types of factors that affect whether an issue is given priority—the power of the actor, the ideas, the political context and the characteristics of the issue.[13] Box 5.1 gives an example from research in China, India and Vietnam that looked at policy processes and the factors that were seen to lead to policy attention related to maternal health.

What is clear in both the research studies referred to above and in the case study is that the process of getting issues onto the agenda is not only 'technical' but is clearly influenced by political (in the widest interpretation) variables. These reflect the power structures and which groups in society are empowered to have their voice heard, and we return to this in Section 5. The wider context and power within this is also reflected in the idea of punctuated equilibrium which suggests that policy processes move in steps.[14]

4.3 Setting Priorities

Within both policies and plans, priorities for action need to be set. This is because the resources available are limited—everywhere but particularly tightly in LMICs. Decisions are needed as to what will be focused

**Box 5.1 Factors affecting policy attention:
Case study from India, Vietnam and China**

Research in China, India and Vietnam looked at policy processes related to maternal health in three countries. The table below summarised the key factors that were seen to lead to policy attention and to policy implementation.

The policy issue	Agenda-setting	Policy development and implementation
Fits within a context of over-arching policy paradigms	✓	
Is classed as a health rather than a social or rights issue	✓	✓
Appears to have clear causes and feasible solutions	✓	✓
Is non-controversial	✓	✓
Has clear and credible indicators	✓	✓
Is seen as 'severe' or important		
Has a global movement to support it, with global targets	✓	✓
Involves only one sector		✓
Is a longstanding and familiar problem		✓
Fits easily within the institutional mandate		✓

Source: Reproduced with permission from Green et al. 2011.[15]

on and, by implication, what will not. The setting of priorities is rarely a formalised and explicit process, though governments may identify priority areas and diseases in policy and plan statements. Furthermore, the allocation of resources and budgets are an effective statement of priorities. Prioritisation is perhaps the most important and value-driven aspect of policymaking and planning as it determines what areas are focused on; yet we may know little about how it occurs in practice.

We suggest two related reasons for the frequent lack of an explicit process for prioritisation, the lack of accepted techniques and the political nature of the process.

There is no single and broadly accepted method or technique for prioritising.[16] Various are attempted, but none captures all the elements that one might expect to be present in considering priorities. Priorities have been set based on relative importance as shown by ranking health indicators, but none of these indicators are satisfactory, both in terms of the availability of appropriate information and the underlying basis for the priority. Indicators of causes of mortality would appear to be relatively straightforward. However, they ignore wider non–life-threatening morbidity and can encounter difficulties of co-morbidity and attribution of cause. By focusing on actual deaths, they may also ignore wider public health implications—for example, potential spread with infectious disease. Ranking according to morbidity is much harder as it assumes that the implications of a single case of one health problem is the same as another; but this is not the case—'flu is not identical to HIV in terms of its impact, in terms of pain, distress, social and economic consequences, ultimate mortality and disability. Some form of judgement as to the relative importance of different health problems is needed. The development of indicators such as the Quality Adjusted Life Year (QALY) or Disability Adjusted Life Years (DALY) has been seen as a means of incorporating the wider effects of a health problem. DALY is increasingly used as a way of measuring the 'Burden of Disease'[17] and bring the effects of disability and mortality together in a single composite indicator. Diseases can then be prioritised according to their contribution to the wider Burden of Disease. However, the use of the DALY does not *avoid* judgements; indeed, it may mask them.[18] For example, any composite indicator such as the DALY requires a judgement as to the relative importance or weight to be given to the different components of the indicator—in this case, disability versus mortality. They also, to be workable, have to make a judgement as to the relative importance of a life year at different ages.

Furthermore, though composite indicators can widen the scope of the priority focus (such as from mortality alone to mortality and disability), no single indicator can include *all* aspects of the implications of a health problem. For example, the DALY, as an indicator by itself, does not take account of wider effects on the community such as transmission of infectious disease or social considerations such as with a problem like alcoholism.

Setting priorities should result in clear objectives for the health system. There is a danger, however, that such objectives are couched in terms that seek overall (average) changes in levels of health or service access. As such there is a danger not only that they ignore issues of equity but also that they may lead to strategies in pursuit of these objectives that run counter to equity. This can occur as implementers, driven by the specific objectives, seek the easiest means to achieve these, which may lie within services aimed at advantaged rather than disadvantaged groups. Gwatkin discusses this danger with the Millennium

Development Goals (MDGs) and calls for disaggregation of such objectives to highlight and incorporate the distributional dimension.[19]

The above has focused on the importance of a health problem in terms of its impact or severity. However, this is generally not accepted as being a sufficient basis for setting priorities for action. The ability to deal with the problem and attendant resource implications are also considerations. Economic appraisal that brings together the health outcomes (often measured in DALYs) and the economic costs of strategies has been seen as a technique for tackling this.[20] The World Bank's reform proposals in 1993[21] proposed this and indeed ranked priorities using data on these aspects. But economic appraisal also masks various value judgements and is selective in the cost implications it considers.[22] Economic appraisal is used both to assist in setting priorities and in selecting between different alternative strategies for responding to priority problems and in the next section we discuss its use and how values are incorporated (often implicitly) in such techniques.

A different framework for setting priorities is that of a rights-based approach.[23] Under such an approach, a minimum set of services would be identified, not on the basis of economic feasibility but arising from a more political agenda. Increasingly, a rights-based agenda is being pursued by civil society activists who, for example, insist on the right of a woman to be able to deliver safely. One of the practical difficulties for rights-based approaches to planning however is the general nature of many formulations of rights. For example, the right to health needs clearer operationalisation if it is to serve as a useful planning approach. Thus it has been argued[24] that whilst a rights-based approach can show how the system failed, it may have less use in planning than in policy setting in part due to a conflict between public health approaches which focus on the community and rights approaches which focus on the individual.

Ultimately then there is a tension in the priority-setting process. On the one hand, there is desire to develop a technique in which measurable indicators can be analysed and which results in an apparently objective set of priorities. On the other, there is recognition that many of the concerns important in setting priorities are not quantifiable without incorporating significant value judgements both in terms of their measurement and the relative weighting given to them. Techniques can also be seen as closed and disempowering; economic appraisal, for example, involves concepts that are not intuitive or clear but that often incorporate values which may or may not be shared. Box 5.2 illustrates this with the concept of discounting, which refers to the process of giving different importance in decision-making to benefits that occur at different

Box 5.2 Economic appraisal, discounting and value judgements

Individuals tend to view benefits (and costs) differently depending on when they occur. In particular, people prefer to delay costs and to receive benefits (including health benefits) as soon as possible. For example, if asked whether the health service should invest to save 100 lives today or 100 lives in 5 years time, many people would opt for the former. This phenomenon is known as *social time preference*. As economic appraisal often compares alternatives which have different streams of benefits and costs occurring at different times in the future, it is often argued that economic appraisal needs to take account of this. Economists may do this by applying a *discount rate* to both benefits and costs that occur in the future which reduces their apparent 'value'. The higher the discount rate, the greater the importance given to the present rather than the future. In contrast, a discount rate of zero would suggest that the appraisal was giving equal value to benefits and costs irrespective of when they occur. The choice of a discount rate may be made based on studies that attempt to measure the overall average view in society about social time preference. However, for some policy-makers, they may feel that they have a responsibility to give the same importance in their policies to future populations as to present populations (a zero discount rate). The choice is then ultimately value-based.

points in time. The use of such a technique in 'discounting' future benefits would run against our stated value of giving equal importance to future benefits.

This then is the second major issue underlying the setting of priorities; the recognition that ultimately values and value judgements are an essential and required ingredient in the process. Those involved in the setting of priorities will bring their own values to the process, including both the criteria that they see as important and their application of the criteria. Box 5.3 gives an illustration of this related to cancer in Ghana.

This suggests that priority-setting needs to be recognised as a more political process—such as that used in the US state of Oregon where the public was involved in setting priorities.[25] Closely linked to this is the tension that exists as to the *level* within the health system at which priorities should be set. National level policymakers may seek to set priorities that span the whole country. They may do this for various reasons. There may be a desire to pursue equity and rights objectives and a need for a national process that clearly prioritises this. Linked to this, there may be a recognition that some aspects of policy need to have a national uniformity—for example, financing of health care—both in terms of

> ## Box 5.3 Priority-setting: Case study of women's cancers in Ghana
>
> A study in Ghana compared the different priority given to two cancers affecting women – breast and cervical cancer. Epidemiological and economic evidence indicated that cervical cancer should be given a higher priority in terms of service responses but, as a result of political pressure spearheaded by powerful advocacy groups including the Ghana First Lady, breast cancer received greater attention. The research concluded that traditional methods of priority setting involving epidemiological and economic evidence need to be set alongside broader political and analysis of the distribution of benefits.
>
> *Source*: Derived from Reichenbach. 2002.[26]

fairness and for practical reasons. There may be concern at the national level as to the existence of capacity, particularly in terms of skills at local levels to set priorities. There may also be less acceptable reasons linked to retention of national or personal power—which may hide behind any of the above reasons. However, a decentralised governance system is predicated on a belief that local priorities should be able to be set by local stakeholders both on grounds of local participation and accountability and on grounds of practicality related to the understanding of local needs. These two different sets of perspectives lead to a tension between nationally set priorities (often in the form of set targets) and local plans. One of the challenges of any national planning system is balancing these competing approaches.

Ultimately what is required, we argue, is a priority-setting approach that has two components.

The first of these is the full and balanced involvement of those actors who are seen to have a legitimate voice in the process at different levels in the system. Health systems decision processes are dominated by a combination of medical perspectives and sociopolitical elites and need to be opened up to greater and more balanced involvement and transparency. We discuss this in Section 5. Second, greater recognition needs to be given to the value-driven nature of setting priorities. Decisions as to what a health system focuses on and by implication what it does *not* focus on as a result of the scarcity of resources have to be led by values. These values need to be made explicit and open to challenge and debate. This requires a more transparent expression of the implicit values in priority-setting and the processes and techniques used within this. As part of this, the techniques that *are* used to assist in setting priorities need to be made as accessible as possible and not comprehensible only to a small group of 'technical experts'. In particular, and related to the previous point, they need to clearly show the values that are incorporated within them.

4.4 Developing the Content of Policies and Plans

A key step in the development of both policies and plan strategies is the identification and appraisal of alternative strategies and policy positions over issues that have been accorded priority and which are on the policy agenda. The issues faced in developing such strategies and the method-ologies deployed are very similar to those used at the final stage of the planning and policy processes—the evaluation.

The choice of alternative strategies to appraise is critical. This is, in some ways, analogous to the issues of 'getting on the policy agenda', discussed in Section 4.2 of the previous chapter. The list of poten-tial strategies for assessment will depend significantly on who is able to suggest possible options. It will also depend on how the interests of different groups are affected by the potential options. For example, options to intervene in HIV/AIDS may reflect medical interests or wider inster-sectoral action for health. The mechanism of, and selection of, participants in, the generation of options has a significant influence, therefore, on the final policies and plans and suggests the need for a very open and transparent process. We return to the issue of inter-sectoral ac-tion for health later in this chapter and discuss it more fully in Chapter 7.

In recent years, economic methods have been increasingly brought to bear on this process, particularly through the use of economic appraisal techniques such as cost-effectiveness and cost-utility analysis. The use of such techniques is not surprising, given that at the heart of economic appraisal lie questions about measuring the effects of interventions and the resources or costs used in achieving them. These two considerations are critical in any health planning or policy decision processes given the health-related objectives of a health system and the resource constraints within which it works. However, there are two dangers in too dominant a focus on economic appraisal techniques. The first relates to the fact that economic appraisal focuses on two considerations—the outcomes (expressed often, though not exclusively, in health measures such as DALYs) and the costs of resources or inputs used. However, there are various other factors that we suggest should be included. The effects of the *process* of turning the resources into benefits should also be consid-ered. There may, for example, be ethical issues in the use of particular interventions which would not be considered by sole focus on costs and outcomes. In particular, the *feasibility* of any policy and its acceptability are key as well as its likely *sustainability*. Though these may be argued to be considered as part of the process of assessing the likely outcomes, this is not always the reality.

Furthermore, the objectives of any strategy may not be solely related to overall health improvements. As we have argued earlier, the distribution of such improvements amongst different groups in the population is also important and is central to our definition of the aim of a health system. The *equity* implications of any strategy may be disregarded in a narrow economic appraisal, though, if the outcomes are adequately specified to incorporate the distributional effect, this can, in principle, be incorporated. The wider objectives of the health system—the empowerment of citizens—and the generation of social cohesion do not however easily lend themselves to incorporation in economic appraisal techniques.

The above should not be interpreted to suggest that economic appraisal does not consider values. It does, but these are often hidden. Figure 5.5 gives an illustration of this, showing the types of value judgements that are required in an economic appraisal of HIV/AIDS alternatives.

The above suggests that in conducting an appraisal of policy options, a critical step is the identification of the criteria for judging it, which may include narrow economic appraisal considerations but should not be confined to these. Instead, they should include consideration of all the values of the health system. Criteria therefore would include the equity effects of the different options and their long-term implications. These criteria indicate the value-driven nature of the process. Different groups with different interests in a particular policy issue will have different expectations as to the nature of the policy and will reflect this in a different set of criteria and relative importance to give to each of them.

Throughout the discussion of the various processes of planning, we have repeatedly referred to the critical difference that involvement by different stakeholders has on the character of the processes and we turn now to more explicit discussion of this.

5 Involvement in Policymaking and Planning by Health System Members

Who makes and implements policies and plans will affect the content and relevance of such policies as well as their likelihood of being implemented. During policymaking and planning, there is potential for the involvement of a wide variety of stakeholders or health system members,

Figure 5.5
Examples of value judgements required in economic appraisal using HIV/AIDS programme example

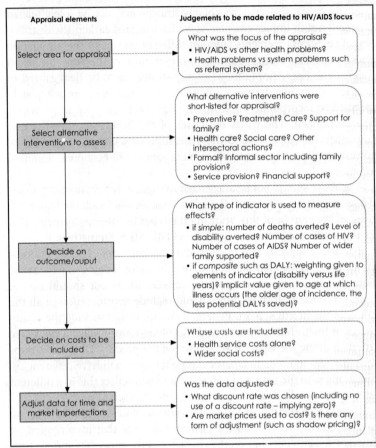

many of whom are referred to in Chapter 2 on governance. These groups will have different levels of power and ability to influence policy.[27] They will also each bring different values and interests to the policy processes. Some will be recognised as having the right to a place at the policy table, whereas others may have to fight for this—what has been called 'claiming a space'. The understanding of the nature of power and how it is exercised in the health sector is still in its infancy, but there is increasing recognition of the differentials in power between different groups.[28] The choice of who a government consults or involves in policy processes will reflect the values of that government. In the UK, for example, the coalition government that came to power in 2010 has been accused of promoting the interests of the drinks industry by changing the composition of the advisory body which focuses on polices on alcohol to include more representatives of the drinks industry, reflecting the commercial interests of the government.[29]

Involvement can take place at different points in the policy and planning process, with implications for its depth and nature.[30] For example, it can occur at the agenda-setting stage or before the contents of a policy or plan has been considered—when, for example, policymakers seek to identify potential alternative policies. It can also occur when (the core group of) policymakers have identified their preferred policy and seek views on this. These forms of consultation have a different objective and implications for the likely response by the policy leaders. The way in which involvement occurs is also likely to affect its quality, speed and effectiveness. A variety of means are possible, including small targeted closed meetings with identified groups, wider open public meetings, web-based mechanisms and formal distribution of draft documents. The form, and language used, can also be significant; highly formalised processes and technical language is likely to discourage broad involvement.

In Chapter 3 we argued in favour of participatory governance. This was not seen as a 'free for all' opening of participation to any group but as correcting the imbalance found all too often in health systems. We suggest the need to simultaneously reduce, modify and open participation to different groups. We outlined the types of group we would typically see in each one of these categories and this selection is clearly influenced by the values we subscribe to. We recognise that the specifics of this will depend on the context and form of the health system concerned and how groups relate to it. There is the need for some sort of method to allow for such an understanding. For example, policymakers and planners may use techniques of stakeholder analysis[31] to identify the power and attitude of different groups in relation to particular policy and planning issues. This may then be used to modify a potential policy or to seek means to address likely opposition to a policy through, for example, persuasion, compromises or seeking to form supportive alliances. This more political nature of policymaking requires different skills to the more technical analysis, which may be associated with the development of health policy.[32] It is clear, however, that the process is likely to be strongly affected by the values of those leading the policymaking process both in terms of the values underpinning the policy content (for example, concern over equity) and in terms of attitudes to the process itself (for example, concern to have a participatory and open process and who are seen as appropriate participants in the process itself). The precise mechanism of participation itself will affect who participates, to what end and to what effect. The term 'participation' also covers a wide range of approaches and objectives, as we saw in Chapter 2.[33]

It is important to recognise that having a more open process of participatory governance does not obviate the need for subsequent 'political' decisions in the process. Policies and plans resulting from such processes, if they are to be real agents of change, are bound to be unattractive to some groups who see their values and interests threatened. As such, they will seek ways either to stop the development of the policy or, if approved, to hinder or slow down its implementation. An example of both of these can be seen in Thailand where attempts to develop a social insurance system for health care started in the 1940s but only resulted in law in 1990; these delays were the result of resistance by groups opposed to its development.[34] Policy leaders will have to determine their attitude to the different positions placed by different groups and mediate these different perspectives—itself a highly 'political' process. This mediation role is an important one.

It is also important to recognise that policy actors rarely act alone but interact with each other. The role of networking (both formalised and informal) within policy processes which can bring new dynamics to the processes is increasingly being recognised and studied. Groups and individuals may also form networks to interact with the policy processes. These may be issue networks (formed around a specific policy issue, such as disability) or policy communities which are often tighter and share values.[35] Such networks may comprise members from across the above groups of actors. Thailand, for example, is a good example of a health system in which a policy community has had a strong influence over policy (see Box 5.4).

**Box 5.4 Example of a policy community:
The Thai Rose Garden Group[36]**

In the early 1970s, a radical period in the Thai struggle for democracy, a group of medical students with a strong commitment to equity and rural development formed a group that later met regularly to discuss how the Thai health system could be improved—with a focus on universal coverage. The members of the Thai Rose Garden Group gradually became senior figures in various parts of the health field in Thailand but retained their joint commitment and meetings effectively forming an influential policy network.

The different actors will also have different roles in the policy process and it is worth exploring these further. Box 5.5 sets out some of the key roles. In practice, these roles may not be clearly defined, and indeed actors may have more than one role. It is helpful however to recognise the different functions being carried out by different actors. It is also important to recognise that each group will approach their task with a potentially different set of values and also different incentives. For example, politicians' interest in the policy process may reflect a desire to maintain their electoral support; managers may have specific performance targets

---

Box 5.5 Roles in policy and planning processes

Policy makers: those who have the final decision power to *make* policy. Such power may reside with different actors depending on the nature of the policy; clinical policies may be made by health professionals, national level policies by politicians, administrative policies by civil servants, operational policies by managers

Policy leaders: those who champion and *lead* the process of setting a policy—this may be the same as policy-makers, but can be different. A civil servant may lead a process yet require political approval for the final decision

Policy facilitators: those who are responsible for *guiding* the processes. These may be mid-level civil servants in a policy or planning unit who are responsible for gathering evidence, conducting consultation and ensuring the process is followed and timely

Policy analysts: those who examine and *analyse* evidence to assess different and present different options to policy makers. This group may overlap with both evidence providers and policy facilitators

Policy advocates: those who have a particular view on a potential policy and seek to *influence* the final policy content. These may for example be NGOs with a specialist interest in the policy field

Evidence providers: those who *gather, analyse and present evidence* to the policy process. This may include academic researchers, NGOs, professional bodies and civil servants

Policy implementers: Those who are responsible for ensuring that the policy is implemented as set; these may include public sector managers and regulators of the private sector

Policy evaluators: this may be a formal process in which specific actors are asked to assess the policy and plans; it may also overlap with policy advocates who maintain an interest, once a policy is set or a plan made, in its implementation

to meet; advocates may have a specific and potentially narrow interest in the policy area.

The above suggests that for policymakers and planners, there is a need for four considerations. They need to develop clear criteria for who should be involved, at what stage and to what degree within the policy processes and then seek ways of applying these criteria. For example, claimed legitimacy by Civil Society Organisations to represent particular interests may need scrutiny and testing. Policymakers also need to consider the detailed processes by which they set policies and plans and the points of interaction with and between interested groups. This interaction is often viewed as *consultation*.[37] Both these suggest the need for a third consideration; the importance of being transparent as to the criteria for involvement and over the processes to be used for developing policies. Transparency is an important (though not sole, as we have seen in Chapter 2) factor in heightening participatory governance. Lastly, and linked to the issue of transparency, is the need to make policies that are currently 'implicit' more explicit in order that they are transparent and can be challenged by stakeholders and health system members.

6 The Role of Evidence in Policymaking and Planning

Decision-making in the areas of policymaking and planning (and management) involves a combination of three broad components, existing knowledge about the issue in question, values and judgement which brings these two components together.

In recent years, there has been an increase in interest in the first of these, with a variety of initiatives (accompanied by new acronyms and terms) to increase the use of evidence in decision-making. The GRIPP acronym (Getting Research into Policy and Practice) reflects a concern that evidence is not sufficiently widely used. The term *evidence-based policy* widens this focus on research evidence to any form of evidence. It has more recently been replaced by *evidence-informed policy*—a subtle shift of emphasis. The term *evidence* itself covers a number of interpretations and we look at these below.

6.1 What is Evidence?

For some, the term *evidence* represents the results of scientific research. However, even the term *scientific* can be contentious. Within the health field, there is still a strong body of opinion that holds that the only 'rigorous' evidence is that derived from randomised trials. This apparent gold standard for rigour is clearly relevant for clinical trials where treatment options are evaluated. However, for much policy and systems research, such an approach is either unfeasible or inappropriate and different research methods are needed. These include both other quantitative economic and social science investigations and qualitative methods. The last two decades has seen a growth in both the number of methods available, and their rigour, for investigating such policy questions.[38]

Evidence (as the term is used above) should meet various scientific criteria such as validity and replicability. However, a second form of 'evidence' is far more subjective and not open to such scrutiny and yet is a major influence on policy. This is the personal experience of policymakers. We all, within our personal lives, use our own bank of personal experience, including that passed on by others, to inform our decisions. This also occurs within the professional lives of policy actors, particularly where there is no clear scientific evidence available to them (we return to the issue of availability below). Ideally, policymakers should declare such personal 'evidence' for scrutiny by others but, in practice, such evidence may not enter the explicit domain of policymaking but still be used implicitly to give weight to particular perspectives or options.

From the above, it is clear that evidence is not 'neutral'. Its derivation, selection and interpretation are heavily dependent on the context within which it is used (or not) and the actors who deploy it in support of their particular case. A case study from the UK illustrates this well; it shows two reports on alcohol with access to the same evidence but reaching different conclusions each influenced by different values.[39]

Evidence alone cannot determine policies and plans; it needs to be analysed for its implications and this requires the further input of both values and judgement. At each stage of the policy and planning cycles, there are points where judgements and value-based criteria are required. We illustrate this with an example from planning (see Box 5.6). Sometimes these decision points may be hidden behind apparently 'neutral' techniques; however, these often have embedded within them values. For example, in the technique of economic appraisal, increasingly used to determine the best strategy to be adopted, there are points at which values are built into the technique as we have seen earlier in Figure 5.5.

6.2 What are the Sources of Evidence?

There are various sources for information which forms the basis of evidence. We have already seen that personal experience or informal

---

Box 5.6 Evidence, values and judgement in planning— an example

A country has set a priority on reducing the number of incidents from road traffic and is developing a plan. It has obtained information about the numbers of deaths, injuries and disabilities arising from such incidents and is examining various alternative option strategies to respond to this. Five options have been shortlisted for further attention:

- Speed calming measures
- Legislation related to motor-bike helmets
- Crossing points on roads near schools
- Enhanced ambulance system
- Educational measures about road safety

Each of these options has different implications in terms of:

- the number of incidents prevented or responded to
- the type of health effect of the incidents (death, injury or disability)
- the group affected by the measure (for example, motorbike drivers or children)
- the distribution of the health benefits over time
- the relative cost both in capital terms and ongoing recurrent costs
- the reliability of the information, given that this is a new set of strategies and information is based on a small pilot in-country and international data which may not be contextually specific

Values are required in terms of assigning criteria for judging:

- the relative importance to different (in terms of age and road user) groups
- the relative importance of benefits occurring in the near future rather than at some point in the future (known by economists as time preference)
- the relative importance of preventing deaths, injuries or disabilities

Evidence is needed on:

- the likely implications of the options particularly in terms of impact and cost
- the attitudes of different stakeholders to the policy options

Judgment is needed as to:

- the interpretation of the evidence
- sensitivity of the data to the country context
- the acceptability of different options in terms of implementation
- the trade-offs between the different criteria

sources may be important ones. More formalised evidence may come from various sources. It may be derived from existing routine information systems.[40] In many countries, however, there are poor information systems which are either collecting inappropriate data or have low levels of accuracy in terms of the data collection or subsequent analysis and transformation into information. Unfortunately, there is the danger of a vicious cycle in such circumstances, where the loss of confidence in poor data can result in a lack of further attention to accuracy. An important, yet often neglected, element of a health system is the design and functioning of such health information systems, both in terms of ongoing regular data collection and analysis and commissioning of occasional data collection through, for example, surveys. A critical issue in the design of an information system is the choice of indicators being collected.[41] There are significant costs involved in such collection and analysis and a built-in reluctance to change existing indicators. As a result, information systems may focus on information which does not reflect current values or concerns. For example, mental ill-health, an area of policy increasingly recognised as neglected, often has indicators reflecting an outdated view of mental illness and its treatment and prevention. Information systems also may have little data on distributional issues which are essential if an equity policy is to be pursued or on the wider health system components including costs or process effects.

Where the routine information system does not capture the information seen as necessary for policy formation, specific efforts may be needed to capture this information through one-off methods such as surveys or through long-term adjustment to the information systems.

Different stakeholders are likely to have their own sources of evidence which will carry different degrees of credibility with policy leaders. Civil Society Organisations, for example, may include testimony of patients or community groups whilst international organisations may bring experience from other health systems.

One particular issue related to evidence is the increasing role of the internet as a source of information. The growth of the internet has led to an exponential growth of information on health issues. This can be viewed positively in terms of opening up access to an area that has traditionally been seen as the preserve of the medical and scientific community; as such it can be a form of empowerment, though clearly restricted to those with access to, and ability to use, the internet. However, the lack of accepted systems of validating information on the internet also carries with it negative implications. The lack of any quality assurance on such information or contextualisation carries dangers with it.

6.3 What is the Capacity of the Health System to Use Evidence?

We turn now to a broader examination of factors affecting the general capacity of a health system to use evidence and particularly that generated by research related to health policy and systems.[42] Figure 5.6 provides a conceptual framework of this.[43] The first level suggests four interlinked functions. The key one in the context of this chapter is that of policymaking, but the use of research within this is affected by the generation of appropriate evidence, which in turn is influenced by the prioritisation process and whether this links to the needs of policymakers. It is also influenced by what the model calls the Filtration and Amplification function, whereby evidence is selected by policy advocates according to their interests and policy stance and the policy message amplified and reinforced through, for example, policy briefs or the use of the media in a format that is likely to be useful to, and accepted by, policy actors. These four functions can be performed by various institutional actors, though the most obvious ones are the health ministry (policy formation), research institutions (generation of evidence), research councils (research prioritisation) and knowledge brokers or advocacy NGOs (filtration and amplification). These actors comprise the second level. The third level in the model relates to components of the capacity of the different institutions to perform the different functions. For example, policymakers may have differing degrees of capacity and willingness to use a range of evidence,[44] and indeed to commission research to fill evidence gaps. Within the health field, policy actors may have come from a technical or clinical background with little training in either policy processes or in the use of non-technical information. Furthermore, the growth of information availability poses increasing challenges for the management of evidence for policy processes. This, together with the time pressures on policymakers and the fact that they may not have been trained in the interpretation of information, may lead to poor use of information. There is an increasing recognition of the need for what are called 'knowledge brokers' who can distil the key elements of complex information into a more useable format. Entrusting this process to such a group does raise issues of their legitimacy and trust, particularly as often such groups are external NGOs who may have a particular policy perspective. Increasingly, however, there are information specialists within public sector organisations who can either conduct such syntheses themselves or are able to judge the quality and perspective of external groups.

The model also suggests a number of other factors influencing the identification and transformation of evidence into policy at the different levels, including external influences, the availability of appropriate methods and the values and interests of the different actors. The model

Figure 5.6
Capacity of health policy and research system

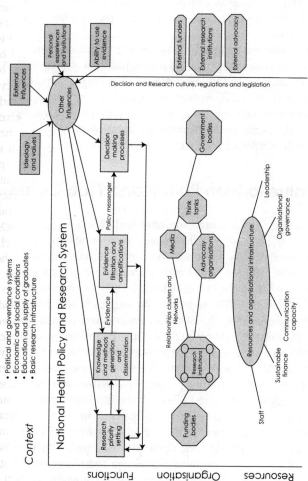

- Political and governance systems
- Economic and social conditions
- Education and supply of graduates
- Basic research infrastructure

Context

National Health Policy and Research System

Functions

Organisation

Resources

Research priority setting

Knowledge and methods generation and dissemination

Evidence filtration and amplifications

Decision making processes

Evidence

Policy messenger

Decision and Research culture, regulations and legislation

Other influences

External influences

Ideology and values

Personal experiences and institutions

Ability to use evidence

External funders

External research institutions

External advocacy

Funding bodies

Research institutions

Relationships clusters and Networks

Media

Advocacy organisations

Think tanks

Government bodies

Resources and organisational infrastructure

Staff

Sustainable finance

Communication capacity

Organisational governance

Leadership

Source: Reproduced from Green and Gadsby. 2007 with permission from WHO.[45]

illustrates the complexity of the different elements involved in the role of evidence in health policy. It suggests that using evidence to 'inform' policy requires a number of actors, judgements and values. For those working within the public sector with responsibilities for policy processes and structures, it may provide a useful starting point for diagnosing the current situation concerning evidence use and how it can be strengthened.

The above has assumed a positive role for information. It is important to recognise that pursuit of information can also be used by actors to slow down or halt a policy process. Opponents of particular policy stances may challenge the accuracy of evidence and demand new forms of evidence as a strategy to delay policy processes. Policymakers need to make judgements about the trade-offs between accuracy, relevance and timeliness of information for any specific policy decision.

7 Value-driven Policy and Plan Content

The outputs from the processes discussed in Section 4 are policies and plans. At the beginning of the chapter, we referred to the range of different types of policies and plans. We suggested that policies may be very specific (for example, within clinical areas such as the stage of pregnancy at which abortion is no longer allowable) or very broad—such as a statement endorsing a PHC approach. We suggest however that there are a number of characteristics of robust and appropriate policies and plans. First, they should, almost self-evidently, be driven by, and reflect, the overall *values* of the health system. Good policies need to be clear and set a direction for the health system that reflects these values. It is essential that the policy and planning processes are well understood and designed consistently with the core values.[46] Ambiguity leads to opportunities for non-action. They need to have unambiguous objectives and clear strategies and implementation details that relate to these objectives.

There is a similarly wide range of policy tools which policies and plans may deploy to encourage or ensure compliance with the policy. Such tools include legislative requirements, provision of budgets and incentives, inclusion in codes of practice and training curricula, setting of targets and regulatory mechanisms related to licensing of practitioners and premises.

We saw in Section 4.4 that the strategies adopted in the policies and plans will depend in part on the choice of alternatives chosen to assess. This suggests two particular challenges. The first relates to the scope of health policies. Many 'health' policies and plans are in fact 'health service' focused with little or only tokenistic reference to wider health policies and inter-sectoral action for health. The second relates to the relative focus on different providers. Health plans have often focused largely on the activities provided within the public sector. We examine each of these aspects of policy content in turn.

7.1 Health Alongside Health Care Policies: Inter-sectoral Action for Health

A paradigm shift is needed away from seeing policies and plans as relating solely to those aspects over which there is direct managerial control and recognising the potential for wider range of policy tools in support of wider change. As Chapter 2 argued, health is clearly the product of a range of determinants of which health services are only one.

Each health system will have different responsibilities, rights and boundaries for the sectoral public agencies such as the health ministry and each country faces a challenge as to how to reconcile the differing objectives of these agencies within an overall health agenda. This attempt to cross sectoral boundaries in pursuit of a broad health agenda is a long-standing challenge to policymakers, and there is no single solution. The PHC strategy of Alma Ata referred to multi-sectoral collaboration and in the 1980s there were attempts to develop coordinated cross-sectoral policies, particularly through the mechanism of national coordinating committees. Such committees had little power however and were often reduced to a role of 'talking-shops'. The challenge of HIV/AIDS and the recognised need for cross-sectoral strategies led to the development of specific institutions in some countries such as National AIDS Commissions organisationally housed at high levels of government such as the President's Office. However, most aspects of life have a health dimension; this solution of involving high-level political leverage cannot be available for all these health issues and governments continue to struggle with seeking ways to discourage what has been called 'silo' mentalities between the different sectoral boundaries. The WHO has, in recent years, raised the profile of the wider determinants of health in two important initiatives. First, the impact of tobacco on health led to the Framework Convention on Tobacco Control in 2005. More recently, the determinants of health have been the subject of a major Commission on Social Determinants of Health. These international initiatives mirror those needed at the national level and indeed are being pursued in some countries. Wider development initiatives such as Poverty Reduction Strategies have attempted to cross-sectoral boundaries and provide an opportunity for raising the wider health profile and related inter-sectoral activities. Some countries and states have gained a reputation for taking a broad view of health and focusing, alongside health care, on the wider determinants of health. Kerala state, for example, in India has an above average (for its income level) set of health indicators which are attributed to its wider strategies in areas such as female education. However, for many health systems, crossing the sectoral boundaries remains a significant policy challenge. This challenge to inter-sectoral action may be reinforced by international funding flows reinforcing specific service strategies on diseases or, even where there are SWAps, a service provision focus. There is a clear need for inter-sectoral action to permeate health policy and planning and financial processes.

From the health ministry's perspective complementary strategies can be identified to developing the cross-sectoral dimension of health policies. We discuss strategies for Inter-sectoral Action for Health further in chapters 3, 6 and 7.

7.2 Policies Encompassing All Health Care Providers

The second major challenge is ensuring that plans and policies developed by the health ministry relate to all providers and not solely those within the public sector or those over whom there is direct managerial control. The internationally led reforms of the 1990s led many countries to both decentralise their health system governance and to give greater provision roles to other agencies outside the direct managerial control of the health ministry. There is a temptation for this to be interpreted as implying reduced policy involvement over areas covered by these providers, but it is essential, if the health system is to achieve the objectives we have suggested in Chapter 2, that a holistic view is taken recognising the multiplicity of providers. However, this suggests that policies and plans have to develop new tools for influencing providers other than the traditional public sector ones of command and control. A range of incentives and controls, contracts and regulatory mechanisms need to be developed to allow the full potential of the heterogeneous health system to be maximised.[47] However, policymakers also have to consider the overall composition of the health sector and be prepared to challenge the conventional wisdom that the private sector is an inevitably more efficient provider and that choice is both desirable and likely to result in greater efficiency. We discuss the role of the private sector in provision of health care in see Chapter 7.

8 Implementing Policies and Plans

The final element of the policy and planning processes is the implementation of the policies and plans. The implementation of plans needs to be closely linked to managerial processes and we discuss these in more detail in Chapter 6. However, there are some general points related to the planning processes which need to be made at this stage.

8.1 Causes of Implementation Failure

Without implementation, plans are, of course, meaningless. However, plans or policies may not result in action—what has been termed *policy evaporation*[48] or the implementation gap.[49] The most apparent cause or symptom of implementation failure is a lack of sufficient funding or other resources—or a more general lack of capacity.[50] We examine this in more detail below both in terms of financial resources and human resources, the two key ones for the health system. However, other causes of an implementation gap are a lack of administrative or legal authority or changes in the wider context since the policy was designed. Implementation may also not occur as planned due to monitoring or management failures and/or lack of administrative authority to make plans and policies. We examine management issues in Chapter 6.

The implementation of policies may also be resisted for various reasons. Interests groups who feel adversely affected by the policies may seek ways to slow or stop implementation. For example, pharmaceutical companies have resisted the implementation of policies around the introduction of generic medicine lists. They may use a variety of techniques to counter implementation including legal mechanisms or political pressure. Resistance may also come from those expected to implement them who may see their interests threatened (for example, doctors concerned about the introduction of greater diagnostic powers to nurse practitioners) or who feel that the policies may not result in the outcomes sought. For example, they may feel that the policies are out of date or unfeasible. As such, they may be ignored. Planning may be unrelated to policies or may, not uncommonly, be either seen as a bureaucratic exercise which has to be completed, but with little worth, or as leading to plans that are rapidly out of date in a swiftly changing context. The format for plans and processes for their development may also reflect a top–down and closed approach to governance that is inappropriate. Policy may be set, or dominated, by an inappropriate set of actors—what is often called policy capture. Such a process is likely to result in policies that do not reflect the core values that we argued for in Chapter 2; furthermore, there may not be general support for, or what is often called ownership, of the policies. Policy may also not be informed by current knowledge. Where there is inadequate consideration of evidence in the setting of policy, then subsequent strategies may not result in the desired policies. Inappropriate policymaking may also result in a set of policies that are not consistent with each other; this can happen, for example, when disease-focused polices are set by different parts of the health ministry with little internal coordination. Such inconsistency may lead to a failure of one or more policies to be implemented as expected, or inefficiently. In Uganda, for example, a pilot to test contracting in hospitals set performance targets which included the use of anti-malarial drugs which were different from those in guidelines from the malaria section of the health ministry; it also set hospitals targets to treat more cases of malaria as well as asking the same hospitals to expand and support the community distributors to treat malaria at the community level.[51] Such inconsistency may lead to a failure of one or both policies to be implemented as expected, or inefficiently.

These problems suggest two interlinked wider underlying causes. First, it suggests poor policy design which did not adequately examine the needs, feasibility and implementation processes. Second, it suggests a lack of support from key actors. In particular, managers or health professionals who do not agree with the policy or plan content may find ways of subverting, ignoring or slowing down implementation. This can lead to what has been described as street bureaucracy[52] where higher level policies are reinterpreted and implemented in a manner which is different to the original intent. These problems can lead to cynicism about planning and more generally about the role of the state.

8.2 Allocation of Financial Resources Including Resource Allocation Formulae and Payment Mechanisms

A lack of adequate financial resources can be a major cause of non-implementation. Chapter 4 focused on the generation of finance for the health system. We turn here to look at how these funds are distributed within the health system—a critical aspect of planning and implementation. Where funding is raised through centralised collective mechanisms such as social insurance and taxation, decisions are needed as to the principles underlying subsequent allocation of these funds to the providers of services. This contrasts, for example, with situations where user fees are used by the same provider who collects them.

International funding is another case in which the donor has different levels of control over the allocation of funding. We have criticised above the tendency for donors such as bilateral aid agencies and Global Health Initiatives to determine the destiny of international funds away from the in-country planning process. We argued in favour of directing these funds through more collective mechanisms (different forms of budget support) that allow for their allocation according to in-country health needs and not agendas set outside the country health system.

One argument in favour of collective prepayment is that they separate the funds from the interests of international donors, health care providers and private companies and locate them, in the first instance, in a separate authority. This allows for their subsequent allocation on the basis of key values, such as equity and efficiency/effectiveness. This, however, is not a simple matter and there are number of mechanisms and issues to be taken into account.

8.2.1 Allocation Within a Managed System

Within a managed 'command and control' system, central decisions are made on an annual basis as to the budgets for lower administrative levels. A 'valued' health system would apply the principles and values set out in Chapter 2 to such a process. The precise manner in which such budgets are set will vary between health systems, but the key determinants frequently found to underpin such decisions are shown in Box 5.7.

8.2.2 Effect of Different Models of Decentralisation on Financing and Allocation

The above form of allocation assumes a managed system from the centre to the periphery. Different models of decentralisation are likely to affect, and be affected by, the financing mechanisms. In a devolved model, a large part of central funding can be channelled directly to local authorities from the central finance ministry or the local government ministry without passing through the health ministry. These funds could be non-conditional, leaving the responsibility to the local government to make sectoral allocations or conditional with the central level requiring a specified level and/or type of sectoral expenditure by the lower level. The decentralisation of decision-making to lower levels may mean that priorities regarding health vary. In Uganda, for example, decentralisation of the responsibility for decision-making on sectoral allocations to the

Box 5.7 Approaches to allocating resources and setting budgets

Current service and resource levels

Budgets may be set taking account of existing service parameters such as the number of facilities or beds or existing resource levels such as the number of staff. This is often linked to set norms for resources related to each of these. Such an approach is administratively simple and 'politically' unchallenging in that it attempts to allocate finance to existing processes, thus maintaining the status quo. For such an approach to be equitable, there would need to be a clear mapping between such services and the underlying needs to which they respond. Unfortunately, many services exist and are located in their current positions, as a result of decisions made long ago, possibly with little interest in equity. Even where this has been a consideration, changes in relative health needs between areas will not be reflected in such an approach to allocation.

Previous budgets

Often, budgets and resource allocations are incrementalist in nature with budget levels being closely influenced by the previous year's budget or, in some cases, expenditure. Such a historical incremental approach to resource allocation inevitably ignores issues of equity. Even if, at some historical point, budgets had been developed based on relative health needs, these are likely to have changed subsequently.

Utilisation data

Budgets may be linked to health service utilisation data. It can be argued that utilisation data can be taken as a proxy for health needs. However, utilisation data will inevitably be higher in areas with existing facilities and lower in poorly served areas. Unless there is a clear linkage between distribution of services and needs (see above), then an approach based on current utilisation may lead to an exacerbation of existing inequity.

Health needs

Some health systems have attempted to introduce an equity-based approach to allocating finance. Most famously the UK NHS changed its allocative criteria in the mid-1970s (and adjusted it subsequently) to reflect population need (using population and standardised mortality rates) adjusted for various other indicators such as relative service costs and any cost differentials involved in providing services in different parts of the country. Other health systems have attempted to develop similar equity-focused formulae,[53] though the paucity of information on population health needs has often meant that population numbers (possibly adjusted to take account of differential costs associated with different age groups) is taken as a proxy for wider needs. Such an approach needs careful introduction into a health system that is currently allocating according to one or more of the above criteria. Given the current inequitable distribution of resources to lower levels of the health system, a shift to a needs-based system is likely to encounter political resistance from areas which have previously, in relative terms, been 'over-provided' and from whom resources will be (relatively) taken away. There may also be issues related to the capacity of the previously under-resourced areas to absorb significant new resources in the short term. A phased approach is almost inevitably required.

district level in the late 1980s led to less funds for primary health care until the central government switched to conditional allocations for health from the centre.

However, devolution has also been used as a way to devolve fiscal responsibility to lower levels. Such devolved funding responsibility may result in either the use of fees or local taxation, which may be inequitable (in addition to any inherent inequity of the local financing mechanisms itself) between different communities with economic capacity.

8.2.3 Finance for Inter-sectoral Action for Health

The above has focused on allocation of resources to health service delivery. However, we have argued that a key function of the health system is also supporting and advocating for health-related activities in other sectors. We discuss IAH in other chapters and particularly in Chapters 3, 6 and 7. It is important that such activities are seen as important in organisations such as the Ministry of Health, disease control programmes and decentralised health authorities. Resources need to be allocated for this purpose. This can include funding for research studies, travel, meetings and conferences and publications advocating for other non-health organisations to take on a health agenda. All this requires funding, as do joint programmes with other sectors. This is most obviously funded through the public collective system of finance and generated though taxes. Allocation mechanisms then need to ensure that IAH including advocacy and joint programmes with other sectors receive required funds. This could be through the regular budgets assigned to organisations and conditional or unconditional grants to health organisations to promote IAH. This needs to be accompanied by these organisations having the authority to spend across sector boundaries with monitoring and evaluation of expenditure to ensure its inter-sectoral nature. Crossing the functional and geographical boundaries of the public sector is not easy. However, we emphasise in Chapter 6 that managers need to be much more conscious of the linking role of management.

8.2.4 Contracting

Centrally and locally raised public sector funds may also be used to contract services from providers including the private and NGO sectors (see Chapter 7 for further discussion of contracting). The terms of such contracts will affect how such providers behave through the reimbursement terms. For example, contracts may be based on total services provided in different categories (with different reimbursement rates attached), total

patients covered (through capitation) or may cover the costs of a number
of specified inputs such as staff. Each of these sets up an incentive for
the provider to react in a different manner to maximise revenue. This is
discussed further in Chapter 6.

8.2.5 Voucher Systems and Cash Incentives

One mechanism that is being tried in various low-income countries involves the provision to potential users of vouchers for specified services.
These focus on the demand rather than supply side constraints to health
care. Ensor[54] assesses various schemes including vouchers aimed at poor
pregnant women in Tanzania (for insecticide treated bed-nets [ITN]) and
in China's Yunnan Province (for free hospital services). Direct financial
incentives are provided in Mexico to poor populations on condition that
they use basic health and education services and in Andhra Pradesh in
India to poor women to deliver in a health facility. Such approaches face
a number of practical constraints (for example, ensuring that *women* in
Tanzania actually end up with the ITN) and that the transactions costs of
the system do not outweigh any additional benefits.

8.2.6 Vertical Programmes and Financing

As we have seen, vertical programmes have often arisen as a result of
external vertical funding. Even where a SWAp has been set up, there are
often still external funding linkages with specific programmes. From the
programme managers' perspective, there may be an incentive to maintain such linkages where the funding appears to be sustainable. This
reinforcement of verticalism through the funding can lead to the difficulties we explore in Chapter 7.

8.3 Human Resources for the Health System

The preceding has looked at implementation mechanisms related to financial resources. This is clearly fundamental to the operation of the
health system. However, finance is only of use when it is translated into
other resources. Within the health system, the key resource is staff and in
particular professionals. The shortage of such staff is a major constraint
on implementation of policies and plans.

We have already referred to the fact that the reforms of the 1990s
largely ignored this issue, focusing instead on structures and, in the area
of resources, on finance. By the turn of the millennium however it was
becoming more evident that for many health systems, there was a critical shortage of professionals in many different groups but particularly of
nurses and doctors (see Table 5.1).[55]

Table 5.1
Estimated critical shortages of doctors, nurses and midwives, by WHO region

WHO Region	No. of countries		In countries with shortages		
	Total	With shortages	Total stock	Estimated shortage	Percentage increase required
Africa	46	36	590,198	817,992	139
Americas	35	5	93,603	37,886	40
South-East Asia	11	6	2,332,054	1,164,001	50
Europe	52	0	n/a	n/a	n/a
Eastern Mediterranean	21	7	312,613	306,031	98
Western Pacific	27	3	27,260	32,560	119
World	192	57	3,355,728	2,358,470	70

Source: Reproduced from WHO. 2006 with permission.[56]

The reasons for this shortage are multiple and complex and include what are often referred to as push and pull factors. Such factors include levels of remuneration, living conditions (such as housing or educational opportunities for children particularly for remote postings) and working conditions (for example, a lack of adequate supplies to provide the professional service for which the staff have been trained). Where there is a thriving private sector, then this may provide opportunities in-country for public sector professionals. Depending on the role of the private sector (see Chapter 7) within a health system, such a shift may have implications both for efficiency and equity. Alternatively, professionals may move out of the health system altogether, with clear losses to the original investment made in them by the health system. The third key destination for some professionals is the health system of another country. Migration can be attractive, particularly where the terms and conditions are (or are perceived to be) significantly better than the home health system. Again, for the 'losing' health system, this is a loss on its earlier investment. Such migration tends to be from poor health systems to rich ones and has clear implications for global inequity as is well demonstrated by Table 5.2.

Table 5.2
Global health workforce, by density

| WHO region | Total health workforce | | | Health service providers | | Health management and support workers | |
	Number	Density (per 1000 population)		Number	Percentage of total health workforce	Number	Percentage of total health workforce
Africa	1,640,000	2.3		1,360,000	83	280,000	17
Eastern Mediter-ranean	2,100,000	4.0		1,580,000	75	520,000	25
South-East Asia	7,040,000	4.3		4,730,000	67	2,300,000	33
Western Pacific	10,070,000	5.8		7,810,000	78	2,260,000	23
Europe	16,630,000	18.9		11,540,000	69	5,090,000	31
Americas	21,740,000	24.8		12,460,000	57	9,280,000	43
World	59,220,000	9.3		39,470,000	67	19,750,000	33

Source: Reproduced from WHO. 2006 with permission from WHO.[57]

There is increasing attention being paid both internationally and nationally as to how to respond to what is, for some health systems, a major crisis. National strategies include increasing the outputs from training institutions, better working conditions to retain staff, changing the roles of staff through task-shifting and the use of multi-purpose workers and mechanisms to minimise losses including bonding after training and focusing on non-internationally marketable cadres such as clinical officers. Such strategies need to be clearly linked to the national policy and planning processes through human resource planning approaches[58] and it needs to be recognised that they will often have a long lead time before they have an impact. However, given the ability of staff in many countries to migrate, and indeed the rights of movement of professionals, international strategies are also needed to complement these national strategies. Richer health systems need to recognise the impact of their recruitment actions and either limit it (as some have, through voluntary codes) or recompense the sending countries for the loss of their staff and investment.[59] International migration is a clear example of the increasing globalisation of health care through the development of an international market for professionals. Such markets need international forms of regulation which respect the needs of individual health systems.

It is important that we recognise that underlying the development and assessment of strategies related to the adequate generation and retention of professionals are values. The key issue of distribution both within and between health systems relates closely to the value of equity; the distribution between the public and private sectors also relates to this and also to issues of efficiency and the general importance associated with the availability of staff links closely to our value of long-term sustainability. The specific strategies chosen will have different effects on the system's values.

9 Value-driven Policy and Planning

In the preceding sections, which have looked at the elements of the conceptual framework set out in Figure 5.2, we have referred to the influence and importance of values on the processes involved. We bring these together now in the form of a table (Table 5.3), which gives examples of the way in which our core values may affect the different elements of the processes.

Table 5.3
Value-driven policy making and planning

	Processes	Evidence	Context	Stakeholders/members	Policies and plans
Equity and the right to health	Do the processes, such as the situational analysis and prioritisation, incorporate equity considerations?	Is evidence collected, including through the information system, and used which reflects these values and in particular equity?	Is the context and its effects on equity and efficiency taken fully into account in policy-making?	Are stakeholders representing disadvantaged groups able to participate?	Do policies and plans reflect the values of equity and efficiency?
Efficiency	Do the processes encourage examination of a wide range of options including inter-sectoral action for health and all providers?	Is evidence which is relevant to the issues actively sought or only passively accepted?	Is social inequality and its impact on health equity considered?	Are the contributions of stakeholders concerning different approaches to policies and plans fully represented?	Do they have an appropriate balance between IAH and health care?
Participative and accountable decision-making	Are the processes open and transparent to allow balanced participation by all stakeholders?	Do the processes ensure that any evidence used (including experiential) is transparent and can be held to account?	Do the processes recognise the effect of the political and social context including inequality on participation?	Are all stakeholders allowed a fair voice?	Are policies and plans explicit and available for scrutiny?

10 Final Thoughts

Long-term perspective	Are there mechanisms to ensure accountability by decision-makers to the health system members?	Do plans give adequate emphasis on future needs of current and future populations?	Does the information system allow for likely future changes and the wider context?	Do the processes, including techniques (such as economic appraisal), encourage a long-term perspective?
Generic	Do the processes facilitate a transparent recognition of values in decisions?		Is the (changing) context adequately reflected in processes and the involvement of stakeholders?	

10 Final Thoughts

In this chapter we have explored aspects of policymaking and planning. We end with a number of summary reflections.

First, it is important to recognise the critical importance of policies and plans and the processes that produce and implement these. These processes should set the direction and tone for the health system and as such are critical precursors to the delivery of services and promotion of inter-sectoral action for health. They also need to be firmly rooted in the values underpinning the health sector.

Second, policies and plans need to be *achievable*, in various respects. They need to be politically feasible—to carry sufficient social and political authority to be able to be implemented. This does not mean that they should not be radical, but the degree of radicalism needs to reflect the ability of the ruling power to overcome inevitable resistance. They also need to be achievable within the resources likely to be available. Policies and plans that are aspirational but non-feasible quickly lose credibility and are ignored. Such resources do not simply refer to financial resources, which is a medium of exchange, but also to real resources such as the availability of skilled professionals.

Third, the strategies incorporated particularly in the plans need to be rooted in *evidence* that shows that they are likely to result in the set objectives.

Fourth, policies and plans need to achieve the appropriate health dimension. Policies and plans emanating from the government (and particularly the health ministry) are often called health policies. However, in practice, many of these policies focus almost entirely on health care rather than wider health. This reflects the institutional focus of many health actors on health care, with less interest in the wider determinants of health. We have, however, argued in this book that a health system should include within it actions by health care agencies (including the health ministry) related to health advocacy towards other sectors. As such policies emanating from the heath system should reflect this. A reproductive health policy might, for example, include both objectives related to the type, quantity and distribution of emergency obstetric care facilities and strategies related to working with the infrastructural agencies of government to develop transport for speedy referral of at-risk mothers, despite the fact that the implementation of this is not the direct responsibility of the health sector. Alternatively, but harder to achieve, there could be a national health policy or plan that incorporated actions by all sectors, and would require leadership from a national authority such as the office of the head of government, rather than the health ministry.

Fifth, policies and plans require resources for their implementation. The mechanisms for allocation need to be infused with key values, particularly in support of equity and efficiency/effectiveness. Allocation needs to be guided by policymaking and planning based on these values.

Last, it is important to recognise that the effectiveness of policymaking and planning cannot be seen in isolation from the *other processes* in the health system. In particular, it depends on being realistic in relation to the resources available and good governance and we have already emphasised this above and in Chapter 2. It also depends on good management and it is to this that we now turn.

Notes and References

1. See Green, A. 2007. *An Introduction to Health Planning for Developing Health Systems*. Oxford: OUP, for a detailed discussion of health planning.
2. Health economics texts explore the role of the market and its imperfections, for example, see Witter, S., Ensor, T. and Jowett, M. 2000. *Health Economics For Developing Countries: A Practical Guide*. London: MacMillan.
3. See, for example, Mintzberg, H. 1993. *The Rise and Fall of Strategic Planning: Reconceiving Roles for Planning, Plans, Planners*. New York: Simon & Schuster. This text criticises formal strategic planning; an example from the health sector of the arguments deployed can be found in Hill, P. 2000. 'Planning and Change: A Cambodian Public Health Case Study', *Social Science and Medicine*, 51(12): 1711–22, which argues against formal strategic planning using these arguments. Much of the debate however depends on the definition of planning and its approach rather than an attack on planning per se.
4. See Walt, G. and Gilson, L. 1994. 'Reforming the Health Sector in Developing Countries: The Central Role of Policy Analysis', *Health Policy and Planning*, 9(4): 353–70.
   For an overview of policy analysis tools and approaches see also:
   Gilson, L. and Raphaely, N. 2008. 'The Terrain of Health Policy Analysis in Low and Middle Income Countries: A Review of Published Literature 1994-2007', *Health Policy and Planning*, 23(5): 294–307.
   Walt, G., Shiffman, J., Schneider, H., Murray, S.F., Brugha, R., Gilson, L. 2008. 'Doing Health Policy Analysis: Methodological and Conceptual Reflections and Challenges', *Health Policy and Planning*, 23(5): 308–17.
5. There are various articles that analyse the role of context in policy processes. See, for example, two related specifically to the context of southern Africa: Gilson, L., Doherty, J., Lake, S., McIntyre, D., Mwikisa, C. and Thomas, S. 2003. 'The SAZA Study: Implementing Health Financing Reform in South Africa and Zambia', *Health Policy and Planning*, 18(1): 31–46.
   Parkhurst, J. and Lush, L. 2004. 'The Political Environment of HIVE: Lessons from a Comparison of Uganda and South Africa', *Social Science and Medicine*, 59(9): 1913–24.

6. See, for example, Gauld, R. 2001. 'Contextual Pressures on Health—Implications for Policy Making and Service Provision', *Policy Studies*, 22(3/4): 167–79.

7. See Special Issue of *International Journal of Health Planning and Management*. 2009. Vol. 24, Issue S1 on Health Planning and Management in the Transition from Humanitarian Emergencies to Development.

8. See, for example, Walford, V. 2002. *Health in Poverty Reduction Strategy Papers*. London: (PRSPs) DFID Health Systems Resource Centre.

9. See, for example, Walt, G., Shiffman, G., Schneider, H., Murray, S.F., Brugha, R. and Gilson, L. 2008. '"Doing" Health Policy Analysis: Methodological and Conceptual Reflections and Challenges', *Health Policy and Planning*, 23(5): 308–17.

10. Green, A. 2007. *An Introduction to Health Planning in Developing Health Systems*, Third Edition. Oxford: OUP.

11. See, for example, Ogden, J., Walt, G. and Lush, L. 2003. 'The Politics of "Branding" in Policy Transfer: The Case of DOTS for Tuberculosis Control', *Social Science and Medicine*, 57(1): 179–88, which is a case study of international policy transfer. See also Walt, G., Lush, L. and Ogden, J. 2004. 'International Organizations in Transfer of Infectious Diseases: Iterative Loops of Adoption, Adaptation, and Marketing Governance', *An International Journal of Policy, Administration, and Institutions*, 17(2): 189–210, which argues that the transfer of technical policies from international bodies to national ones undergoes various loops.

12. Kingdon, J.W. 1995. *Agendas, Alternatives, and Public Policies*. New York: Harper Collins. See also Shiffman, J. and Ved, R. 2007. 'The State of Political Priority for Safe Motherhood in India', *BJOG*, 114(7): 785–90 and Ridde, V. 2009. 'Policy Implementation in an African State: An Extension of Kingdon's Multiple-streams Approach', *Public Administration*, 87(4): 938–54.

13. Shiffman, J. and Smith, S. 2007. 'Generation of Political Priority for Global Health Initiatives: A Framework and Case Study of Maternal Mortality', *The Lancet*, 370(9595): 1370–79.

14. See Baumgartner, F.R. and Jones, B.D. 1993. *Agendas and Instability in American Politics*. Chicago: University of Chicago Press and Shiffman, J., Beer, T. and Wu, Y. 2002. 'The Emergence of Global Disease Control Priorities', *Health Policy and Planning*, 17(3): 225–34 who in a case study of the treatment of international priorities suggest the punctuated equilibrium model most appropriate.

15. Green, A. et al. 2011. Health Policy Processes in Maternal Health: A Comparison of Vietnam, India and China. *Health Policy* 100(2–3) pp. 167–173.

16. See a discussion of various approaches and tools for development planning in general in Dale, R. 2005. *Development Planning: Concepts And Tools For Planners, Managers And Facilitators*. London: Zed Press.

17. See, for example, Jamison, D., Breman, J., Measham, A., Alleyne, G., Claeson, M., Evans, D., Jha, P., Mills, A. and Musgrove, P. (eds). *Disease Control Priorities in Developing Countries*, 2nd ed., pp. 1–1400. Washington DC, New York: The World Bank, Oxford University Press.

18. Barker, C. and Green, A. 1996. 'Opening the Debate on DALYs', *Health Policy and Planning*, 11(2): 179–83.
19. Gwatkin, D. 2005. 'How Much Would Poor People Gain From Faster Progress Towards The Millennium Development Goals For Health', *The Lancet*, 365 (9461): 813–7.
20. See, for example, Mitton, C. and Donaldson, C. 2004. 'Health Care Priority Setting: Principles, Practice And Challenges', *Cost Effectiveness And Resource Allocation*, 2: 3.
21. World Bank. 1993. *World Development Report: An Agenda for Reform*. New York: OUP.
22. Green, A. 1990. 'Health Economics: Are We Being Realistic About Its Value?' *Health Policy and Planning*, 5(3): 274–79.
23. See, for example,
    Aim for human rights. 2008. *Health Rights of Women Assessment Instrument P.O. Box 114,3500 AC Utrecht*. Available at http://www.humanrightsimpact. org/themes/womens-human-rights/herwai/herwai-home/ (accessed on 18 September 2012) which provides an instrument for advocacy groups using a rights approach.
    Patel, V. 2007. 'Mental Health In Low- And Middle-Income Countries', *Br Med Bull*, 81–82(1): 81–96 also draws on rights in the area of mental health and Cook, R. 2001. *Advancing Safe Motherhood Through Human Rights WHO Occasional Paper 5*. WHO. Available at www.searo.who.int/LinkFiles/ Publications_Advancing_Safe_Motherhood_through_Human_Rights.pdf (accessed 9 November 2010).
    Backman, G., Hunt, P., Khosla, R., Jaramillo – Strouss, C., Mekuria Fikre, B., Rumble, C. et al. 2008. 'Health Systems and the Right to Health: An Assessment Of 194 Countries', *The Lancet*, 13 December, 372(9655): 2047–85.
    Frisancho, A. and Goulden, J. 2008. 'Rights-based Approaches To Improve People's Health in Peru', *The Lancet*, 13 December, 372(9655): 2007–08.
    Belhadj, H. and Toure, A. 2008. 'Gender Equality and the Right to Health', *The Lancet*, 13 December, 372(9655): 2008–09.
24. D'Ambuoso, L., Byass, P. and Qomariyah, S. 2008. 'Can the Right to Health Inform Public Health Planning in Developing Countries? A Case Study for Maternal Healthcare from Indonesia', *Global Health Action*. Available online at http://www.globalhealthaction.net/index.php/gha/issue/view/281.
25. Dixon, J. and Welch, H.G. 1991. 'Priority-setting: Lessons from Oregon', *The Lancet*, 337(8746), 891–4.
26. Source: Reichenbach, L. 2002. 'The Politics of Priority Setting for Reproductive Health: Breast and Cervical Cancer in Ghana', *Reproductive Health Matters*, 10(20): 47–58.
27. See, for example, for a discussion of the roles of NGOs as activists in South Africa: Klugman, B. 2000. 'The Role of NGOs as Agents for Change', *Development Dialogue*, 1–2: 95–120.
28. For a discussion of tools for analysing power, see
    Gaventa, J. 2005. *Reflections on the Uses of the 'Power Cube' Approach for Analyzing the Spaces, Places and Dynamics Of Civil Society*. Participation

and Engagement Institute of Development Studies, University of Sussex, Sussex.

Erasmus, E. and Gilson, L. 2008. 'How to Start Thinking About Investigating Power in the Organizational Settings of Policy Implementation', *Health Policy and Planning*, 23(5): 361–68.

Buse, K., Dickinson, C., Gilson, L., Murray, S.F. 2009. 'How Can the Analysis of Power and Process in Policy-making Improve Health Outcomes?' *World Hospitals Health Services*, 45(1): 4–8.

29. See, for example, http://www.independent.co.uk/news/uk/politics/drinks-industry-takes-a-hold-on-government-alcohol-policy-2329676.html (accessed 4 September 2011).

30. See, for example, a case study of the involvement of the public in planning in Kapiriri, L., Norheim, O. and Heggenhougen, K. 2003. 'Public Participation in Health Planning and Priority Setting at the District Level in Uganda', *Health Policy and Planning*, 18(2): 205–13.

31. Varvasovszky, Z. and Brugha, R. 2000. 'How to do (or not to do) a Stakeholder Analysis', *Health Policy and Planning*, 15(3): 338–45.

32. See, for example, Thomas, S. and Gilson, L. 2004. 'Actor Management in the Development of Health Financing Reform: Health Insurance in South Africa, 1994-1999', *Health Policy and Planning*, 19(5): 279–91.

33. For example, see Shiffman, J. 2002. The Construction of Community Participation: Village Family Planning Groups and the Indonesian State', *Social Science and Medicine*, 54(8): 1199–1214, who argues that family planning community groups (which have been seen as part of the successful family planning programme) are in fact state-dominated.

34. Green, A. 2000. 'Reforming the Health Sector in Thailand: The Role of the Policy Actors on the Policy Stage', *International Journal of Health Planning and Management*, 14(15): 39–59.

35. Tantivess, S. and Walt, G. 2008. 'The Role of State and Non-state Actors in the Policy Process: The Contribution of Policy Networks to the Scale-up of Antiretroviral Therapy in Thailand,' *Health Policy and Planning*, 23(5): 328–38.

36. One of the key members of the group, Dr Sanguan Nitayarumphong, who died in 2008 wrote a fascinating account of the policy development of universal coverage: Nitayarumphong, S. 2006. *Struggling Along the Path to Universal Health Care for All National Health Security Office*. Available at http://www.nhso.go.th/eng/content/uploads/files/publication_struggling.pdf (accessed 20 May 2010).

37. The term *consultation* is the subject of much discussion and analysis. A classic analysis of this is given in Arnstein's concept of a ladder of participation: Arnstein, S.R. 1969. 'A Ladder of Citizen Participation', *Journal of the American Planning Association*, July, 35(4): 216–24.

38. For a review of research approaches in the area of health policy analysis, see Gilson L. and Raphaely, N. 2008. 'The Terrain of Health Policy Analysis in Low and Middle Income Countries: A Review of Published Literature 1994-2007', *Health Policy and Planning*, 23(5): 294–307.

39. Marmot, M. 2004. 'Evidence-based Policy or Policy-based Evidence', *BMJ*, 328(7445): 906–7.

40. Health Metrics Network. 2008. *Framework and Standards for Country Health Information Systems*. Geneva: Health Metrics Network, World Health Organization. Available at http://www.who.int/healthmetrics/tools/Version_4.00_Assessment_Tool.pdf (accessed on 18 September 2012). WHO. 2004. *Developing Health Management Information Systems. A Practical Guide for Developing Countries*. Geneva: World Health Organization. HMIS_Introduction_2010.doc Available at http://whqlibdoc.who.int/publications/2004/9290611650.pdf (accessed on 18 September 2012).

41. See, for example, Kapiriri, L., Norheim, O. and Heggenhougen, K. 2003. 'Using Burden of Disease Information for Health Planning in Developing Countries: The Experience from Uganda', *Social Science and Medicine*, 56(12): 2433–41, which brings out the difficulties of a Burden of Disease approach to planning.

42. See WHO. 2004. *World Report on Knowledge for better Health: Strengthening Health systems*. Geneva: WHO and Bulletin of the WHO Special theme Bridging the Know-Do Gap in global Health, 82(10), October, for an overview of the issues.

43. This framework was originally presented in Green, A. and Gadsby, E. 2007. 'A Framework of Evidence-informed Health Policy-making', Chapter 3 in Green, A. and Bennett, S. (eds), *Sound Choices: Enhancing Capacity for Evidence-Informed Health Policy*, pp. 1–172. Geneva: WHO Alliance for Health Policy and Systems Research. Available online at http://www.who.int/alliance-hpsr/resources/Alliance_BR.pdf (accessed on 18 September 2012).

44. See, for example, Innvaer, S., Vist, G., Trommald, M. and Oxman, A. 2002. 'Health Policy-makers' Perceptions of their use of Evidence: A Systematic Review', *J Health Services Research Policy*, 7(4): 239–44.

45. Green, A. and Gadsby, E. 2007. 'A Framework of Evidence – informed Health Policy-making', chapter 3, in A. Green and S. Bennett (eds), *Sound Choices: Enhancing Capacity for Evidence – informed Health Policy*, pp. 1–172. Geneva: WHO Alliance for Health Policy and Systems Research. Available online at http://www.who.int/alliance-hpsr/resources/Alliance_BR. pdf (accessed on 18 September 2012).

46. See, for example, Gwatkin, D., Bhuiya, A. and Victora, C. 2004. 'Making Health Systems more Equitable', *The Lancet*, 364(9441), 1273–80.

47. See, for example, Bennett S., Dakpallah, G., Garner, P., Gilson, L., Nittayaramphong, S., Zurita, B. and Zwi, A. 1994. 'Carrot and Stick: State Mechanisms to Influence Private Provider Behaviour', *Health Policy and Planning*, 9(1): 1–13.

48. Derbyshire, H. 2002. *Gender Manual: A Practical Guide for Development Policy Makers and Practitioners*. Social Development Division, DFID.

49. Pressman, J.L. and Wildavsky, A.B. 1973. *Implementation: How Great Expectations in Washington are Dashed in Oakland; Or, Why It's Amazing that Federal Programs Work at All*. Berkeley: University of California Press.

50. See, for example, Duckett, J. 2001. 'Political Interests and the Implementation of China's Urban Health Insurance Reform', *Social Policy and Administration*, 35(3): 290–306.

51. Ssengooba, F. 2010. *Performance-based Contracting: The Case Study of Non-profit Hospitals in Uganda*, Doctoral thesis, London School of Hygiene and Tropical Medicine, UK.

52. Lipsky, M. 1980. *Street-Level Bureaucracy: Dilemmas Of The Individual In Public Services*. New York: Russel Sage Foundation.
   Walker, L. and Gilson, L. 2004. '"We are Bitter but We are Satisfied": Nurses as Street-level Bureaucrats in South Africa', *Social Science and Medicine*, 59(6): 1251–61.
   Kamuzora, P. and Gilson, L. 2007. 'Factors Influencing Implementation of the Community Health Fund in Tanzania', *Health Policy and Planning*, 22(2), 95–102.

53. For an example of a low-middle-income country, see McIntyre, D.E., Taylor, S.P., Pick, W.M., Bourne, D.E. and Klopper, J.M. 1991. 'A Methodology for Resource Allocation in Health Care for South Africa. Part IV – Application of South African Health Resource Allocation Formula (SAHRA)', *South African Medical Journal*, 80, 139–45.

54. Ensor, T. 2004. 'Consumer-led Demand Side Financing in Health and Education and its Relevance for Low and Middle Income Countries', *International Journal of Health Planning and Management*, 19(3): 267–285.

55. See WHO. 2006. *The World Health Report 2006: Working Together for Health*. Geneva: WHO, for a good overview of the key issues facing health systems.

56. WHO. 2006. *The World Health Report 2006: Working Together for Health*. Geneva: WHO, p. 13, Table 1.3.

57. WHO. 2006. *The World Health Report 2006: Working Together for Health*. Geneva: WHO, p. 5, Table 1.1.

58. See, for example, Green, A. 2007. 'Planning Human Resources', in A. Green (ed.), *An Introduction to Health Planning for Developing Health Systems*. Oxford: OUP; Dreesch, N., Dolea, C., Dal Poz, M., Goubarev, A., Adams, O., Aregawi, M., Bergstrom, K., Fogstad, H., Sberatt, D., Linkins, J., Scherpbier R. and Youseff-Fox, M. 2005. 'An Approach to Estimating Human Resource Requirements to Achieve the Millennium Development Goals', *Health Policy and Planning*, 20(5): 267–76.

59. Some 'losing' countries such as the Philippines have, for many years, deliberately trained health staff for the export market in recognition of the income remittances arising from this.

6
Valuing Management

This chapter[1] starts by discussing what we mean by 'management' and introduces the themes which run through it. It then discusses separately the management of organisational structure, resources, external linkages and culture. Throughout the analysis we emphasise the importance of values and how they can shape the way in which we look at and practice management. Management has often been interpreted in a universalistic manner: a view that there are rules of good management—a one best way—irrespective of context. We take a different approach. We look to understand the importance of both context and values in determining the management process. Throughout this book we have sought to make explicit our own values and these permeate our interpretation of the management process. Far from management being a set of procedures to be learned as universal recipes, we emphasise the importance of management *analysis* and *adaptability* in understanding context and values and how they permeate the management of health systems.

1 Understanding Management

1.1 What Do We Mean By Management

Management is an elusive term, used differently in different contexts. Our own definition is that it is a systematic process of mobilising, combining and using resources with a view to moving efficiently towards agreed objectives.[2] There is no clear-cut demarcation between management and other forms of activity discussed in this book. Indeed, we should expect overlap and interdependence between these activities. Policy focuses on expressions of intent over the long term, although it clearly needs to take account of the feasibility of implementation. Policies can also be both strategic and operational. Planning is focused on the future and is concerned with marrying resources to objectives which will allow the achievement of strategic policies and as such should be a bridge between policy and operational management. Management is concerned primarily with more immediate operational decisions though it clearly needs to provide an input into both policymaking and planning to ensure a perspective of management feasibility. Figure 6.1 illustrates the overlapping interrelations.

Figure 6.1
Relations between policy-making, planning and management

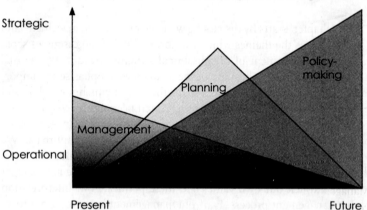

Administration is a term often confused with management; again, there is no neat line between the two. However, administration, in contrast to management, can be seen as a more rule-bound, formal and routine activity and as such often more passive to the wider contextual environment. It is not primarily concerned with resources and objectives but in securing adherence to particular procedures and rules. Management is more proactive and can seek to change the environment and the rules and procedures under which the system operates.

The overview definition of management can be broken down into the interrelated sub-processes illustrated in Figure 6.2. In short, all management takes place in a context and interacts with it. This interaction takes four forms: managers need to interpret the context and how it relates to management; they adapt to policies (that take place in policymaking and planning analysed in Chapter 5); they respond to societal values; and they establish links with groups and organisations in the management process. This underpinning allows the management of structures, resources and culture with a view to producing services and activities to meet objectives. All the processes are monitored so as to learn from the experience and modify, if necessary, subsequent action. Interspersed throughout the processes is decision-making. Situations present different alternative actions which need to be assessed to ensure consistency with overall objectives. Although Figure 6.2 could suggest a sequential and logical flow, we recognise that this is rarely the case. At the same time, all the processes are interrelated and in constant flow.

Figure 6.2
Processes in management

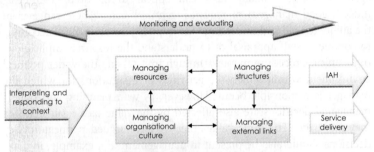

1.1.1 Interpreting and Responding to the Context

Management does not take place in a vacuum but needs to take into account, and adapt to, the context in which it operates. For the manager, the context can appear to consist of three overlapping areas. First, there are the natural, social, economic and political features of the country in which management takes place. The natural features require the manager to think of issues such as topography and seasonal changes and how this affects service delivery. Social, economic and political features, such as fragility of the state, a downturn in the economy and the political consciousness of social groups will also have a potential impact on the management process.

Second, there are the policies and objectives from the policymaking and planning processes. Ideally, the management process would respond to the objectives and the overall direction of travel set from the policymaking and planning processes. In practice, deficiencies in planning and policymaking (discussed in Chapter 5) mean that such objectives may be lacking, unclear or inconsistent. Furthermore, even where there is a robust policy process, management overlaps with policymaking and planning (see above); as such it needs to adopt a strategic perspective and be involved in the formulation of objectives. Moreover, the process of implementation may require adaptation of initial objectives which may be found not to be feasible. Although objectives appear as the *end* result of management, we should not downplay the *means* to achieve them. In particular, we should not assume that the end can necessarily justify the means. We should seek compatibility between ends and means. In particular, the processes should reflect the values that underpin the health system. For example, the implementation of a policy to empower the community in health should itself be implemented as far as possible in a participatory and equitable fashion.

Third, there are the values in society and how they affect the management process. Management can appear to be quite 'technical'; indeed, good management requires technical skills. These range from the ability to read and understand the implications of financial accounts, to conduct a staff appraisal or to understand the resource implications of a clinical procedure manual through to assessing the wider political environment within which the activities or institutions for which the manager is responsible occur. However, as with planning and policy, managerial decisions are also affected by the value base against which they are made. The same values that we have argued permeate policy decisions should also be present in management. For example, in making a staff appointment, a manager may have to assess both the technical competencies of applicants and be aware of wider equity implications which may be written in equal opportunity policies. Values associated with equity, participation and accountability will require new structures and processes to bring the poor, disempowered and underserved into decision-making processes for the health system to understand their needs and tailor interventions to meet these. Managers therefore need to be aware of the dominant values of a health system, where appropriate attempt to influence these and work to respond to them through the management process in ways set out in this chapter.

1.1.2 Managing Resources

A key function for management is ensuring the availability of money, staff-time, equipment and medicines. Resources are scarce and considerable effort can be expended in getting the right types of resources in the right combinations at the right time, and in the right place. Resources also need to be maintained (such as buildings and equipment), retained, retrained and developed (such as staff) and combined.

1.1.3 Managing Structures

Managers work within organisational structures that confer responsibilities, scope of action, resources and authority to the different levels and actors within the health system. Decisions on the organisational levels and relations of authority are ultimately political decisions which should correspond to broad policies both within and outwith the health system. Such decisions may be, for example, about the form of decentralisation. Managers play an important role in developing these organisational infrastructures of levels and relations of authority and may have delegated authority to develop detailed lower structures and systems. These may, for example, be laid down in operational policies. Ideally, these would be agreed statements for a particular organisation (such as a Ministry of Health or a health centre) and would indicate the basic meaning and practice in a particular area of work (such as planning and staff management). They could include objectives, context, underlying values, key policies, activities and procedures, responsibilities, success criteria, monitoring and evaluation and links with other operational policies.

1.1.4 Managing Organisational Culture

Managers also have a role in developing and leading an organisational culture which respects the underlying values of the health system and furthers performance. For example, domineering and autocratic styles of management can lead to a culture of bullying and fear which is both at odds with the values that we are arguing for and which are unlikely to be productive. In contrast, an emphasis on teamwork can improve efficiency, generate a shared feeling of ownership and allow for more participative management.

1.1.5 Managing External Links

The objectives of an organisation, or part of the organisation, are rarely attainable solely by its own efforts. Better health and health care are the result off multi-organisational activity. Managers need to look outwards to, and develop relations with, other organisations or parts of the same organisation. This outward looking approach to management is also evident in the links that need to be made with civil society groups such as associations of users and community groups. This is sometimes referred to as working through and using networks.

1.1.6 Monitoring and Evaluating

The management process requires constant reflection to determine the manner in which the various processes are relating to each other and the extent to which they are moving in the direction of the objectives. Monitoring and evaluating, which have been explained in Chapter 5, require a learning approach to management whereby information is fed into the management processes.

As with policymaking and planning, there are constraints to the workings of this apparently rational process of management, which in practice can be messy. These constraints range from problems related to lack of authority, lack of capacity (such as lack of skills and resources) to political patronage and corruption. Managers require a mixture of realism about the constraints, optimism about the possibility of achieving objectives and purposefulness about working on the constraints. Some problems may be overbearing and even lead to the departure of managers. Others may not be so immovable and immutable. An important skill of a manager is the ability to understand their position in relation to constraints and their area of manoeuvre within their responsibilities. They also have to interpret the extent to which this field of manoeuvre can be manipulated and expanded by seeking additional resources, improving the skill capacity around them or gaining extra support from user and community groups.

The distribution of these management activities varies according to the manager. Managers occupy different positions in organisations and management responsibilities are distributed accordingly. Their position will determine the content of management responsibilities they have; senior managers will have a more strategic responsibility while junior managers will be more restricted and focused in their responsibilities on managing service provision. At the same time, staff may specialise in specific aspects of management, such as financial or staff management. The structure and culture of the organisation in question will also impact on the distribution of management responsibilities. More centralised and authoritarian organisations will adopt an institutional form that concentrates responsibilities within a small dominant group. In contrast, more open and democratic organisations will seek to adopt an institutional form that spreads management responsibilities among staff at different levels in the organisation.

As organisations change, the demands on management also change. New responsibilities and greater organisational autonomy require shifts in management and also who exercises management responsibilities. For example, the granting of delegated semi-autonomy to tertiary hospitals in many countries raises challenges including how management in the hospital relates to the professional nature of a large number of staff who have particular expectations about their roles, responsibilities and clinical rights (see Box 6.1). Both managers and medical professionals can hold their own values and ethical approaches which can lead to tension in the organisation.

Box 6.1 Management and professional autonomy in hospitals

An important issue in the working of a hospital is that of combining management processes with the autonomy of professions. The latter involves decision-making on the care given to individuals and groups of patients. The former is concerned with ensuring the availability and use of resources in an organisational setting to make that treatment possible. Tension between management and professional autonomy can arise, for example, around the cost implications of individual treatments and the extent to which they fit into the resource constraints imposed on the hospital. These tensions can express different values and priorities. While the physician may focus on the high quality of care to individual patients, the manager may be more concerned in ensuring care to the community as a whole, ensuring a balanced allocation of resources across different activities of the hospital and/or ensuring the maintenance of budget stability. How the tension is dealt with, if at all, will vary from hospital to hospital. For example, cost centres in some hospitals are created at a divisional level (for example, surgery or ENT) and the divisions are led by physicians. The division has to combine high levels of care with working within a cost centre budget. In other hospitals physicians adopt a semi-autonomous position; they focus on ensuring the best level of care for their individual patients but are mainly separated from the cost considerations of what they prescribe in terms of care.

1.2 Themes in Management

The previous section gives an overview of management. However, management is practised in many different contexts and it is not surprising to find that it differs in its practice in different settings. In this section, we set out themes that we argue should run through management in health systems in LMICs.

1.2.1 Management Styles

Managers can adopt different styles in carrying out their responsibilities; some may be more appropriate in some circumstances than others. For example, management in an emergency situation is different from management in a routine environment. We examine here different management styles and their attributes.

Managers, particularly in health systems, need to be *outward looking*, linking up with other individuals, groups and organisations. Later in this chapter we examine the importance of managers linking with stakeholders. This requires an open approach whereby managers recognise the rights of individuals and groups to participate in decision-making and the benefits this can provide to the quality of decision-making. Underlying this is a participative approach to management.

Given a commitment to equity in our values, an approach of *fairness* should underlie a manager's style. In dealing with others, including staff and the general public, there should be no discrimination—such as gender, racial and religious discrimination—with fairness guiding action. The justification for this lies in the dual arguments of rights, and the more pragmatic point that, for staff relations and team work to be effective, relations based on trust and fairness are necessary.

Managers need to be *proactive* through, for example, interpreting the changing environment, generating new resources, making decisions, motivating others, innovating new ways of doing things, making links with others and gathering new evidence. Managers may however put on a show of activity through unnecessary haste, multiple tasking and the desire for constant change. Such a style can lead to a lack of analysis in decision-making, poor decisions due to overwork and disruption in service delivery. It can also lead to an inappropriate culture of 'workaholism'.

There are rarely simple answers to complex and changing problems. The practice of management can require a degree of *innovation and risk-taking*. These break with the existing way of doing things and point staff in the direction of unknown territory. There are, of course, limits to this; managers should not risk people's health. The use of reasonable and acceptable risk needs to be practiced. This is not easy and careful judgement is required. There is also a need for clear and agreed technical work and ethical standards to guide managers in innovation and risk-taking. There can also be many constraints. In some organisations, for example, a punitive regime may exist; staff are not rewarded for their successes but blamed for their failures. The culture may be risk-averse, with penalties for risk-taking. Good supervision and constructive support for staff will help staff in exercising innovation.

Problem solving is an important responsibility of management; managers need to develop skills, structures, systems and a culture to allow this. However, a style of management that does not see beyond immediate problems can limit the organisation to a 'fire-fighting' role. A balance is needed between current problems and a more strategic approach that looks to the potential of the organisation and the emerging and future needs, and indeed to foreseeing and preventing future problems.

Lastly, a balance is needed between adherence to certain styles of management and *flexibility* to adapt to the circumstances. For example, where there are time or resource constraints for decision-making, managers might have to adopt a less consultative style of management. The type of staff can also determine the style of management; the way managers delegate activity and supervise staff will vary according to their capacity to work independently and not under close supervision.[3]

1.2.2 Management in Health Systems

The management process needs to recognise three major points of working within a health system. First, actions within the health system are interrelated. Therefore, management changes in one part of the health system can have effects on other parts.[4] Sometimes, these consequences may be unwanted and unintended. For example, improving the rewards and conditions of some health workers may result in the demotivation of other groups of health workers. At the same time, planned changes within the health system frequently require a broad range of interventions. For example, improving the productivity of health workers cannot be simply achieved by a training course. Change may be required in their jobs, remuneration, working conditions and supervision for the improved skills to be reinforced and enabled.

Second, the open nature of the health system means that management action takes place within a context and, in turn, can have an impact on that context. This is a theme throughout this book—and it has implications for the approach to management and its outward looking characteristics.

Last, although managers specialise, they should not lose sight of how their own work fits into the broader system aims and objectives. For example, a malaria programme manager needs to know not just how s/he contributes to the aim of reducing malaria morbidity and mortality but how this relates to the broader system aim of improving the population's health. Scaling up a malaria control programme through, for example, the channelling of additional international money allows the manager to be more successful in achieving malaria control and meeting targets. However, other programmes with greater priority may be left with declining finances and also lose valuable staff to the malaria control programme. Similarly, a human resource manager needs to see his/her work in the context of other resource specialisms such as financial management or more general programme management.

1.2.3 The Political Nature of Management

The context of the health system and its management can be one of contradiction, tension and change. This is born out of the unequal access to, and use of resources and benefits in, society. Managers cannot abstract themselves from this social and political reality. The management process uses resources to achieve objectives which are in themselves political in that they affect the access of groups to health and health care. It also affects the relative access to employment and resources by different health workers. Management involves making decisions which have a political impact and are therefore subject to pressure from these interests.

We have already suggested that the management process overlaps with the processes of policymaking and planning. We have also seen management as an active relation between resources and objectives; to achieve objectives requires getting involved in policy advocacy and mobilising political coalitions of support. The management process needs to recognise the sort of activities suggested by Shiffman's[5] research into the role of advocacy in developing priorities for reducing maternal mortality in Guatemala, Honduras, India, Indonesia and Nigeria. The research revealed, among other things, the importance of working within policy communities, developing 'political entrepreneurs', the use of data to increase the visibility of maternal mortality problems, creating events (for example, conferences and marches) to make visible what is hidden and clarifying policy options.

1.2.4 Public and Private Sector Management

The neo-liberal approach to health systems reform, as outlined in Chapter 2, suggested the superiority of 'private-for-profit' approaches over public sector management. While the former is characterised as relying on performance-related incentives, the latter is often perceived as having in-built tendencies towards budget-guzzling bureaucratic expansion and inefficiency. This has led to attempts not only to reduce the public sector but also to import the management style of the private sector into the public sector. Managed competition, making health facilities generate their own income and performance-based rewards are three such examples. Such reforms raise the questions: is it appropriate to import such mechanisms into the public sector? What differences should exist between management in the public and private-for-profit sectors?

Any attempt to answer these questions is constrained by two problems. First, there is considerable diversity within both the public and private sectors; this point is emphasised in chapters 2 and 7. This means that any argument must recognise that we are referring to general *tendencies* and not universal statements. Second, recent years have seen a blurring of the distinction between the public and private sectors, often as a response to neo-liberal policies. For example, the private sector can be contracted to take on public provision of health services and the public sector health facility may be required to generate surpluses to achieve self-sufficiency.

The way management in the public and private sectors is interpreted depends to a large extent on the values held.[6] We believe that while it is possible to suggest that there is some scope for both sectors to learn from each other, some fundamental differences exist between the two. In the first place, there are differences in the objectives of management: the ultimate goal of private (for profit) sector management is, not surprisingly, that of profit. This clarity of the aims of the private sector contrasts with the politically determined and more obtuse goals of the public sector. The latter are the subject of political negotiation and/or contradiction. Management skills in dealing with such contradictions are critical in the public sector where the ultimate goals may lack a clear single definition and are subject to change. Yet central to these public sector goals should be that of improved and more equitable health. The public sector also needs to adopt a more collaborative and longer term strategy (important for sustainability in the health system) than the private sector with competitive and shorter term frameworks. The two sectors also operate different forms of accountability; the complexity of public sector accountability is outlined below and differs from the shareholder and more market-based accountability of the private sector. In summary, while there may be overlap between the public and private sectors, there are also fundamental differences which need to be reflected in different approaches to management. This does not mean that cross-sector learning is not possible; in some situations, the public sector can learn important lessons from the private sector in, for example, quality assurance, provider–patient relations, staff management and budget management.

So far we have restricted our interpretation of the private sector to 'for-profit organisations'. How do private 'not-for-profit' organisations fit in to the above? The differences within this latter sector do not allow us to make any easy generalisation.[7] The type of time perspective they adopt and their forms of accountability will vary greatly. It might, however, be expected that they have a social objective more akin to that of the public sector, as opposed to giving the owners of capital a return through profit. There may however be a tension between their objectives related to their ideals and those of the public sector. This can be seen, for example, in the case of some faith-based organisations which see pursuit of religious objectives as primary.

1.2.5 Use of Evidence in Management

In managing, staff may rightly aspire to base their work on good evidence. Existing evidence needs to be drawn upon and new evidence through, for example, action research brought in. Whether this occurs will depend, however, on conditions. First, it is important that a culture of generating, storing, analysing and using evidence permeates the organisation in its decision-making. Bureaucratic inertia may dominate; furthermore, key stakeholders may have a vested interest in hiding certain evidence from decision-makers. Many of these issues are discussed in Chapter 5. Second, there is always a concern (particularly, but not solely, in resource poor countries) that data is unreliable and/or too costly to collect and store. It is of course important that managers take care in the evidence they use; it should meet standards of accuracy, relevance and validity for making decisions. However, determining the appropriate level is not straightforward and will depend on the type of decision. Seeking overly accurate levels of evidence may stymie decision-making—and indeed can be used by opponents of change to delay decision-making.

The pursuit of evidence-informed management should not be interpreted to imply value-free processes. As we have suggested above, values will continue, appropriately, to be set alongside evidence in the same way that we have discussed in relation to policy and planning in Chapter 5. This serves to underline the importance of judgement in decision-making and the capacity to determine what information is required and how it needs to be analysed.

We turn now to examine the different structures and processes involved in management.

2 Managing Organisational Structures and Processes[8]

An important responsibility of management is to develop organisational structures and processes. This involves setting out the formal responsibilities of organisations such as health programmes and projects, defining the nature of the organisational hierarchy and spans of control, defining the relations of authority and accountability in the organisation, arranging the internal division of labour around, for example, departments and divisions, setting up mechanisms of internal coordination and defining jobs. This constitutes the formal framework within which services are delivered. A distinction should be made at this juncture between institutions and organisations.[9] The former are usually seen as the formal and informal rules which determine behaviour. For example, these could be the way in which staff are promoted in an organisation, the informal customs that guide the way in which staff in health teams work together or the rules and procedures determining the development of a budget. We will see in this section that there is a strong interrelation between institutional and organisational factors.

In order to explain this management responsibility, we will illustrate this with the case of a District Health Authority (DHA) in an LMIC and work through a review of its organisational structure. Box 6.2 sets out five features of a review and breaks these down into questions which are considered in the text. The need for such a review may be provoked by

---

Box 6.2 Features and key questions of a review of a District Health Authority

Feature	Key questions
1. **Contextual analysis**	What is the social, political and economic context of the DHA? How does the DHA fit into the national health system? How does the DHA fit into the district health system?
2. **Analysis of objectives and responsibilities**	What are the underlying values of the DHA and how are they operationalised through the aims and objectives of the DHA? What should be the basic responsibilities of the DHA?
3. **Analysis of organisational structure**	What is the form of the hierarchy and spans of control? Are they appropriate? What are the relations of authority? How is accountability ensured? How is the division of labour brought into the organisational structure? How is internal and external linking done? Where is responsibility for decision-making located?
4. **Integrating change**	How is complementary and supportive change achieved?
5. **Process of the review and change**	How is consultation with stakeholders done? What is the timing of change? How is change monitored?

Source: Adapted from Manning and Parison. 2003; Nunberg and Nellis. 1995.[10]

events such as a major cut in resources, conflict in the organisation and incidents of poor performance. The process of management, however, includes monitoring and it is advisable that any organisation should conduct routine checks on its performance and, as a result, be prepared to periodically review its organisational structure.

2.1 Contextual Analysis

The key issue concerning contextual analysis relates to the impact of the economic, social and political context of the DHA on its internal organisational structure. The work of the DHA and how it fits into the national and district health systems will be determined by a range of factors such as the epidemiological and demographic profile of the district, the form of decentralisation operating in the country and the financing and provider roles of the public and private sectors. Of importance also is the relative strength or fragility of the state and how this impinges on the organisational structure. For example, in Chapter 7 we refer to the position of fragile states and how this affects the balance between an approach based on PHC and one based on emergency medical assistance. While the former would lead to a longer term perspective based on district integrated services, the latter may emphasise a shorter time project format.[11]

2.2 Analysis of Objectives and Responsibilities

Box 6.3 sets out a range of broad responsibilities of a DHA; the precise nature would depend on the contextual setting and the degree of autonomy exercised.

Box 6.3 Range of responsibilities for a DHA

- formulation and implementation of a **district health plan** providing a strategic direction for health in the district;
- collection, compilation, transmission and analysis of **health information;**
- delivery, in an integrated fashion, of **community health programmes;**
- **management of government health units** such as the district hospital, health centres and health posts;
- the development of constructive links with the **private sector,** including the co-ordination, regulation, support and supervision of all non-governmental health facilities;
- **management and development of health human resources** through, for example, supervision, control and in-service training;
- **financial management** through receipt of central funds, raising of local funds and budget management of district health funds;

Box 6.3 continued

Box 6.3 continued

- **logistics management** for the health district;
- promotion of **links with other sectors,** such as education and agriculture, in pursuit of common development objectives;
- promotion of **community participation** in the district health system

We see the values enunciated in Chapter 2 permeating the aims and responsibilities and the organisational structure of the DHA. Empowerment and participation call for the representative bodies, such as District Health Councils (or similar bodies) to be given authority and responsibilities to make participation a reality; the exercise of accountability requires clarity in the distribution of responsibilities in the organisation, health improvement and equity require strong organisational links to be developed with other sectors; efficiency requires an effective planning function to be incorporated into the DHA.

2.3 Analysis of Organisational Structure[12]

The organisational structure and its analysis consists of six interrelated issues; the form of the organisational hierarchy and how this leads to a consideration of the spans of control, the relations of authority, the forms of accountability, the division of responsibilities between the horizontal groupings in the organisation, internal and external linking and defining decision-making responsibility. We examine each one of these.

2.3.1 Hierarchy and Spans of Control

The DHA, in common with most other organisations such as a Ministry of Health or a hospital, is likely to operate some form of hierarchy that tapers at the strategic top and has a broader productive base. It consists of hierarchical levels, each of which has a specific depth of authority (deeper as one gets towards the top of the hierarchy and more shallow as one moves towards the base) and breadth of vision (wider towards the top and more specific towards the base) (see Figure 6.3). It is important that the design of the hierarchy incorporates the values enunciated in this book. Efficiency is a key issue in organisational design which seeks to link objectives, responsibilities and organisational structure. At the same time, a participative approach and accountability should be brought into the organisational structure.

There are two broad types of hierarchies that could be adopted by a DHA. They could be tall and thin and quite bureaucratic with a narrow hierarchical shape in which successive levels of the hierarchy rigidly enforce a chain of disciplined command. Such rigidity would be

Figure 6.3
Characteristics of levels of management

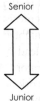

inappropriate for many DHAs; multiple management levels would enforce a costly straitjacket on innovative and flexible action. Alternatively,
the DHA could adopt a flatter and more flexible hierarchy with less management levels. This restriction or reduction in the management levels is
often viewed favourably.[13] For a DHA, it would reduce the organisational
distance between the top levels and the point of service provision, ease
up communication within the hierarchy and facilitate greater appreciation of community needs and service impact. However, reducing the
levels of an existing hierarchy can be difficult as the interests of multiple
managers may appear threatened.

One reason why the number of levels in an organisation may have expanded might be to ensure parity between organisational levels and the
public sector grading system. Developing a system in which each level
can accommodate more than one grade is important to make the system
flatter and more flexible. Decentralisation within the hierarchy can also
reduce the need for middle-level managers to exercise control. Another
option is to widen the spans of control in the organisation, allowing
the number of levels to be reduced whilst employing the same number of staff.[14] However, there are constraints on doing this. Widening
spans of control should not be undertaken without considering variables
such as the burden it places on the line manager who is required to
manage more staff. Before widening the spans of control, attention also
needs to be paid to the nature of the work being done by health workers
(some types of work are easier to manage than others) and the capacity of both managers and subordinates to operate in widened spans of
control.[15]

2.3.2 Authority Relations
Health care organisations use different forms of authority, including strategic authority, main line managerial authority, supervisory authority,

professional authority, coordinating authority and technical authority.[16] Strategic authority is very important in making decisions that provide direction to the organisation or a constituent of it. In Africa, this is often represented by the role of the District Health Management Team which might include, amongst others, the District Health Officer, the District Head Nurse, the District Hospital Manager and the District Administrator. Main line management refers to the authority to give a remit of work and instructions to staff over whom the superior has had a say in their appointment together with possible transfer and dismissal and in the review of their performance. This may be combined or separated from supervisory authority which can be a more day-to-day direction and technical support form of authority. Quite often, the same manager exercises both main line and supervisory authority, although it may be split between two managers. Other forms of authority are referred to below.

How these different and overlapping forms of authority are combined in a health care organisation is important. A poorly designed organisation could be a major constraint on health system values; for example, excessive top-down authority could be both inefficient and impose decisions from the top instead of listening to those nearer the community. Authority relations are a complex area as staff fall under more than one form of authority. For example, the health worker responsible for the delivery of TB control in a health district may lie under dual authority, as depicted in Figure 6.4. The Regional TB Officer may exercise a technical supervisory authority while the District Health Manager will have main line management authority. There is clearly room for variations in the relative power of these two authorities over the field officer; the relative strength of the main line authority relationship indicates the overall level of authority of the district over national health programmes such as the National TB Programme. The changing nature of these relations over time and the personal characteristics of the staff involved add complexity to how these relations are understood and practiced.

Widening the spans of control through the use of dual authority relations is a way to reduce the number of levels in the hierarchy. Figure 6.5 illustrates this. Staff are subject to two forms of authority. First, there is the main line managerial authority of the Director of Community Health. S/he is able to manage a larger number of outreach health staff because s/he has the help of a public health nurse acting as a supervisor or staff person providing day-to-day supervision and support. The supervisor/staff person is under the main line management direction of the line manager but could exercise supervisory authority over the staff providing

Figure 6.4
Dual authority relations for a district TB officer

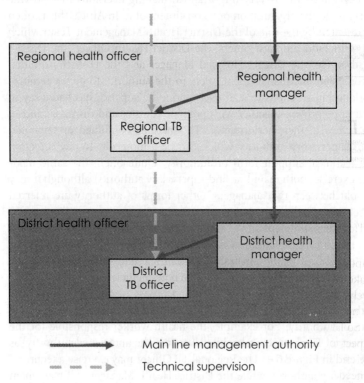

Source: Adapted from Rowbottom and Billis. 1987.[17]

technical and day-to-day support. The staff are able to maintain contact with the manager and do not necessarily have to go through the supervisor for contact with him/her. The need to create another management level has been avoided.

However, the mixing of different forms of authority in health organisations can lead to confusion and inefficiency. In order to avoid this, managers need to be clear what they mean by the different types of responsibility and authority and ensure all managers and staff members have a single and clear understanding of this. These responsibilities include tasks such as appointment, induction, technical supervision and performance review.[18] It is also important that there are specified mechanisms for resolution of any tensions that arise from these dual relations. These could include involvement of a 'grandparent' manager higher in the managerial chain. We also point out below the

Figure 6.5
Dual authority and managing the spans of control

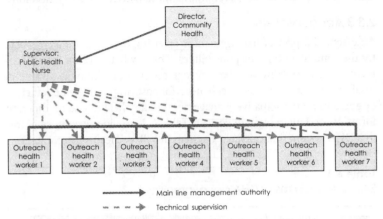

Source: Adapted from Rowbottom and Billis. 1987.[19]

importance of combining institutional and organisational change; to make dual authority (and other structures such as teams) work effectively, relations based on trust, transparency, compromise and collegiality need to be fostered in the DHA.

So far we have focused on the formal skeleton of authority we would expect to develop in a DHA. While this is important, it is far from being the endpoint of developing an effective organisational structure. Clarity is needed on three issues.

First, relations of authority are not simply about top-down instructions and technical authority associated with main line and supervisory authority. Staff interrelate through various forms of authority; some staff may have coordinating and monitoring authority, physicians in a district hospital can have prescribing authority in that they direct other health workers on patient treatment; professional authority also exists within and between professional groups.[20] Second, relations of authority are not omnipresent in the organisation. Many relations with work colleagues are ones of working together as co-workers without reference to status and authority; indeed, we should see it as a strength of a DHA that staff are able to develop such informal and creative relations. These are relations based on trust, respect, collegiality, support and compromise and help make the organisation work effectively. Third, we do not see authority relations as simply involving communication from above and in one direction. The channels of authority in an organisation need to be a two-way communication, so the front line health workers feel they are able to transmit their needs and the needs of communities to higher level staff. This is a step in the direction of a more participative organisation.

2.3.3 Accountability

An essential aspect of management is ensuring that staff are answerable for the conduct of their responsibilities. This is what is meant in management by *accountability*. We have recognised accountability as a value in itself and it is an important mechanism for ensuring both greater efficiency and a more participative management. In any health system, different forms of accountability will coexist. Table 6.1 provides examples of this in a DHA system that operates a system of Village Health Committees.

Table 6.1
Examples of forms of DHA accountability

Features of accountability		Forms of accountability		
	Managerial	*Community*	*Political*	*Professional*
Focus	Use of district health vehicles transport by staff	Operation of village health post	Performance of District Health Services	Quality and ethical standards of nurses' health care practice
Desired impact	Efficient and effective use of transport to meet health service needs	Continuity of care provided by village health post	Performance meets the objectives set out by the health team	High level of ethical standards by nursing profession
Accountability mechanism	Check on key transport indicators	Check by Village Health Committee on staff attendance	Annual report to locally elected District Council	Periodic professional inspections to supplement on-going supervision
Who is accountable?	District transport manager	Staff in village health post	District Health Team	Nurses
To whom are they accountable?	District Health Officer	Village Health Committee	District Council and through them to the electorate	Nursing Council

Table 6.1 continued

Table 6.1 continued

Features of accountability	Forms of accountability			
	Managerial	*Community*	*Political*	*Professional*
Possible action or sanction	Training, or discipline such as dismissal	Recommendation to district authorities to discipline or transfer poor performers	Change in budget allocations	Ongoing continuous professional development or discipline including strike off nurse's register

Table 6.1 includes forms of accountability that are consistent with the values that we have set out. Other forms of accountability also exist however, and in particular, those related to the market. In particular, the mechanisms of consumer choice and the loss of potential fee income may be seen as accountability processes. Such market forms of accountability raise important challenges, such as the asymmetry of information between users and providers and the possibility of supplier-induced demand, the lack of alternative providers for competition to exist, the impact of co-payments on equity and the impact of provider competition on collaboration between health facilities. The use of markets and choice is discussed in Chapter 7.

Balance is required in developing accountability mechanisms. Robust and meaningful accountability is required to ensure, for example, that health needs are being met, quality of care is ensured and communities can exercise a right to monitor health service provision. However, staff also have to be able to get on with their work and not spend inordinate amounts of time satisfying multiple forms of accountability. It is important to synchronise the different forms of accountability to ensure adequate, consistent and coordinated coverage of the different forms of management activity. For example, in Table 6.1, community and managerial accountability are related—the Village Health Committee would ask the District Health Team to take action on absentee staff.

2.3.4 Horizontal Divisions

Within organisations, there is often division of labour with individuals put into horizontal groupings, such as directorates, departments and units. In such cases, the criteria upon which these groupings are created are important. In a decentralised system, *geographical location* will be important and the DHA may split the district into sub-districts with coordinators for each sub-district, possibly focused around a health centre. In Uganda, for example, devolved districts are divided into sub-districts which are run from Health Centres (termed Level 4) and headed by Medical Officers who report to the District Director of Health Services. *Function* may also be used as a criterion for grouping, as in the case of divisions into health programmes. We discuss the appropriateness of both health programmes and projects in the Chapter 7. *Professional and occupational groupings* can be used, as in the case of a department of nursing. In fact, a high-level division of labour could be introduced in a DHA between planning (including health planning, health information and overall coordination), service provision (covering primary health care, district hospital(s) and disease control activities), support (including financial management, personnel management, and logistics management) and regulation (including formulation and implementation of standards and quality assurance mechanisms). In making these divisions, it is important to maintain balance in terms of size, relevance to the organisation and authority. One problem of grouping in this way is fragmentation and the difficulty of getting the organisation to work cohesively towards common goals. For this reason, organisations need to consider their internal form of linking to which we now turn.

2.3.5 Internal and External Linking

As we have seen, the structure of an organisation can lead to fragmentation. It therefore needs to develop a cohesive and collaborative style. Vertical forms of authority can be useful in ensuring a coherent vision, and planning can be one important mechanism for this. Operational policies and procedures need to be developed which also take account of this. These provide common ways of doing work in the organisation, particularly in resource management of finance, staff and supplies (see next section). Job descriptions can highlight the liaison and collaborating roles individuals are required to carry out. Structures can also be created, such as interdepartmental committees and working groups, and staff can be assigned specific linking roles with other departments. Lastly, matrix systems also allow staff to work on cross-departmental projects and programmes while remaining in their line departments. However, such systems need to be approached with caution particularly given the possibility of confusion; the dual lines of authority in a matrix can be a source of problems when responsibilities are not clearly defined and there is little trust between staff.

2.3.6 Defining Responsibility for Decision-making

Defining responsibility for decision-making follows on from the process of determining the work levels/authority relations in the hierarchy and the division of responsibilities in the horizontal structure of the organisation. These processes will go some way to defining the location of decision-making authority in the organisation. Job descriptions should also give clarity as to who is responsible for what. It is also important that the role of committees be clarified through terms of reference. This clarity is essential if the exercise of effective accountability is to be achieved. This point has already been underlined in the section on accountability in Chapter 3.

2.4 Complementary and Supportive Change

Changes in organisational structure do not stand alone; they need to be complemented by supportive changes in other areas. For example, the development of District Management Teams needs to be complemented by effective management and planning systems, new skills in resource management and shared approaches to teamwork. Changes in organisational structure also need to be complemented and supported by institutional change through, for example, changes in the organisational culture. Thus, the development of a more collaborative culture in the organisation can help in the effective operation of dual authority relations. A more participative culture of decision-making can also allow for authority relations to incorporate a two-way process of communication.

2.5 Process of Review and Change

The preceding has been built round an example of conducting a review into a DHA. There are key process issues concerning such a review—and in particular, how it is formulated and implemented through consultation, timing and monitoring. We refer the reader to other sections of this book and particularly to stakeholder consultation in Chapter 3 and monitoring and evaluation in Chapter 5. However, we emphasise here the importance of involving front line health workers in the process as organisational change can be a stressful and confusing period for them. It is also important that change should not divert attention and disrupt the continuity of service delivery. Incessant organisational change can be expensive, divert attention from the core activities and focus attention of staff on the present at the expense of providing a longer term perspective to work. Community representatives also need to be consulted over the governance issues of the changes.

3 Managing Resources

We turn now to look at how three resources—finance, staff and supplies—are managed. What is sometimes viewed as a fourth (and critical) resource—information—is discussed in Chapter 5. For each resource, we begin by asking what the management of that particular resource involves. We then examine the particular problems and constraints that management faces. Finally, we ask what needs to be done to improve effectiveness, drawing on the three levels of capacity referred to in Chapter 2.

3.1 Finance Management

3.1.1 Defining the Activities

The management of finance involves eight key functions outlined in Table 6.2. The generation and allocation of funds has already been

Table 6.2
Financial management activities

Activity	Characteristics
Income generation	The raising of income from sources such as fees, loans and grants to supplement any centrally allocated resources
Resource allocation	The distribution of financial lump sum resources from a central to a lower authority
Budgeting	The determination of intended future expenditure within a specified time period (often a year) and within a financial envelope determined by central resource allocation, local income generation and loans or grant-aid
Expenditure (drawing and disbursing)	The commitment of funds to purchase a particular service or good consistent with the set budget
Accounting	The maintenance of records of financial transactions (income and expenditure)
Expenditure and income monitoring and control	The periodic and regular monitoring of expenditure and income monitoring against the budget to ensure appropriate, timely spending and income generation and to determine management action where an imbalance is detected
Virement	The authorisation of a change in the budget items during a budget period without an overall change in the budget totals

Table 6.2 continued

Table 6.2 continued

Activity	Characteristics
Auditing	The scrutiny of expenditure and income accounts to validate their accuracy and that appropriate spending and income generation occurred against the set budget and satisfying legal requirements

discussed in chapters 4 and 5. We do not have the space to elaborate in detail on all the other activities in the table; we will however draw out some key challenges and areas for capacity strengthening in the area.

3.1.2 Challenges for Financial Management

There are a number of problems with financial management faced by health systems. For low-income health systems (and indeed some middle-income systems such as India), the levels of resources available to public sector managers are very low. At such low levels, there are particular challenges in attempting to use resources to meet needs efficiently. Furthermore, even these low levels of resources may not be predictable, causing a different set of challenges for financial management— that related to uncertainty.

Financial management systems may not link sufficiently closely to the other key decision-making subsystems and in particular policy and planning and human resource management. This almost inevitably leads to inconsistencies between the stated intention of the health system and its implementation.

The overall financial management system may also face specific constraints where there is significant external funding. Donors frequently insist on financial management procedures in areas such as budgeting, procurement and accounting which are specific to their own needs and timetables thus requiring the health system to set up multiple parallel subsystems. The transactions costs of such parallel subsystems can be significant and this, together with the danger of fragmentation, has led to the attempts to get greater aid harmonisation through mechanisms such as SWAps.

In many countries, financial management is seen as part of a centralised system. As a result, health facilities and district health authorities may have limited authority to manage their own financial affairs thus constraining effective decentralisation. Even where there is apparent decentralised financial authority, this may only apply to the non-staffing costs. Yet these staffing costs typically account for 50–70 per cent of the recurrent budget and provide the main opportunity for genuine decentralised decision-making. This reluctance to decentralise may stem from a desire of the centre to maintain full control, or it may be a response to a lack of financial management capacity, particularly in the form of skills and systems. If a health system is to be able to respond to local needs however, decentralised financial management is essential.

Investment in financial capacity has not been seen as a priority in many health systems and, where the skills do exist, there are inevitably better paid opportunities outside the public system leading to recruitment difficulties or attrition of skilled financial managers. Low levels of financial management skill within both specialist financial managers and general managers may lead to mismanagement (which should be distinguished from corruption). Good information on income and expenditure can be lacking while unpredictable flows of income can disrupt the flow of expenditure. In many low income countries, international funding, for example, can come in tranches that respond to the decision-making processes of the international agencies and not the expenditure priorities of the recipient.

An important issue for financial management is the method of payment used for professionals and service providers. The payment formula can send particular signals to them and result in different performance. This is also true within a system of contracting whereby, in economic terms, a 'principal' contracts with an 'agent' (for example, a public or private health facility) to perform certain activities. In both cases, the criteria for payment can affect performance. Payments could be made in a number of different ways including:

- By volume of activity (for example, the number of immunisations conducted)
- By the number of patients covered for specified health care (often called capitation)
- By the level of health achieved (for example, the incidence of malaria within an area)
- By the inputs used (for example, the salaries of a specified number of doctors)
- By the type of diagnosis of patients (for example, some volume contracts may be specified in terms of Diagnostic Related Groups [DRGs] with different costs and payments associated with each DRG)

There are various issues related to the different mechanisms. Some of these involve sophisticated information systems which are excessively costly and/or not always present. There is also a need for reporting and monitoring systems to validate that activities have taken place. It is also likely that each of these mechanisms will lead to incentives for the contractee to react in different ways and these are explored in Box 6.4.

Box 6.4 Possible reactions to payment incentives by health care providers

How health professionals and managers of health facilities react to the different forms of payment is difficult to predict both within and between health systems. A wide range of possibilities exist ranging from self-seeking behaviour for more monetary gain irrespective of the consequences for the patient to those who practice a strong ethical code respecting the health needs of the patient. In the case of the former, reactions to the various incentives could be as follows:

- Payment by volume of activity may lead to falsification of the figures or unnecessary treatment given to the patients.
- Payment by the number of patients registered at a health facility covered could lead to the health staff/facility rejecting registration of ill patients and searching for 'healthy' patients to maximise the difference between income and revenue.
- Payment by the level of health achieved among patients could lead to a focus on easier targets that can have quick outcomes and avoidance of the more challenging and resource intensive activities which could be shunted on to other health facilities.
- Payments by the inputs used could lead to the hiring of less experienced and less costly staff.
- Low salaries could lead to a de-motivated staff and the emergence of dual practice as health staff seek to supplement their activity with outside work. This could lead to health staff channelling patients to their own private practice and even using the resources of the facility for their own personal patients.
- DRGs, which mean that a fixed payment is made for specific types of patients with the same diagnosis, may lead to the facility lowering quality of care to make a surplus/profit or incorrectly diagnosing patients into more lucrative DRGs.

Lastly, the low salaries of health staff put them under particular personal financial pressure and some may seek to abuse the financial system to supplement their salaries. Such inappropriate behaviour may range from under-the-table payments to clinicians and pharmacists through to improper purchasing. All health systems have to guard against such inappropriate behaviour; weak health systems face a particular challenge as a result of the lack of robust financial management systems and monitoring skills.

3.1.3 Developing Capacity for Effective and Value-driven Financial Management

The values of a health system will have an important impact on how financial management is conducted.

The development of a broad health agenda is likely to require greater flexibility between budgetary boundaries and organisations. Mechanisms such as joint funding for inter-sectoral initiatives need to be developed. This may be more feasible at lower levels where there is devolution than within centralised budgeting systems even where there are deconcentrated responsibilities. However, even here it is possible with appropriate leadership and signals from the centre.

Planning the priorities for health action and budgeting for the necessary activities to promote an equity driven approach to health often requires a rethink as to how the health care budget is formulated. Frequently, budgeting is based on historical incrementalism in which budgets are set based on previous allocations. A focus on equity requires a radical shift away from such incrementalism based on existing institutions and historical patterns of spending to an assessment of the needs of a population. This is similar to the principles of a needs-based resource allocation system discussed in Chapter 5.

A needs-based approach also requires greater decentralised authority to allow local responses to needs. Decentralisation implies the transfer of the responsibilities and authority of financial management from the centre to the periphery. Hospitals and district health authorities become responsible for financial management. This raises issues. First, we need to clarify how these decentralised budgets respond to national planning and expenditure priorities. Table 6.4, for example, sets out the interrelationship between the centre and district in budget formulation. Central approval for expenditure above a certain level may be required and a central auditing process can be used.

Second, there is the issue of financial management capacity in the decentralised agency already referred to above. Active investment in these skills and systems is needed. Capacity, as indicated in previous chapters, can be viewed at three levels: enabling environment, the organisation and the individual.[21] Table 6.3 outlines the key areas of financial management capacity in the example of a tertiary hospital.

Decentralisation of financial management responsibilities can also be practiced *within* organisations. In hospitals, for example, budget management responsibilities are often centralised in a single budget. The

Table 6.3
Levels of capacity and financial management in a tertiary hospital

Levels of capacity	Effective financial management
Enabling environment	• Delegated responsibility to the hospital for managing its own financial management and clear regulations setting out the regulatory boundaries of this transfer • Management support on important technical issues relating to finance and external and/or central support for financial management capacity development • External funders meet their obligations in allocating funds on time • Appropriate auditing of the hospital by an external auditing body
Organisational	• Clear systems for the organisation setting out procedures for budgeting, making expenditure, accounting and auditing and responding to income uncertainties and cuts in a manner consistent with the plans and values of the hospital • Effective links between the hospital plan that sets out the priorities for future action and the planned budget • Transparency in the organisation in the exercise of financial management including published budgets and accounts • Capacity in the organisation to collect and manage information on finance • Transfer of appropriate responsibilities within the hospital of financial management responsibilities to directorates or similar units • Appropriate mixes of methods for provider payments linking them to the values sought for in the system and avoiding the perverse incentives outlined in Box 4
Individual	• Skills in financial management located in the organisation according to the internal spread of responsibilities • Sense of ownership in the overall hospital plans and resultant budgets

development of a divisionalised structure in hospitals would involve the transfer of budget management to a number of specialised divisions within the hospital.

Greater inclusiveness in decision-making, another of our core values, suggests the need for a more open approach to consulting with stakeholders, including staff, on the budget. Greater transparency calls for a

Table 6.4
Annual budget cycle for a three level deconcentrated health system

Month	Activity
1	Financial year begins.
5	Health ministry receives provisional allocation for following year from central government, together with any special constraints or conditions.
6	Health ministry issues broad resource allocation guidance to regions* on the basis of provisional allocation.
7	Regions issue broad allocations to districts on similar basis.
8	Budget holders develop and return proposals showing; • Review of service targets in line with plan • Estimated expenditure for the previous year • Estimated expenditure out-turn for current year • Reasons for under/overspending • Budget proposals for following year, costed and showing how they will meet planned service targets.
8	Budgets totalled and reconciled at regional level and then at health ministry.
9	Adjustments made: • To reflect national policy • To reconcile with other budget proposals • To reflect constraints • To reconcile with central government allocations.
9	Discussions with central governments.
10	Adjustments with service managers.
11	Informal approval.
12	Government approves budget.
13	Budgets issued to budget holders.

Source: Reproduced from Green. 1999 with permission from Oxford University Press.[22]

*Where an organisational structure does not include regions or provinces, adjustments will be needed.

shift away from budget secrecy to presenting a more exposed, intelligible and clearer format. While this will not get rid of corruption, it is likely to make corruption harder and enhances the potential for accountability.

3.2 Staff Management

In the past, the management of the workforce has often been neglected in health systems and their reform. However, given the staff-intensive and professional nature of health services together with the important impact staff can have on the performance of the system it is an area of great importance. In recent years, there has been a revival in policy and research. An expression of this was the World Health Report 2006 of the WHO which was devoted to the issues surrounding health workers. We have already, in Chapter 5, raised some issues relating to the importance of staff in the implementation of policies and plans. We focus here on issues related to management, though there is some overlap with the discussion in Chapter 5.

3.2.1 Defining the Activities

A useful way of portraying the breadth of health workforce management is shown in Table 6.5, which outlines the areas of staff management and illustrates these with examples of typical activities. These responsibilities are shared between specialists occupying positions in, for example, departments of human resources and, increasingly, line managers.

Table 6.5
Areas of staff management and typical activities

Area of staff management	Typical activities include …
Ensuring an adequate numbers of staff with appropriate skills	… staff planning, training, staff review, job analysis and definition, task shifting, employing and deploying, managing attrition …
Achieving appropriate staff performance	… rewarding and motivating staff, supervising and supporting staff, developing teamwork and good interpersonal relations, reviewing staff performance, improving working and living conditions, training, managing conflict and change …
Administering staff	… personnel functions such as keeping staff records, ensuring compliance with regulations …

3.2.2 Challenges for Staff Management

The challenges facing LMICs in the area of health staffing are immense; indeed, it is not unusual for managers to see the management of staff as the most challenging part of their job. People vary in their motivation and values; their future behaviour is difficult to predict; they cannot be kept for future use; attempts to increase staff numbers can be delayed by lengthy training. Furthermore, within the health system, there are specific challenges related to the management of professionals. These include inter- and intra-professional relations in addition to reconciling management authority in health care organisations with the autonomy required by health professionals in the exercise of their responsibilities.

Health Workforce Imbalances and Inequities

While the Americas has 10 per cent of the global burden of disease, 37 per cent of the world's health workforce and 50 per cent of the world's funding on health, Africa has 24 per cent of the global burden of disease but only 3 per cent of the world's health workforce and 1 per cent of the world funding on health.[23] Within poor countries, this is made even worse as health staff are often unwilling to live and work in poor urban and particularly rural areas leading to geographical imbalances. Major imbalances in gender, ethnicity and social class can be found among health staff employment. These imbalances relate primarily to issues of inequity (though diversity in background of staff can be important also in terms of effectiveness of service delivery). However, there may also be imbalances between different staff categories (such as between doctors and nurses) which are inefficient.

Low Staff Attraction and Retention

Within poor countries, there are difficulties attracting and retaining people in the public health system. This can be the result of various reasons—the counter attractions of private health sector facilities (who rarely train their own health staff) or non-health-related employment (wasting the professional training) for better rewards and geographical location. Recruitment by richer country health systems is also a major cause of staff losses again raising inter-national equity issues. Research in Uganda found that only 8 per cent of nurse students surveyed were not likely to migrate in the five years after training.[24]

Poor and Unethical Staff Performance

Poor staff performance can be linked to the lack of effective management practices and systems such as defining job responsibilities, supervision, performance appraisal, training, teamwork and remuneration. In five provinces of Indonesia, 47 per cent of nurses and 71 per cent of mid-wives had no job description and no in-service training in the last five years.[25] This lack of staff management skills and systems is compounded by the lack of resources to remunerate adequately, to travel for supervision and to allow staff the required complementary equipment and supplies. Poor staff management leads to poor performance. A study in Cameroon found that 73 per cent of staff time in health centres was of an unproductive nature (16 per cent explained absences, 34 per cent unexplained absences, 4 per cent social visits and 46 per cent in waiting).[26]

Other pressures on health staff may also constrain their performance; in Tanzania, for example, District Medical Officers spend 40–50 per cent of their time writing reports and 20 per cent dealing with mission visits.[27] This is not to suggest that managers should not write reports or meet mission visits; rather, it raises issues on their time efficiency and their availability for other work. Poor performance can also be linked to more unethical causes. There may be informal payments demanded for clinical services or more sophisticated corruption in procurement practice. Where there is pressure to raise income (either for personal reward or institutional income generation), there may be an incentive to over-diagnose or treat. The increased blurring of the boundaries between public and private sectors can also lead to inappropriate referral of public patients to the private sector for monetary gain.

3.2.3 Developing Capacity for Effective and Value-driven Staff Management

Table 6.6 takes the case of a district health system intent on improving its workforce management and looks at the three levels of capacity development. Consistent with our analysis throughout this book, we see staff management as an area in which the values of the health system are developed. Because of the importance of context, the table cannot be comprehensive; the example highlights, however, the interplay between the different dimensions of the process by reviewing a range of possible options.

Table 6.6
Levels of capacity development and examples of options for developing staff management in a district health authority

Level of capacity development	Options for improving staff management
Enabling environment	Agreeing international regulation and agreements to limit the international migration of health workers from low- to middle- to high-income countries
	Strengthening the authority of the DHA to manage and develop its own staff according to local context and needs (for example, local recruitment and selection of staff and staff allocation to priority areas in the district)
	Allocating sufficient central resources for improved remuneration of health staff and complementary resources
	Agreeing national regulations as a framework in which the DHA meets common quality standards in terms of how they manage health staff

Table 6.6 continued

Table 6.6 continued

Level of capacity development	Options for improving staff management
Organisational level	Strengthening an organisational culture that rests on a public sector ethos—staff working for an organisation that seeks to represent and meet the needs of the public
	Strengthening an organisational culture that provides a collaborative and innovative environment in which to work
	Strengthening an organisational culture in which staff are valued and are recognised as people with needs, values and aspirations and who are more than just a resource input (those responsible for staff management would need to find out how staff feel, their level of motivation, their problems and challenges and what health workers feel needs to be done for improved performance)
	Distribute health staff between health facilities and pro-grammes in such a way as to ensure that they are in place to meet the priority health and health care needs of the district
	Strengthening the supervision system by recognising its importance, providing resources (including time and transport for supervision) and ensuring responsibility for it is included in job descriptions and appraisal systems
	Establish systems of staff performance management allowing staff to understand the nature of their work and the standards for effective performance and monitor work through qualitative and quantitative standards (where standards are not met, then action would be taken to improve performance)
	Ensuring channels and fora of staff communication and involvement so that their experience, expertise and needs are recognised in the decision-making process
	Ensuring appropriate procedures and resources exist for local recruitment and selection in line with principles of fairness and transparency
	Setting clear promotion and disciplinary criteria and procedures with appeal mechanisms
Individual and group level	Making sure that all staff have job descriptions, that these are the result of some appropriate form of job analysis, that staff understand their responsibilities and are clear what performing well means (defining jobs would take into account task-shifting and the extent to which staff are specialised and/or multifunctional in their roles)

Table 6.6 continued

Table 6.6 continued

Level of capacity development	Options for improving staff management
	Identifying the needs for, and improving the skills of staff through in-service training
	Motivating staff through the use of measures such as adequate remuneration, teamwork, managing promotion, training opportunities and giving them a belief that better performance is feasible
	Developing opportunities for teamwork
	Delegating authority to staff to make decisions in their area of expertise

Box 6.5 looks at a particular issue of change—the retention of Community Health Workers in Bangladesh. It suggests the need to combine a range of measures to improve retention and points to the important role of management in doing this.

Adopting a health systems approach requires us to understand the interrelationships between the different resources and forms of management. It makes little sense trying to improve staff management in isolation from issues of financing and supplies. Staff performance in

---

Box 6.5 Community health worker retention in a newborn care intervention in Bangladesh

A study researched the recruitment and retention of female CHWs in northeast Bangladesh by focusing on a newborn care intervention. High levels of attrition can have a negative impact on performance of the intervention. The research used employment records, a survey and qualitative data. Of 73 CHWs in the programme, 40 worked through the project period, while 26 and 7 left as a result of actions by the CHW/family and the project, respectively.

Two key points are raised. First, the decisions of staff to continue their work or leave are complex and multi-factoral. They nevertheless need to be understood. The key factors were job satisfaction (for example level of pay, self pride, improving community health), other job opportunities, life events (for example, childbirth), values held by the community relating to CHW work and degree to which CHW expectations were met. Second, staff management can be used to manage attrition. Money is an issue and attention needs to be paid to compatibility in pay, increments, allowances, incentives need to be considered. Conditions such as sick leave need to be recognised while the importance of clarifying roles and responsibilities need to be understood and clarified.

Source: Rahman et al. 2010.[28]

a health facility will clearly be low in situations of inadequate supplies. We now turn to supplies management, recognising the importance of a systemic approach to improving resource management.

3.3 Supplies Management

3.3.1 Defining Supplies Management

Although in this section we focus primarily on medicines, supplies management also covers medical equipment and other medical (such as bandages) and non-medical (such as cleaning substances, office and food) supplies. Table 6.7 sets out the four main activities associated with medicines management and their characteristics.

3.3.2 Challenges in Supplies Management

An important issue related to supplies managements is the political and international context in which it operates. At stake is 'big money'

Table 6.7
Characteristics of medicines management

Activity	Characteristics
Selection	Selection should consider the needs of the health units and programs in addition to understanding the health situation of the particular communities concerned, their unmet needs, and the way in which these factors affect medicine requirements. Among the key considerations are the medicine requirements of the different levels of health care, priorities set, targeting of specific groups (e.g., children younger than 5 years), the use of an essential medicines list and generic medicines, and the design and implementation of quality assurance specifications.
	The quantities required need to be estimated. Such estimates can be constructed via methods that use (1) population-based data on morbidity and mortality complemented by norms, (2) service-based data on diagnoses (and frequency) complemented by standard treatment norms, or (3) historical consumption data. Each of these methods has both pros and cons. For example, the second method fails to take into account unmet demand, and the third method may be the easiest to use but fails to account for changes. Adequate supplies have to be maintained over time; thus attention needs to be paid to issues such as consumption patterns over time, lead time for procurement, safety stocks, and reconciliation of medicine needs with available resources.

Table 6.7 continued

Table 6.7 continued

Activity	Characteristics
Procurement	Medicines are obtained through a procurement process, which involves actions such as following purchase procedures (e.g., tendering, negotiating), selecting the supplier (according to criteria such as price and quality through inspections), clarifying the terms of supply and supply periods (fixed or variable intervals), monitoring order status, and receiving and checking the medicines.
Distribution	Distribution can be based on either a "push" (kits) system or a "pull" (inventory) system. In the former system, quantities of medicines are sent at regular intervals, based on estimates of anticipated usage. The latter system requires the health unit to order medicines according to need. Use of this approach assumes, for example, the existence of an adequate stock control system and good communications for ordering and delivering. Among the issues to be considered are the simplicity, regularity, and reliability of the push system, in addition to how it compares with the greater sophistication and adaptability of a pull system.
Use	The use stage involves "diagnosis", "prescribing", "dispensing", and "patient compliance". A variety of indicators can be developed to monitor and evaluate medicine use.

Source: Reproduced from Green, Collins and Mirzoev. 2011 with permission from Jones and Bartlett Learning.[29]

involving national and international pharmaceutical companies, issues around 'branded' and 'generic' medicines, the role of international agreements in facilitating trade in medicines and the trade in counterfeit medicines. As Global Health Watch point out:

> *The combined worth of the world's top five drug companies is twice the combined GNP of all Sub-Saharan Africa and their influence on the rules of world trade is many times stronger because they bring their wealth to bear directly on the levels of western* power.[30]

Added to this are the special and sporadic funding LMICs receive for specific medicine purchasing through global health initiatives. In these circumstances, it is often difficult for national purchasers to assume a needs-based coherent approach, operating through rational systems of effective supplies management that allow improved access of medicines to the poor in LMICs. Oxfam, for example, point to international intellectual property rights, pricing regimes and failure to focus research on diseases affecting the poor.[31] Dealing with these problems requires both national and international action.

In addition to the above, a wide range of problems can affect supplies management. These include inadequate needs determination, corruption (particularly in purchasing), poor supply system (due to, for example, lack of an efficient operational policy of procedures and lack of transport), over- and under-prescribing by health care providers, poor storage and stock control, lack of regulatory effectiveness (in areas such as essential medicines lists and quality control (particularly, but not solely, for street vendors and private pharmacists), poor funding for drugs and low-patient compliance.

3.3.3 Developing Capacity for Effective and Value-driven Supplies Management

Table 6.8 outlines some of the key options for improving supplies management covering the enabling environment and the organisational and staff levels.

We finish this section on resource management by emphasising once again the importance of a systems approach. By this we mean that it makes little sense treating the issues in resource management in isolation. Within each form of resource management we need to think in

Table 6.8
Levels of capacity development and options for developing supplies management

Level of capacity development	Options for improving supplies management
Enabling environment	Improving regulatory control by national government through, for example, an essential medicines list and controls on who prescribes drugs
	Engaging in WTO negotiations around Intellectual Property Rights and public health issues
Organisational level	Developing guidelines for standard treatments
	Developing guidelines for protocols for stock management and distribution
Individual and group level	Developing skills in medicine management and prescribing
	Improving staff supervision in medicines management through training and guidance

terms of packages of change which bring together complementary and supporting processes. This is important for the sustainability of change. Increasing the responsibilities of health staff, for example, requires the manager to think of a package of changes in staff management in terms of training and new forms of supervision and performance review. At the same time, the manager needs to move across the specialisations of resource management and see change in a broader perspective. Thus, financial issues need to be considered, such as a revised rewards structure to take into account the new responsibilities. Logistics and supplies are also important—staff may need to travel further to carry out the new responsibilities and added supplies of medicines may also be required. The manager needs to adopt imaginative approaches that go beyond the immediate object of change; a systemic package of complementary and supportive change needs to be considered.

4 Managing External Linkages

We have argued that management is an outward looking process in that those who practice it must relate to a wide variety of groups and organisations to achieve their objectives. We refer to this as managing external linkages. We use again our example of a DHA and the sort of external linkages that we regard as essential to the different district-level health system processes. These are set out in Table 6.9.

The linkages in the table are multiple and range from regulations based on legal statutes through contracting service provision to planning and allocation processes and links with community groups. Many of these types of external linkages are analysed in the respective chapters of the health system processes; for example, regulation and inter-sectoral linking are discussed in Chapter 3, while contracting, the referral process and service delivery through market systems and user choice are covered in Chapter 7 and planning in Chapter 5. It is important that managers recognise the gregarious and outward-looking character of management, developing a network of relations appropriate to their aims and responsibilities. Managers need to be conscious of this wide field of linking and develop the different forms of relations appropriate to each one. In this section, we look at another feature of linking—collaboration between organisations.

Collaboration is about working together. Managers in, for example, a DHA have to work together with other organisations, such as other health care providers, health planning organisations or water and sanitation agencies. This might be for reasons of developing health services and/or improving inter-sectoral action for health. How can such

Table 6.9

Typical examples of external linking for district health authority management

District health system processes	Examples of external linking
Governance	• Inter–organisational relations to achieve inter-sectoral action for health • DHA regulation of the private sector • Involvement of community groups and civil society in district decision-making
Funding	• Discussion and agreements with Ministry of Health and/or Ministry of Finance over the allocations made to the district • Negotiating for specific grants with funding agencies • Ensuring insurance payments to district health facilities from the social health insurance fund(s)
Policy-making	• Guidance on national health priorities from the Ministry of Health to be adapted to the district's own determination of health priorities • Involvement of stakeholder organisations in DHA decision-making
Planning	• Integration of district health planning with the national health planning process • National, regional and district flow of information on determinants of health, health status and health care for health planning
Management	• National auditing of the district financial accounts • Relationships with the Civil Service Commission (or similar body) for the appointment and dismissal of staff • Supply of medicines from Central (and regional) Medical Stores and/or the private sector
Service delivery	• Responding to policy guidelines from national health programmes in specific areas • Contractual relations between the DHA and NGOs for health care delivery • Ensuring the operation of the referral system within and between districts • External quality assurance of district health care • Involvement of the community in service delivery • Service delivery through market choice and managed markets

Figure 6.6
Making collaboration between organisations more feasible

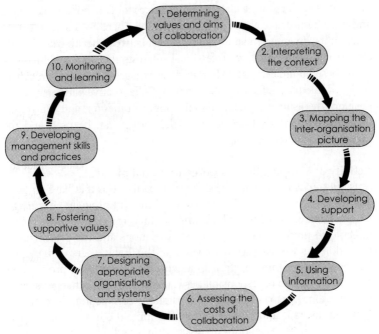

collaboration be developed? Figure 6.6 suggests a sequence of 10 activities that can contribute to make collaboration more feasible which we describe in the following text. Although we present the activities in the form of a sequence, this is not rigid; managers need to show judgement and innovation in adapting the process to particular situations.

Activity 1: Determining the values and aims of collaboration
The type of linkages developed in management and their relative priority depends to a large extent on the values underlying them. Valuing equity places an onus on developing community participation and tackling the inequality in the social determinants of health through inter-sectoral action for health. Efficiency through responding to the health needs of the community should raise the need for collaboration above the interests of professional and occupational groups and the bureaucratic interests of defending organisational autonomy. Values such as equity and inclusiveness should inform the aims of the collaboration. It is important that these aims are consciously recognised by the participants to guide the collaborative activities.

Activity 2: Interpreting the context of collaboration

Collaboration between organisations is conditioned by contextual opportunities such as the availability of resources for collaborative activities and the extent of social and political stability. There are also contextual constraints; an environment of competition between health care providers, strong and dominant professional interests that find it difficult to cross these boundaries, staff shortages, patronage and corruption can be major problems to effective collaboration. Collaborative partners need to develop a realistic interpretation of the opportunities for, and constraints to, collaboration, working out how the former can be used and the impact of the latter reduced.

Activity 3: Mapping the inter-organisational picture

A useful step is to map out the different organisations that have an obvious relevance to the health organisation. This will provide the manager with a framework within which to determine the degree of inclusiveness of the present inter-organisational relations and the priority areas for action. As we have seen elsewhere in this book, there is increasing fragmentation within the health systems. Organisational proliferation and fragmentation of responsibilities can occur through changes such as privatisation, purchaser–provider separation, contracting, decentralisation and diversification of the forms of funding the health system. This fragmentation places an onus on organisations and staff to manage inter-organisational relations, though its complexity can make this difficult.

In developing collaborative links—including for IAH—managers will work with a wide range of groups in civil society, some of which have a particular interest in the health system, including its management. We refer to groups such as associations of private health providers, professional and occupational associations (such as the Nursing and Midwives Association), NGOs (both national and international), community-based organisations, cause-based groups (such as advocates for disability rights) and groups representing patient groups (such as people living with AIDS). Other groups with interests include external donor partners and the media. All these groups have an interest in the management process and gaining access to the points of decision-making. Through their actions, they can influence decisions. Managers can also be interested in these groups to the extent that they can gain valuable information on needs, conditions and the impact of policies from them, gain legitimacy, political support and approval for the management decisions and generate additional resources from them. Similar issues are discussed in relation to planning and policymaking in Chapter 5.

The management process is never politically neutral in providing equal access to interested groups; inevitably, it shows a bias by allowing greater access to some. The broader context of social, economic and political power will be important in shaping this preferred access. In Chapter 3, we referred to the 'hollowed out' and the 'patronage' states as two instances where the relations of power and society mean that the health system, and in this case its management, are open to dominant interests in society. We suggest in Chapter 3 a process of 'shifting the bias' to a more equity-based linking between the state and social groups.

Activity 4: Developing support
Collaboration needs political backing for it to be effective. Those responsible for collaborating across organisational boundaries face many challenges. Organisations can talk different professional languages, follow different cultural norms, operate under different relations of funding, authority and accountability and meet the needs of different service users. These differences have to be bridged so as to make working together possible. To do so, they need backing and support from both within their own organisation and the collaborating one. We consider this in chapters 3, 7 and below.

Activity 5: Using information
Information can be important in managing inter-organisational relations. Health managers interested in establishing alliances with other providers will gain from knowledge both about the aims and objectives of the latter and their resources base, working culture, values and whom in the organisation to relate to. Such knowledge can smooth the way to better organisational links. District health managers developing health-related activities will gain from district health information that have cross-sectoral content and include information about issues such as educational level and households without good water and sanitation services.

Activity 6: Assessing the costs of collaboration
Collaboration is not a good in itself. It can only be justified by its results for health and the health system. It does however take up valuable and scarce resources. Managers have to be able to justify the effort and resources put into it. For this reason, managers must examine opportunities for collaboration to see if the benefits are worth the resources. For example, a two-hour 'collaboration' meeting (with two extra hours per person for travel and preparation) of six staff is the equivalent of three working days. Was it really necessary? If it is worth it, then organisations need a measure of 'slack' in their operation. There needs to be some

resource space in the organisation to take advantage of opportunities for collaboration in new and innovative ways.

Activity 7: Designing appropriate organisations and systems

The way we design the structure of organisations and the relationships between them is important in facilitating positive inter-organisational relations. Table 6.10 suggests some forms of organisational design that can promote good inter-organisational relations.

Operational policies also need to be developed in collaborative resource management. Funding is a key issue in collaboration. For example, district level mechanisms of funding and resource allocation need to allow for locally based inter-sectoral action for health. Organisations seeking to collaborate may operate different systems of

Table 6.10
Examples of organisational design for developing inter-organisational relations

Organisational design	Commentary
Over-arching policy-making bodies	These bodies, such as a National or District Health Councils, can provide a common strategic direction for other organisations, such as national health programmes.
Joint bodies for pooled funding and allocation, in addition to decision-making	Where funding from various sources is pooled in one fund, then the agency allocating these funds can require collaborative action as a precondition for funding. Organisational arrangements for a SWAp are an example of this. Cross organisational committees can also provide the contact necessary to make decisions, implement services and monitor their impact.
Decentralisation	To make decisions in collaboration with other agencies, a degree of authority is required. District Health Authorities interested in joint programmes with the district educational agencies need authority to commit resources to joint endeavours.
Collaboration as a departmental or staff responsibility	Organisations may designate a particular department or staff member to collaborate with other organisations. These must have sufficient authority, status and support to carry out their collaboration responsibilities. Job descriptions should make clear to the job-holder the relations of authority in the job and the forms of liaison and collaboration required.

budgeting and decision-making and this can hinder the use of resources in joint activities. These systems need to be not only compatible with each other but also to spell out who does what when, why and how in inter-organisational relations. Decision-making in, for example, joint appointments, the shared use of transport and patient transfer in a referral system need to be clarified in jointly agreed operational policies.

Activity 8: Fostering supportive values
Values play an important part in securing effective and trust-based inter-organisational collaboration. We have already pointed out that agreement around the values that underlie policy, such as equity, can facilitate collaboration. Open recognition by stakeholders that no single agency can control diseases or promote health is a critical ingredient of collaboration.

Collaboration involves risk as organisations rely on other agencies to contribute to solutions to common problems. Staff seeking collaboration across organisational boundaries need to believe in the sincerity of their collaborators. Trust is necessary to accept the risk. To develop trust, the risk involved in trusting needs to be assessed. Starting with small ventures may build up confidence, develop personal and more stable relations and help maintain 'principled conduct'.[32] Fair and decent behaviour by managers can be essential in building up trust. As we argued earlier, the attitude to risk is important. Health staff will not be willing to take on appropriate levels of risk through collaboration if a blame culture dominates; if successful collaboration is ignored or taken for granted by higher levels but unsuccessful collaboration is excessively criticised, then the values and preconditions for good collaboration are unlikely to be present. The possibility of developing trust is also dependent on the resonance between the values underpinning the two organisations in question. Where one organisation sees health care as a citizen's right and another sees it is a market commodity, then trust will be in short supply. In such cases, more formal and legally based relations such as regulation and contracts may be required to manage the inter-organisational relations (see Chapters 3 on regulation and 7 on contracting).

Activity 9: Developing management skills and practices
Managers need to develop skills and practices to facilitate collaboration. Professional divisions linked to differences in staff status (for example, clinicians who see themselves as belonging to a 'superior' profession) can make collaboration difficult. The personality and skills of the manager in problem-solving and negotiation will be important in overcoming such

constraints. Support needs to be given to innovators, who can take the initiative in collaboration, can advocate for collaboration to meet health and health care objectives, are able to instil trust among collaborators, can mobilise support among interested stakeholders and are experienced in presenting the way forward.

Activity 10: Monitoring and learning
Monitoring of and learning from the collaboration can be important for the process (for example, do both organisations have joint decision-making?), outputs (for example, is the collaboration leading to new services?) and outcomes (for example, does the new service meet health needs?). In assessing the relative benefits and costs it is important to recognise that the benefits may not be immediate—there may need to be a period of investment in the relationship before the benefits are visible. The monitoring needs to be used in showing what works and what does not work. This assumes a degree of flexibility in developing the collaboration as solutions to new problems are met and adjustments are made to meet the changing interests and positions of collaborators.

5 Managing Organisational Culture

Individuals and groups in organisations share understandings, values and expectations and we refer to these as organisational culture. While it may not always be accepted by everyone in the organisation, a prevailing culture frequently exists and will affect the management process and the performance of an organisation. Two questions related to this are relevant to our analysis.

First, there is a need to ask about the *type* of organisational culture to be promulgated in health system organisations. We would argue that it should be founded on the values expressed in this book: equity and right to health, efficiency, participative and accountable decision-making and long-term perspective. These fundamental values relate to the key objective of the health system—to promote and maintain the health of its citizens/members equitably to their full biological and social potential. Secondary objectives are also recognised—to promote social mutuality amongst citizens/health system members, and to empower health system members in terms of decisions about their own health, the wider health system and society. Consistent with this approach, we view management as including the acceptance and development of these values among stakeholders. It is also about developing supporting values. For example, we have stressed the importance of 'working together' in the analysis of structure, linking and resource management in this chapter. It is also critical to achieving inter-sectoral action for health and maximising the capacities of individuals and groups through teamwork.

Second, we need to ask what management can do to promote these values. Changing organisational culture is not easy, although there are actions managers can take in that direction. Table 6.11 outlines actions that can be taken. We see these actions as overlapping and supporting each other.

Table 6.11
Areas of management action for developing organisational culture

Area of management action in creating organisational culture	Commentary
Creating a strong understanding and acceptance of the organisation's values, aims and objectives	This can be developed by creating opportunities for staff to participate in the development of these values, aims and objectives, communicating them to staff, showing how individual and group responsibilities are linked to realising them, and transparent monitoring of their achievement.
Creating systems and structures that are permeated by the values	The values can be strengthened in the organisation by ensuring they are embodied in structures and systems. For example, channels for staff involvement in decision-making can be created. Striving for more collective decision-making makes sense given both the knowledge and expertise of the staff and the sense of ownership this can generate in the organisation. There is also a need for an organisational structure and management systems that recognise the need for a two-way process in the organisational hierarchy. Supervision and performance assessment can also express cultural norms through the mechanisms and criteria used.
Identifying the criteria to be used in decision-making	Managers need to explain and reiterate the criteria and how they can be used in decision-making. For example, equity is a key criterion to be used in decision-making. It should permeate service delivery to the community. It should also be recognised in promoting equality of opportunities in staff management. Equity is important in providing staff with the support they need to achieve good performance; staff should be supported according to their work needs and the context in which they are working.

Table 6.11 continued

Table 6.11 continued

Area of management action in creating organisational culture	Commentary
Leading by example	Managers should not only espouse the values but put into effect the values through demonstration. In areas such as making decisions, supervising, and working in teams their work should demonstrate to all staff the desired organisational culture.
Training	This can be done not only through the practice and context of formal training courses but also through using practices such as supervision, induction, mentoring, managed delegation and shadowing to explain the 'what' and the how' of the organisational culture.
Linking staff interests to organisational interests	Performance management in the organisation needs to link individual and organisational effectiveness. Staff need to feel that there is a connection between their own rewards and career and the effectiveness of the organisation operating according to a desired culture. This increases the sense of ownership felt by staff in the organisation.

6 Final Thoughts: Valuing Management

Mangers need to reflect upon what management actually is; we have argued for a management style that it outward looking, fair, proactive, innovative, problem-solving, flexible and evidence-based. The systems, political and public (or private) aspects of management need to be understood. Most of all, we have argued for a value-based approach to management which should permeate managing structures, processes, resources, culture and external linkages. How those involved in the management process define and realise the values that underpin the health system is vital. In this book, we emphasise the importance of values. While it would be naïve to ignore the constraints on realising these values, it is equally unacceptable to ignore the possibilities open to managers. To this end, we conclude this chapter by bringing together the ways in which the management process can be developed in such a way as to provide a more equitable, inclusive and empowerment based approach in a local health system. This is laid out in Table 6.12.

Table 6.12
The management process for improved equity, inclusiveness and empowerment: Some measures for change in a district health system

Measures	Commentary
Understanding management among district	A break is required with universalism in the approach to management; it needs to be seen as value based, contextually driven and analytical as an important precondition for permeating particular values in the management process. The outward looking perspective of management needs to be emphasised, allowing managers to link up with other agencies in pursuing an inter-sectoral agenda for health to deal with the inequitable social conditioning of health and health care. This outward looking perspective is also required to forge the links between the management process and the organisations and groups of civil society to pursue progressive policies. The overlap between management, policymaking and planning brings advocacy and political relations into the management process in pursuit of political objectives such as equity.
Promoting management efficiency	Resources are scarce and need to be used efficiently ensuring the maximum return with a view to improved and more equitable health and health care.
Decentralising the district	The district health system needs to practise its own internal decentralisation and formally authorise the transfer of authority, responsibility and resources to the localities nearer the community. This helps in bringing decision-making nearer the community and helps in the understanding of community health needs.
Using district information	The information system should bring to the fore the areas of health and health care needs and inequities and include the social determinants of these. Data has to be presented and made clear to funding agencies, political bodies, community groups and health staff.
Managing money	Where the district is responsible for some of its income generation, equity considerations and ability to pay need to be brought to the fore, particularly in the case of user fees. Budgeting and expenditure should adopt a needs based approach and consider the impact on equity, particularly meeting the health and health care needs of the poor. Funds need to be channelled in such a way as to allow for inter-sectoral action for health that tackles the underlying inequality in the district.

Table 6.12 continued

Table 6.12 continued

Measures	Commentary
Understanding communities in the district	Managers need to understand the communities they work in; their social, political and economic relations. They need to understand the networks of communities and groups, their needs, resources and power together with their potential involvement in the management process. This requires not only the capacity to interpret communities but greater stability of local staff to allow such familiarity.[33]
Developing progressive policy communities	These were referred to in Chapter 5. They can play an important role in policymaking and implementation when organised around a progressive coalition of local groups interested in promoting equity, inclusiveness and empowerment—and with support from regional and national groups and organisations.
Management structures and processes for community participation	This requires advocating for and/or practicing management in such a way as to allow greater access to groups that promote equity, to develop management in such a way as to allow access to decision-making to those often excluded and to promote the empowerment of excluded groups.
Supporting local groups	The district health authority can provide resources such as information, finance, co-opted staff, transport to local groups to the extent that they play a positive role in the local health system.
Developing organisational culture	Developing capacity in staff for a more inclusive management needs to challenge the attitudes and practices of managers based on bureaucratic, gender, professional, urban or class-based notions of superiority. This needs to be replaced by a more open, needs-based, equity-driven perspective that seeks to empower communities to gain greater control over their future.
Developing systems and structures	The systems and structures of the district health system need to be analysed to look for openings for more inclusiveness. The role of the community in assessing community health needs and in monitoring and evaluating service delivery should be examined.

Notes and References

1. Parts of this chapter draw on Green, A. and Collins, C. 2006. 'Management and Planning for Public Health', in Merson, M., Black, R. and Mills, A. (eds), *International Public Health: Diseases, Programs, Systems and Policies* (pp. 553–599). USA: Jones and Bartlett Publishers.
2. This definition and the differences between management and administration (below) build on Keeling, D. 1972. *Management in Government*. London: Allen & Unwin.

3. See, for example, Hersey, P., Blanchard, K.H. and LaMonica, E.L. 1978. 'A Situational Response to Supervision: Leadership Theory and the Supervising Nurse', in Rackich, J.S. and Darr, K. (eds), *Hospital Organisation and Management: Text and Readings* (pp. 184–191). New York: Spectrum.
4. See, for example, de Savigny, D. and Adam, T. 2009. *Systems Thinking for Health Systems Strengthening.* Geneva: Alliance for Health Policy and Systems Research, WHO.
5. Shiffman, P. 2007. 'Generating Political Priority for Maternal Mortality Reduction in 5 Developing Countries', *American Journal of Public Health*, 97(5): 796–80.
6. Particular aspects of this analysis referring to the public sector and its characteristics and contradictions draw on and develop issues in Stewart, J. and Ranson, S. 1994. 'Management in the Public Domain', in McKevitt, D. and Lawto, A. (eds), *Public Sector Management Theory, Critique and Practice* (pp. 54–70). London: SAGE Publications.
7. See Green, A. and Matthias, A. 1997. *Non-governmental Organisations and Health in Developing Countries.* London, England: MacMillan.
8. Parts of this section draw on Green, A. and Collins, C. 2006. 'Management and Planning for Public Health', in Merson, M., Black, R. and Mills, A. (eds), *International Public Health: Diseases, Programs, Systems and Policies* (pp. 553–599). USA: Jones and Bartlett Publishers.
9. See, for example, UNDP. 2008. *Practice Note: Capacity Development.* New York: United Nations Development Programme.
10. Manning, N. and Parison, N. 2003. *Institutional Public Administration Reform: Implications for the Russian Federation, Poverty Reduction and Economic Management Unit.* Europe and Central Asia Region: World Bank; Nunberg, B. and Nellis, J. 1995. 'Civil Service Reform and the World Bank', World Bank Discussion Papers Number 161, World Bank, Washington. Available at www.gdrc.com (accessed on 15 November 2007).
11. See, for example, Van Damme, W., Van Lerberghe, W. and Boelaert, M. 2002. 'Primary Health Care Versus Emergency Medical Assistance: A Conceptual Framework', *Health Policy and Planning*, 17(1): 49–60.
12. Particularly important references for the development of this section are Child, J. 1984. *Organisation. A Guide to Problems and Practice.* London: Harper and Row; Collins, C.D. 1994. *Management and Organisation in Developing Health Systems.* Oxford: Oxford University Press; Green, A. and Collins, C. 2006. 'Management and Planning for Public Health', in Merson, M., Black, R. and Mills, A. (eds), *International Public Health: Diseases, Programs, Systems and Policies* (pp. 553–599). USA: Jones and Bartlett Publishers; Rowbottom, R. and Billis, D. 1987. *Organisational Design, the Work Level Approach.* Aldershot, U.K. Gower.
13. See, for example, Child, J. 1984. *Organisation. A Guide to Problems and Practice.* Harper and Row.
14. Child, J. 1984. *Organisation. A Guide to Problems and Practice.* Harper and Row.
15. For deeper analysis, see Child, J. 1984. *Organisation. A Guide to Problems and Practice.* Harper and Row.

16. Rowbottom, R. and Billis, D. 1987. *Organisational Design: The Work Level Approach*. Aldershot, England: Gower.
17. Rowbottom, R. and Billis, D. 1987. *Organisational Design: The Work Level Approach*. Aldershot, England: Gower.
18. Rowbottom, R. and Billis, D. 1987. *Organisational Design: The Work Level Approach*. Aldershot, England: Gower.
19. Rowbottom, R. and Billis, D. 1987. *Organisational Design: The Work Level Approach*. Aldershot, England: Gower, p. 16.
20. Rowbottom, R. and Billis, D. 1987. *Organisational Design: The Work Level Approach*. Aldershot, England: Gower.
21. UNDP. 2008. *Practice Note: Capacity Development*. New York: United Nations Development Programme.
22. Green, A. 1999. *An Introduction to Health Planning in Developing Countries*. Oxford: OUP, Second Edition, p. 230, Box 11.3.
23. WHO. 2006. *The World Health Report 2006: Working Together for Health*. Geneva: WHO.
24. Nguyen, L., Ropers, S., Nderitu, E., Zuyderduin, A., Luboga, S., Hagopian, A. 2008. 'Intent to Migrate among Nursing Students in Uganda: Measures of the Brain Drain in the Next Generation of Health Professionals', *Human Resources for Health*, 6: 5.
25. WHO. 2006. *The World Health Report 2006: Working Together for Health*. Geneva: WHO, p. 74.
26. Bryant, M. and Essomba, A.R.O. 1995. 'Measuring Time Utilisation in Rural Health Centres', *Health Policy and Planning*, 10(4): 415–21.
27. WHO. 2006. *The World Health Report 2006: Working Together for Health*. Geneva: WHO, p. 74.
28. Rahman, S.M., Ali, N.A., Jennings, L., Seraji, M., Habibur, R., Mannan, Ishtiyaq, Shah, Rashedduzaman, et al 2010. 'Factors Affecting Recruitment and Retention of Community Health Workers in a Newborn Care Intervention in Bangladesh', *Human Resources for Health*, 8: 12.
29. Green, A., Collins, C. and Mirzoev, T. 2011. in Merson, M., Black, R. and Mills, A. (eds), *Global health: Diseases, Programs, Systems, and Policies* Third Edition Exhibit 13–5, p. 687 USA: Jones and Bartlett Learning.
30. Global Health Watch. 2005. *Global Health Watch 2005-6*. Zed Books, p. 103.
31. Oxfam. 2007. *Investing for Life. Meeting Poor People's Needs for Access to Medicines through Responsible Business Practices*, Oxfam Briefing Paper 109, Oxfam International, November.
32. Hudson, B., Hardy, B., Henwood, M. and Wistow, G. 1999. 'In Pursuit of Inter-agency Collaboration in the Public Sector. What is the Contribution of Theory and Research?' *Public Management*, 1(2): 235–60.
33. See Korten, F.F. 1983. 'Community Participation. A Management Perspective on Obstacles and Options', in D.C. Korten and F.B. Alonso (eds), *Bureaucracy and the Poor. Closing the Gap* (pp. 181–200). West Hartford, Connecticut Kumarian Press.

7

Inter-sectoral Action for Health and Health Service Delivery

1 Introduction

In the framework set out in Chapter 2 for understanding a health system, we describe the parts of the health system as processes. Since then we have analysed these constituent processes—governance (including regulation), financing, policymaking, planning and management. We are now in a position to discuss what comes out of the operation of these processes, namely, the activities that directly affect health in the form of IAH and health service delivery. These are the culmination of the working of the processes studied so far and should be designed to lead on to better and more equitable health.

The chapter is divided into three parts. First, we refer to IAH. This pays particular attention to developing interpretations of health and its determinants, governance, financing, policymaking, planning and management. These need to be combined in such a way as to lead to effective action that spans other sectors through joint programmes, effective legislative action and advocacy.

Second, the chapter looks at health service delivery. It does this in more detail than its coverage of IAH—not because we wish to downplay the importance of IAH but because service delivery continues to be the main preoccupation and resource consumer in all health systems. We identify and focus on five current key issues in service delivery: health programmes, health projects, scaling up health services, public–private providers and relations and the referral system. These issues raise important points relating to the broad processes we have already discussed and illustrate how other delivery issues can be analysed in similar ways.

Third, we analyse the manner in which the values championed in this book are brought into these two overarching outputs of the health system—IAH and health service delivery. In part this is answered by making the values permeate the processes in the ways previously analysed in this book. It is also answered by analysing the specific issues relating to IAH and health services delivery explored in the first two parts of this chapter.

Consistent with the analysis of this book, we recognise the importance of context in IAH and health service delivery. For example, service delivery will be affected by the extent of urbanisation, the degree of concentration in rural settlement, the political mobilisation of groups, the extent to which communities are conscious of their needs and the role of religious groups in relation to the health system. Also, where there is civil and political upheaval, there will be a difficult environment to build a comprehensive network of service delivery. Not only does ill-health flourish in such environments but health workers fear for their lives, health facilities are attacked and destroyed, equipment and medicines stolen, and supply lines disrupted. Natural disasters can also be highly disruptive and destroy the very infrastructure of health services delivery. In such circumstances, the more immediate needs to ensure emergency health care can compete with, and even jeopardise, a longer term strategy of developing a sustainable network of service delivery. This is recognised by NGOs such as Médecins Sans Frontières (MSF),[1] which see their expertise as relating to emergency situations and deliberately seek to move out of the country when a more stable development phase is entered. Between the extremes of stability and upheaval, there is a wide variety of non-developmental and non-emergency situations and these require innovative compromises and adjustments of the two approaches taking the local context into account.[2]

2 Inter-sectoral Action for Health

In Chapter 3, we reminded readers that the causes of ill-health lie largely outside the health system. As such, we argued that if the health system has, as its objective, the maximisation of health, then it needs to take action to promote healthy actions in other sectors. These sectors, by definition, lie outside the direct managerial control of the health system and as such different strategies are required. To develop IAH, we present a simple framework in Figure 7.1 for guiding the work of organisations such as the Ministry of Health.

Figure 7.1
Framework for inter-sectoral action for health

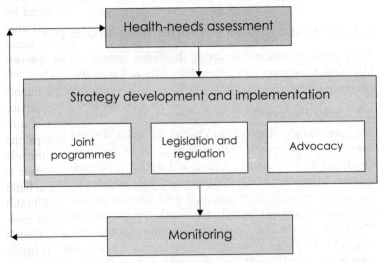

Underlying this framework is the importance of politics. We make no apologies for emphasising this once again. The challenges to be faced in IAH should not be underestimated; it crosses sectors, affects group interests and reduces inequalities. Challenging these inequalities will bring resistance from those who see themselves as losers in this process. Also, narrow bureaucratic and professional jurisdictions can be found throughout the public sector. This inevitable resistance to progressive change is why we have consistently recognised the political nature of the values and their development. It is also why we have emphasised the role of political coalitions of groups to champion the cause of IAH.

2.1 Understanding Inter-sectoral Health Needs

It is important to know *how* social determinants and inequalities affect health. Without this basic understanding, it is difficult to take the health agenda forward. This places on onus on research, information systems and the capacity to link with a wide range of stakeholders (particularly community groups) to understand these. The WHO Commission on Social Determinants[3] provides a clear demonstration of how health needs can be approached from the perspective of social determinants and inequalities. The report not only indicates the key social determinants (such as housing and employment) but also provides ways in which research, training and monitoring can be developed. For example, a useful tool for developing information systems is provided by a national system of health equity surveillance.[4]

2.2 Developing and Implementing Strategies

Three types of strategies involving the health system can be used for IAH; joint programmes of action, legislative and regulatory action and advocacy.

2.2.1 Joint Programmes of Action

We have already classified, in chapter 2, health services as curative, 'carative' and preventive. *Inter-sectoral action for health services* can be developed in, for example, schools and district health services coming together to develop health education activities among children. Spraying against mosquitoes might need joint programmes of action with organisations formally outside the health system, such as agriculture. This requires inter-organisational collaboration, which was discussed in Chapter 6. While the above forms of inter-sectoral action improve health services delivery through joint programmes, it is also important to develop joint programmes between sectors to work on inequities and the determinants of health. For example, a school and a DHA might work together to fund a joint programme to improve road safety for children near local schools or the DHA and the police force could come together to restrict drug trafficking.

2.2.2 Legislative and Regulatory Role

The regulatory process was discussed in Chapter 3 and can be an important means to IAH. The MoH, for example, may be responsible for setting and enforcing environmental health and food standards. When other ministries, such as transport, are making decisions with health implications then, at a minimum, consultation with the MoH may be required in legislation. An example of this could be a requirement in law that the Ministry of Health (or equivalent body) is required to conduct a health impact assessment on the environmental implications of the construction of new roads.

As we discuss in Chapter 3, regulation is an important aspect of governance in the health system. The MoH and associated organisations need authority in the system to ensure the legislative body passes an appropriate legislative framework and the political legitimacy to implement the regulations. Blas et al. (2008) point out that '*Typical characteristics of*

successful frameworks are that they outline roles and responsibilities (includ-
ing legal responsibilities, such as those related to human rights) of every sector,
how collaboration will proceed, and what resources will be available.'[5]

The regulatory competence of, for example, the Ministry of Health
requires resources of staff and logistics to inspect standards and impose
penalties if required. It also requires the ministry to develop good liaison
with politicians in the legislature and advocate amongst them for legislative frameworks that allow the Ministry of Health to operate effectively
in the areas referred to in this section.

2.2.3 Advocacy

Advocacy occurs throughout the health system. It refers to activities by
social and professional groups which aim to change the behaviour of
other groups over whom there is no direct control. It is perhaps best
known in areas of political lobbying where interest groups attempt to
persuade politicians as to the merits of a particular policy espoused
by the lobbyists. Policymakers, planners, managers, providers, users
and non-users may also advocate, for example, for more funding, different allocations, additional staff. Indeed, an essential tool of all these
groups is the ability to persuade other groups to adopt their position.
IAH will need advocacy by a number of different actors within the
health system to push for health-related activities in other sectors. Given
the importance of social determinants on health, it is important that
health system actors have a clear and active strategy and role in initiat-
ing, advising on and supporting activities in other sectors alongside their
more traditional health service delivery activities.

Effective advocacy by health actors requires appropriate underlying processes—those we have already discussed—governance, financing, policymaking, planning and management. These health system
processes should be developed in such a way as to allow for effective
advocacy. This allows health system actors to demand, persuade and
support other systems to take IAH. In Chapter 3, for example, we see the
role of health system actors in accepting and championing an interpretation of health that emphasises its social determinants and inequities.
Actors within the health system frequently adopt, however, a restrictive
medical interpretation of health and downplay the importance of wider
IAH; as such, they may not see a role for health-related advocacy. Furthermore, those working in other systems have objectives that do not include, or supersede, the health of the population; private companies are
primarily interested in profits, while other government departments are
interested in meeting their primary goals, such as education or industrial
growth. They can easily think that health is the problem of the Ministry

of Health and not theirs. To collaborate with those in the health system assumes that they both have an interest and the resources to do so. The WHO Commission on Social Determinants[6] emphasised the importance of education on the social determinants on health. This is important for actors both within and outwith the health system.

We also argue in Chapter 3 that governance runs through the health system and the power and authority relations need to be able to provide strong support for health-related advocacy. Although health advocates have no direct control over those working in other systems, they nevertheless have to alter the latter's behaviour to make what they do more 'health friendly'. Power 'speaks' and advocates of health need to be active in developing their political backing. A theme of this book has been the importance of the coalition of individuals and groups politically supporting a progressive approach to health and health care. This is vital in health-related advocacy.

To appreciate the breadth of advocacy in the health system, it is worthwhile recalling how it comes into our analysis in the previous chapters. In Chapter 5, we stress the importance of conducting policymaking and planning through an approach that espouses consultation and broad health perspectives and allows for the consideration of other system activities as potential interventions. We emphasise planning for health and not just for health care. Chapter 5 refers to the politics behind policymaking, the role of actors, stakeholders and health system members in the process, the stages of policymaking and the role of policy advocates. The financing of the health system, discussed in Chapter 4, can also provide both an opportunity and a constraint to health-related advocacy. The practice of advocacy in the health system uses up resources; it is staff intensive and staff need space to be able to carry out the activities of advocacy, including research, policy analysis, publications and networking. The financing processes needs to ensure the resources for this.

In Chapter 6, we emphasise an interpretation of management that is political, outward-looking, proactive and evidence-informed. We also emphasise the importance of, and steps to, ongoing inter-organisational collaboration within which advocacy can take place.

So far we have set out the foundations for advocacy within the health system; without this, it will flounder. Yet we still need to think through the form of activities that advocacy involves. These can be wide-ranging and Table 7.1 lists these.

Three points are important to consider in the development of effective and sustainable advocacy.

First, we stress the importance of values in advocacy. The right to health and equity underpins health-related advocacy and IAH and

Table 7.1
Advocacy activities

Means of advocacy	Details
Evidence generation	Research can play an important role in understanding the determinants of health and showing the effectiveness of different interventions to deal with these determinants.
Evidence presentation	Where robust data is available that highlights the wider determinants of health and inequalities, this needs to be presented in a clear and accessible manner. This highlights the problems, helps policy-makers to analyse options for IAH, and provides support to stakeholders including civil society groups pressing for action on the social determinants of health.
	Publications cover a wide range of options from hard copies to electronically based and social media. Particular attention needs to be paid to the message to be conveyed, to whom it is directed and the impact sought. These factors will determine the type and style of the published matter. For example, a Policy Brief on tobacco consumption could be a way of indicating: the nature of the problem in the link between tobacco and ill-health, a range of options to deal with the problem, reasons for a preferred set of options, and what the expected readership, such as Parliamentarians, could do in terms of legislation. Such a brief would be written in a style that Parliamentarians can connect with.
	Advocates can play an important role in persuading the media to highlight particular problems and to create a body of opinion that shows the links between health and social and economic determinants.
Policy analysis	Advocacy involves opening up the range of policy options, and inviting the consideration of policies and activities to deal with inequality and the social determinants of health. It can also mean inverting the causality; not just saying what other systems can do for health but showing what better health can do for other systems' aims—such as better education, agricultural and industrial productivity, family welfare, and social cohesion.

Table 7.1 continued

Table 7.1 continued

Means of advocacy	Details
Linking	Stakeholder analysis, networking, building links with policy groups and communities, making political contacts, working with trade unions, community groups and social movements protesting particular inequities and social problems are all activities of an advocate. Networking in the form of meetings, conferences, workshops, and working through social media can provide opportunities to open up the way in which health and its determinants are perceived, to negotiate IAH, develop networks of contacts, and create trust.
Negotiating	Advocates need to bargain, find common ground, reach agreement, and call in previous favours.

Source: Drawing on Chapman and Wameyo. 2001, Coates and David. 2002, Shiffman. 2007.[7]

should inform the activities chosen to focus on. Advocacy on IAH can also be an efficient use of resources in the health system. We also emphasise the importance of linking advocacy to participatory governance, as discussed in Chapter 2, which may be seen as a constructive step to empowerment of communities.

Second, advocacy requires certain skills and characteristic behaviours; advocates need to be good at communication, persuasive in discussion and trustworthy in their relations. The capacity to be outward-going and to put forward common values, such as the right to health and equity, is also important in identifying common ground and generating enthusiasm among actors from different sectors. The ability to interpret the context is also important. This can suggest the changing positions of stakeholders, the feasibility of advocacy pressure and the political opportunities for change.[8]

Lastly, advocates for health need backing and legitimacy from within their own organisation. The role of advocacy needs to be firmly embedded in the formal responsibilities of organisations and included as a recognised responsibility for which staff are held accountable. It involves risks in that the advocate seeks changes outside both the organisation and the system s/he works with. Advocates often work in unfamiliar territory in the space between organisations. As such, they need to be trusted both within and outside their organisation and receive strong support from their own organisation. This means receiving good data and policy options, resources and organisational space to be able to work outside the organisation and assurances of career development and security in their support.

2.2.4 Monitoring IAH

Monitoring IAH is the final step in our approach and links back to the assessment of inter-sectoral health needs. It requires similar approaches and skills such as research and information on the impact of strategies on IAH. We argue in Chapter 3 that IAH activities in, for example, a Ministry of Health need to be clarified and subject to accountability. The latter requires that the processes, outputs and outcomes of IAH need to be monitored and evaluated. In these circumstances, it might well be appropriate to have a separate unit within a Ministry of Health to ensure that there is organisational identity and responsibility for this function. We also draw attention once again to the WHO Commission on Social Determinants and the importance attached in that document to the monitoring of inter-sectoral health needs and the actions (or lack of) taken to develop IAH. The report stresses the importance of strengthening routine information systems for the surveillance of equity and improved systems of civil registration.

We have argued for the development and implementation of IAH strategy taking the form of joint programmes, legislation and regulation and advocacy. This needs to be based on needs assessment and should be the subject of monitoring. This rather tidy framework allows us to view IAH in a rational and methodical way. The process, however, is fused with values and politics and faces constraints, such as professional and bureaucratic divisions and political opposition. Working through this process of IAH from the perspective of the health system, it is easy to see how it can be criticised and dismissed as a lot of 'desk work' and interminable meetings. Indeed, IAH is not suitable work for those who like to see immediate results from interventions. Rather, it is for those who can see beyond the 'immediate' to the structural and longer term causes of the problem, for those who have a broader vision of how health and social change work together and for those with the virtues of patience and persuasion.

We now move on to look at health service delivery.

3 Health Service Delivery

In this section we look at five key topics in health service delivery: health programmes, health projects, scaling up health services, public–private providers and relations and the referral system. We have chosen these on the basis that in our judgement, they reflect key current issues in health service delivery. However, they are clearly not comprehensive. Furthermore, for some health systems, some will be more important than others. They are context- and time-specific. We foresee, for example, that future concerns over service delivery will bring new delivery challenges. These could include, for example, the appropriate use of tele-medicine and its integration into the main health delivery activities, ethical issues related to genomic-based medicine and issues arising from increasing delivery of health care across countries. We do not address these here but hope that our approach will provider pointers for the analysis of other key service delivery policy issues such as these.

We also recognise that health service delivery takes place in quite different organisational settings such as hospitals, health centres, health programmes and in the public and private sectors. Given the space limits of this book, we cannot cover all these settings and changes in service delivery. We aim to give a general analysis with a range of examples from different situations, albeit, given our stance, mostly in the public sector, leaving the reader to use the analytical approaches themselves to understand specific situations.

As will be seen, the topics we have chosen raise important points relating to governance, financing, policymaking, planning and management. The final section will relate the analysis to the values championed in this book.

3.1 Health Programmes

The most visible application of the programme format in the health system of LMICs is that of the national health programmes usually associated with the one or more diseases—such as a TB control programme or an EPI programme. The use of a programme organisation means that a degree of organisational separation or particularity is recognised usually around a problem(s)/service(s); spec fic activities are defined and given their own organisational identity with specific resources, objectives, management structure and relations.

In the public sector health system, a distinction is made between the more specific health programmes with their exclusive agendas around, for example, the control of a disease, and the general health services delivered by the rest of the public sector health system. A programme may be set up for various reasons: the severity and nature of the problem, such as a disease, may require the concerted and specialised action of expert and increased resources or the broader organisation may be considered ineffective to deal with the problem and a separate structure is required. This may be linked to stakeholder pressures, such as international funding bodies, users of the service and professional groups who wish a degree of identity and separation to maintain and develop service delivery. As will be seen below, the relationships between such programmes and the rest of the health system are critical.

The development of national disease programmes and their relationship with general service delivery has polarised debates in health systems. The national health programmes are often seen as more vertical top–down structures with general service delivery being seen as more horizontal and integrated systems dealing with all the other health service needs. What might be characterised as more vertical interventions tend to be more centralised, specialised in staff and single disease control forms of organising exclusive service delivery with specific allocations. In contrast, more integrated or horizontal forms tend to be broader and multifunctional in their scope covering a wide range of primary health care services. The arguments for the appropriate mix of integrated and vertical delivery modes involve more than strictly service delivery considerations but also involve other issues of health systems, for example, governance and financing.

Chapter 2 discussed three policy areas where concern about the vertical nature of service delivery has been raised: the debate about the comprehensive and/or vertical nature of the PHC approach following the Alma Ata Declaration, the emphasis on prioritising in the health sector reform movement of the 1990s leading to a disease and technocratic focus of vertical health programmes and the disease-centred character of international funding, such as the GHIs, leading to a strengthening of vertical service delivery. Given this, it is not surprising that we also should express concern over the support given to vertical disease programmes.

Vertical programmes can segment health and health care so that health care users are required to fit into the organisational convenience of the division of labour practiced by exclusive top–down hierarchies. Service delivery descends upon the community; it does not emerge from a close understanding of the health needs and their context. The importance and strength of vertical programmes can be set by international aid flows which show preference for control and eradication of diseases determined by international funding bodies and their financial backers. Priorities are set according to the availability of money and not the determination of health needs, particularly of the poor. It is interesting to note the findings of a review[9] which explored the extent to which infectious disease control programmes show a pro-poor slant. Despite important exceptions, the results were not encouraging:

... the pro-poor effectiveness of infectious disease interventions has neither been a priority in programme development nor has it been addressed articulately in research. In order for an infectious disease programme to be considered pro-poor, the endpoints should be measurable as long-term health gains for the poor and vulnerable. Programmes designed as integrated approaches addressing environmental factors, health risks, health care and poverty alleviation have the most potential to yield pro-poor outcomes.

Duplication of financial, logistical and human resource systems by vertical health programmes and the general health services can result in confusion and a waste of scarce resources. Better staff rewards and career development opportunities in national health programmes leads to a drain on the general health services and their ultimate weakening. This can create a major problem given the difficulties in staff retention in the public sector and the overall scarcity in health workers felt by many LICs. The priority given to national programmes in service delivery can take health staff away from their responsibilities in the general health services. Box 7.1 illustrates some of these problems in Mali for its Neglected Tropical Diseases Control Programme.

Box 7.1 Neglected tropical diseases control programme and the health system in Mali

Research carried out in Mali sought to understand the interaction between the country's health system and the NTD control programme, focusing on how this interaction is played out in health centres. The programme, funded mostly by USAID, was implemented from 2007 and provided 'mass preventive chemotherapy' for trachoma, soil-transmitted helminthiasis, schistosomiasis, lymphatic filariasis and onchocerciasis. Although there was an improvement in the mass chemotherapy, the programme also diverted district energies from the general health services, and different systems were developed and used by the programme for managing supplies, monitoring and evaluation and governance structures. Concerns were expressed by respondents around the sustainability of funding, the external decision-making system, the distorting consequences of the priority-setting and the contradiction between the programme and the ongoing work of the health district. Health centres showed differing capacities to: a) deal with the additional work required by the programme by maintaining general health service delivery and b) take advantage of the programme and use it to improve their own capacity.

The findings of the research suggest important challenges for health systems such as: the extent to which programmes can be used for capacity development of the health system; the differential capacities of health centres to both take advantage of programmes for capacity development and for implementing programme activities; and the collective weakening many programmes can have on a health system.

Source: Cavalli et al. 2010.[10]

Though there are arguments for national programmes in terms of their ability to focus, marshal resources and develop disease-specific expertise, the problems associated with vertical programmes have led to the call for their integration into general health services. Strong arguments can be advanced for favouring an integrated and more horizontal approach to service delivery. Such an approach recognises the integrated problems of ill-health and diseases and therefore enhances the efficiency of service delivery.[11] At the same time, it can lead to easier access for users to seek treatment for their health problems and thereby contributes to the pursuit of equity.[12] The approach fits in with the organisation of health care from a decentralised district base and, following our analysis of decentralisation, is consistent with a better adjustment to the health needs of communities and brings decision-making on service delivery closer to the community.

It has been argued that national health programmes can have beneficial 'knock on' effects on the general health services.[13] Their superior funding can allow for improved availability of equipment (such as in laboratories and information technology) and trained staff while their more efficient management systems can similarly lead to better management of the general health services. It is argued that national programmes thereby become catalysts for wider health systems change. While not wishing to suggest that this could never be the case, whether such a role is widespread is a matter for research and will probably depend on the capacity of the general health services to change[14] and the extent to which the national programme has the capacity to take on a broader health systems strengthening role. It is difficult, for example, to understand how a specialised national health programme could provide expertise in areas such as district health planning and priority setting. Even where a link can be demonstrated between a vertical programme and wider health system strengthening, it is also unclear whether investment in such programmes is the most efficient way to promote wider health system strengthening.

The precise meaning of what integration actually means is not always clear. Table 7.2 exemplifies this by suggesting a number of forms in which the integration of mental health programmes into the health system can be interpreted.

For some, integration is seen mainly as a service delivery issue whereby a 'one stop' system of service delivery is provided through multipurpose health workers at the point of delivery. Such a restricted view could however still lead to the continued exclusiveness of national health programmes, pressuring the frequently overburdened primary care workers to give priority to their own specific disease control. The separate funding and duplicated systems of the national programme

Table 7.2

Forms of integration of mental health activities into the health system

Form of integration	Degree of integration Degree to which....
Policy-making and planning	...mental health policies and plans are part of, or separate to, general health plans
Technical guidance, monitoring and control	...there is a separate function and organisational mechanism for providing managerial control, technical guidance, performance monitoring
Information	...a separate mental health information system (HIS) exists or one which is integrated into the broader HIS
Professional and staff	...separate mental health cadres or services provided by general cadres who have some mental health training
Finance	...mental health funding is from separate sources to the general funding of the health system ...there is a separate vertical mental health budget with separate financial management or is integrated into the general budget and its management (and at what level and for which items)
Service delivery in facilities	...mental health services are offered separately or alongside, and at the same time, as other services
Patient pathways	...the patients are treated separately or there are integrated patient pathways
Integration between health and health services	...services are co-ordinated between different health system providers

would be maintained. A more developed form of integration would mean the integration of the programme into a district health system with its own authority and control over resources. In this case, the national programmes, if they continue to exist, would take on a more technical support role for the district health systems. The processes of governance, funding, management and planning would no longer be separate and exclusive activities of the national programme but form part of a more cohesive district-based system.

The process by which integration is implemented can be difficult. As with any change in the organisational structure of the public sector, the interests of individuals and groups are affected. Associations representing those affected by a particular disease and specialised providers can oppose such a change—seeing it, sometimes correctly, as lowering the priority and potential quality of the service. The process of change faces challenges, such as improving the overall capacity of, for example, district health systems to take on the responsibilities for disease control, and develop new forms of governance, priority-setting and resource management. Multipurpose workers need to be trained, new staff recruited and new systems of supervision and referral set up. Revised forms of national resource allocation need to be developed to take account of the shift in disease control responsibilities together with regulatory authority to ensure the quality of disease control. There are difficult issues. For example, the superior funding of some national health programmes in LMICs, particularly from international agencies, has meant that they may provide relatively better quality health care than resource-starved district health services. The process of transition to a more decentralised and integrated approach needs to maintain or at least minimise the loss of the advantages of the superior resources received by the national health programmes; any such loss needs to be outweighed by the advantages to be gained through integration.

Although we argue in favour of a general shift to integration, there are cases in which a more vertical type programme may be appropriate. It has been argued[15] that there are situations in which a degree of verticality is required, such as epidemics, rare diseases, outreach to specific groups and epidemiological surveillance. Contingent variables need to be analysed to identify the extent to which a set of disease control activities needs to adopt a vertical or integrated form. Atun et al.,[16] for example, look at a range of issues such as the high urgency of a health problem: '*At times a rapid response may necessitate speedy introduction of an intervention with limited integration, followed by gradual assimilation as the problem is better controlled.*'

Many of the issues on health programmes are relevant to our next topic, health projects.

3.2 Health Projects

Projects are separate organisational units based on specific tasks, dedicated resources, defined and sequenced activities, are temporary in nature and operate according to initial appraisal and monitoring/ evaluation procedures.[17] Whilst they have often been seen as ways of injecting new approaches to a service, particularly through capital invest-ment or training, they can become vehicles for funding streams aimed at ongoing service delivery. Projects may also have many of the same characteristics as programmes, although the latter are designed as longer term organisational structures without the same degree of exclusiveness.

Projects can have advantages,[18] such as making sure resources are directed to priority problems and targets which put into effect broader planning objectives. They can be aimed at producing tangible benefits and allow for the by-passing of possibly inefficient and corrupt public bureaucracies, though they may set up opportunities for new forms of inefficiency and corruption. They can delineate between an investment in a service (and the one-off costs associated with this—such as capital expenditure on buildings) and the ongoing running of the service.

The project format is often favoured by international funding bodies as it allows for control through separate implementation agencies following the funding body's own accounting procedures, defined monitoring and evaluation procedures, financial audits and controlled contracting and procurement. This raises issues of accountability—whether it is to outside controlling interests or to national bodies and also issues of potential inefficiency through duplication and increased managerial costs.

The project format may also be favoured by some politicians as they can offer tangible outputs to refer to during elections and may also of-fer an opportunity for their own patronage. Their time-limited nature, however, raises question marks over the sustainability of service provi-sion. They can also divert funds away from the established health system structures, such as a District Health Authority, sucking in resources such as scarce staff (their 'freedom' from mainstream bureaucratic control can result in their ability to offer attractive remuneration) away from general service delivery or planning and management roles. The defined and lim-ited tasks of projects can interrupt policies that look for a more integrated and inter-sectoral approach to health and health care. Nor are projects immune from common management problems such as corruption and poor capacity. Their often top-down structures can represent an imposi-tion on a community and their time-limited nature may militate against longer term continuity for the development of community participation.

Organisational design needs to be subordinated to the tasks to be performed and the underlying values of the health system, as indicated in the review process we describe in Chapter 6. These criteria need to be used for deciding *when* to use projects. Korten's[19] analysis is instructive: blueprint style projects are viewed as appropriate to those situations in which there is a clear definition of the task involved, the output can be achieved within a defined time, the environment is stable and the costs may be predicted. This might, for example, occur in engineering and physical construction work. As he points out: '*However in rural development, objectives are more often multiple, ill-defined and subject to negotiated change, task requirements unclear, outcomes unbounded by time, environments unstable, and costs unpredictable*'. The same may be said to apply to areas of health development.

Projects do not have to follow the rigid stereotype presented at the beginning of this section. They do not have to be isolated objects; rather, they should fit into the continuous and long-term work of the organisation. They need to emerge from, and blend into, this work. They need to build into their funding and timing the means by which their achievements (but not necessarily the project itself) are made sustainable. For example, projects to build new facilities or immunise a particular community should incorporate the means by which the advances will not only be sustained but can be developed. Unfortunately, projects can easily outlive their reason for existence and develop a political momentum for self-preservation. Neither do projects have to follow the stereotype of imposed top-down provision of a service. Rather, they can be based on established mechanisms for involving the community in identifying needs, deciding on options and monitoring implementation. As far as possible, these forms of community involvement should not be sporadic add-ons that disappear when the project has finished but be part of the continued work of the district health system.

A key issue related to the existence of health programmes and projects is how the size of the interventions can be expanded and scaled up. We now turn to this issue.

3.3 Scaling up Services

Scaling up involves the often rapid expansion of activities to a larger scale. The move from small-scale activities and coverage to wider systemic coverage is one of the major health systems challenges today. When service interventions, perhaps introduced on a relatively small scale and/or on a pilot basis to test new interventions or service approaches, are viewed as efficacious and cost-effective, there is likely to be a desire to increase (sometimes rapidly) the scope of the interventions to cover more social groups, range of interventions and/or a broader geographical area. The scope of scaling up may vary; at a smaller level, a district health service may wish to scale up a health education programme from one community to others; at the national level, scaling up may occur to meet unmet national needs in disease control.

Considerations about the health system values should underlie scaling up. Appropriateness to priority needs is a key consideration. It is important that the initial success of the pilot or small-scale intervention be verified through robust evaluation and that consideration is given as to whether this efficacy is likely to be maintained when the scale is expanded. Closely linked to this are issues of cost; scaling up may ideally see the capture of economies of scale; however, it is also possible that any efficiency possible at low scale are lost through the expansion—a form of diseconomies of scale.

A separate but linked issue relates to how the service and its expansion is viewed by the wider constituency of stakeholders and its impact on the overall health system. Does the expansion mean that resources need to be cut from other priority programmes? Scaling up a particular intervention takes place in a broader health system and can have both negative and positive effects on the other parts of this system. On the positive side, scaling up services to meet, for example, the HIV/AIDS pandemic is clearly important for communities that have been affected by this disease; the significant influx of resources through local, national and international channels has been important in this respect. It has also been argued, as we saw in the discussion of programmes, that this significant scaling up of disease-specific resources can have an important and positive impact on the wider health system. For example, by strengthening disease control, it can strengthen community organisations, laboratory systems and staff training.[20] However, we should also be concerned when scaling up adopts a vertical structure and has a negative impact on the priority-setting process in the country, detracts the health system from dealing with the other priority health systems needs, diverts resources (such as staff) away from such priority needs and sets up parallel management systems.

We also need to consider the equity effects; how will scaling up affect who pays for the additional resources and how will it affect access and utilisation of services by different groups? Mangham and Hanson,[21] for example, discuss the need to analyse the relationship in scaling up between maximizing coverage of health care '... *across all population groups* ...' or targeting '... *poor and vulnerable groups, which tend to be the hardest to reach* ...' However, not to scale up can also lead to inequity in that services remain restricted to a particular small scale operation.

Scaling up also needs to be consonant with the developing forms of district health services and governance. Indeed, decisions on scaling up themselves will be affected by who decides on the scaling up; provider and funder stakeholders may politically push certain interventions for scaling up that are not necessarily responding to priority needs.

Scaling up can take place through the expansion of an organisation to a larger size and/or the expansion of inter-organisational relations. Table 7.3 outlines some challenges faced in doing this; it requires us to

Table 7.3
Challenges in scaling-up

Health system element	Commentary
Policy-making	• Although the initial experience may be deemed successful, there are inevitably lessons to learn and these have to be brought into the policymaking process for the expansion phase.
	• Scaling-up will have an impact on policies such as those pursuing equity and may require reassessment of priorities.
Planning new resource flows	• The scaled-up activities may have to move from time-limited project funding to a sustainable mainstream budget.
	• There are various costing issues such as additional administrative costs, different costing for populations in urban and rural areas and 'economies and diseconomies of scale'.[22]
	• The new resource flows have to be converted into new staff and other resources and there may be a time delay. This needs to be taken into account.
	• The scarcity of trained health staff in many LICs is a major constraint on scaling-up service provision; this is referred to in Chapter 6.
Management challenges	• Management capacity for the expansion needs to be developed in areas such as staff supervision.[23] Weaknesses in the areas of management referred to in Chapter 6 can be important problems in scaling-up.
	• Informal and flexible relations developed on a small scale may not be possible on a larger scale; new more formal work relations and patterns, systems and organisational structures may have to be developed.
	• The organisational expansion may result in new cultural norms which can affect motivation, values and enthusiasm. New staff may not show the same level of commitment to the values that inspired and underpinned the initial intervention.
Character-istics of the intervention and service delivery	• Each health care intervention has its own specific approach to controlling a disease and this complexity needs to be recognised and considered in scaling-up.[24]
	• Scaling-up needs to consider the issues raised in this chapter concerning targeting, achieving efficiency and equity and deciding on the degree of verticality/integration.[25]

Table 7.3 continued

Table 7.3 continued

Health system element	Commentary
	• Scaling-up service delivery can take place through new forms of inter-organisational relations (such as contracting and franchising).[26] • Scaling-up can face constraints at the community and household levels in terms of problems in utilisation and also low demand for the services.[27]
Context	• The first intervention was developed in a specific context of social, economic and political relations; this might have played an important part in accounting for its success. Scaling-up moves the intervention into uncharted social, economic and political territory which might be more challenging than the first intervention.
Stakeholders and commu-nity link	• Expansion involves a new range of stakeholders and possible strains on relations with existing stakeholders. Systems change needs to be based on a new coalition of stakeholders that has to be developed and sustained. • Expansion from service provision in one community to many communities might threaten the participation nurtured on a small scale and near to the community in the initial intervention. Larger organisations may have less contact with the community.

consider how the scaling up affects key elements of a health system set out in Chapter 2 and covers health system processes such as policymaking, planning, funding, management and service delivery in addition to context and stakeholder and community links.

We turn now to discuss the different forms and combinations of health service providers and then, in the subsequent section, how they can relate to each other through market competition.

3.4 Public and Private Providers and Relations

This section considers changes in the range of service providers and the relations between them. In many health systems, there has been a trend of greater heterogeneity among service providers. Different types of providers exist with different funding streams, forms of payment, range of service provision, inter-provider relations, quality of care, accessibility to users and, underpinning these and affecting them, different values. At the same time, the separation and differences between some categories of service providers has become less defined. To appreciate this, Table 7.4 sets out a description of the different types of service providers. Each category indicates a wide range of different providers.

Table 7.4
Providers of health care

Provider	Commentary
Public sector health care provider	These are employed by Ministries of Health, other ministries with provider functions (such as ministries of higher education with teaching hospitals), social security agencies and sub-national governments.
Private for profit health care provider	This category ranges from a registered single nurse, paramedic and/or doctor providing primary care in private practice to large scale private hospitals. It also covers commercial companies offering primary care services.[28]
National NGOs	These not-for-profit organisations include national NGOs, such as faith based organisations (FBOs) and secular voluntary organisations, and may include clinics, hospital services or specialised services in programmatic areas such as disability or maternal health.
International NGOs	This includes international foundations such as the Aga Khan Foundation and agencies such as Médecins Sans Frontières.
Donor agencies	Some donor agencies may implement their own projects and programmes.
Employment-related health provider	Organisations (for example, a mining company or university) may provide either or both general health care and occupational health services to its employees/members.
Traditional providers	These include traditional healers using non-allopathic medicine and traditional birth attendants, some of whom may have some allopathic training.
Other informal providers (trained and untrained)	These include trained pharmacists who, in addition to the sale of medicines, may also offer medical advice. There are also untrained and non-registered informal providers, such as street sellers and failed or present medical students.
Self and family care	Much health care is provided by the family/friends or the individual patient self-treating.[29]

There are large differences both between and within country health systems in the range, type and importance of different health service providers. For example, in LMICs it is not unusual to find a large number of informal providers as shown in the survey sample taken by in Bangladesh shown in Table 7.5.

Table 7.5
Types of health care providers in study sample in Bangladesh (%)

Types of health provider	Sub-types of health provider (professional and non-professional)	Percentage and location of providers		
		Rural	Urban	Total %
Qualified allopathic professionals	Physicians	0.7	22.6	3.7
	Nurses	0.4	7.1	1.3
	Dentists	0.1	1.0	0.2
Semi-qualified allopathic providers	Allopathic paraprofessionals	0.6	5.5	1.3
	Community health workers	6.5	7.7	6.7
Unqualified health providers	Village doctors	8.1	11.0	8.5
	Drugstore salespeople	6.4	16.4	7.7
	Traditional birth attendants, untrained and trained	24.8	7.6	22.5
	Traditional healers (including faith healers)	48.6	10.8	43.5
	Homeopaths	3.3	8.7	4.0
	Others (for example, circumcision practitioners, ear cleaners, tooth extractors)	0.5	1.7	0.7
Total		100	100	100

Source: Adapted from Bangladesh Health Watch. 2008 with permission from the authors.[30]
N.B. The table does not include self and family care as a separate catagory.

Five aspects of service provision through public and private providers are worth drawing attention to in order to capture the heterogeneity of service provision and the complexity in public–private relations. These are hybrid providers, values and providers, staff fluidity between public and private providers, contracts and market competition.

3.4.1 Hybrid Providers

First there are new hybrid providers that bring together the categories set out in Table 7.4 in new provider organisations. For example, a new organisation may be created with shareholding between public and private agencies. The new Shanghai Sino-German Friendship Hospital in China, for example, has a share structure involving Tongji University (a public university) (46 per cent), Siemens (a private company) (40 per cent) and the private hospital group of Asklepios Kliniken (14 per cent).[31] Joint ventures between public and private agencies for service provision usually involve, as with this example, some form of formal agreement and contract.

3.4.2 Values and Providers

Public and private sector providers are not always what they appear to be. The formal legal position of the provider in the public or private sector does not always correspond with their ostensible values as public or private providers. For example, there are cases of public providers who exhibit private-for-profit values. The current tendency for government hospitals to be more self-funding through the application of user fees or reliance on insurance payments can be associated with staff bonus payments and hence supplier-induced demand and unnecessary treatment to the user. Box 7.2 gives an example of this from China. There can also be specific cases of private providers, such as NGOs such as Oxfam, showing more recognition of public values than parts of the formal public sector.

Box 7.2 Case-study of public providers and private values

In China, public hospitals are only able to cover part of their resource requirements through government allocations and have to rely on user fees and government insurance payments. To motivate hospital staff to increase productivity, various forms of incentive payments are made to staff by the hospital. Research conducted in six hospitals among appendicitis and pneumonia patients identified approximately 18 per cent of average expenditure per patient as unnecessary expenditure; 34–8 per cent of the expenditure on medicines was also considered as unnecessary expenditure.

Source: Liu and Mills. 2005.[32]

3.4.3 Staff Permeability between Sectors

There is permeability in staff between the public and private sectors. In many countries, public sector health staff also have employment in the private sector, either as independent practitioners or working for a

private health care organisation. This is often referred to as 'dual practice'. How this operates will vary a great deal between different professions and occupations, their responsibilities, the structure and dynamics
of the public sector and the broader context. This permeability, however,
is often based on the low wages paid in the public sector and staff looking to supplement these by working in the private sector. Their public
sector employment potentially allows them to maintain a regular salary
and a secure career, pension and benefits, prestige of an official position, training (for example, Continuous Professional Development) and
contact with patients to feed into their own private practices.[33] It does,
however, raise critical issues for the health system. It can mean that the
public sector is subsidising the private sector through a steady stream of
well-trained professionals. Dual staff may use the public sector as a mere
platform for their private sector activity, engaging in unethical practices
(for example, channelling patients and resources to the private sector)
and 'resting' in their government jobs to give them energy for their more
lucrative private work.

3.4.4 Contracts between Sectors

Contracts have become important means for linking the public and private sectors. Contracts are arranged agreements between two or more
parties wherein payments are made by a purchaser(s) to a provider(s) for
the provision of specified services. They are arrangements that put into
effect the purchaser (or commissioner as they are often referred to) and
provider separation we refer to in Chapter 2.

Figure 7.2 illustrates the key elements in such a contract. The regulatory body may or may not be independent of the purchaser or commissioner. The context particularly refers to whether the contracting is
carried out in a competitive environment or not.

There is a wide variety of possibilities for contracting with
different combinations of the variables involved which are described in
Table 7.6. Typical examples of contracting by the public sector are hospitals contracting out the provision of support services (such as cleaning,
car parking, catering services or transport) to the private sector. However, aspects of clinical care or even the whole hospital could be contracted to the private sector. Government agencies may also contract
out other health care services, such as primary health care through a
particular organisation, facility or over a geographic area. This has hap-
pened in the contracting out of primary care facilities in Pakistan and is
also explored in studies conducted in Central America.[36] We refer to the
appropriateness of public sector contracting with the private sector in
our analysis of service delivery and values later in the chapter. Closely

Figure 7.2
Contracting between commissioner and service provider

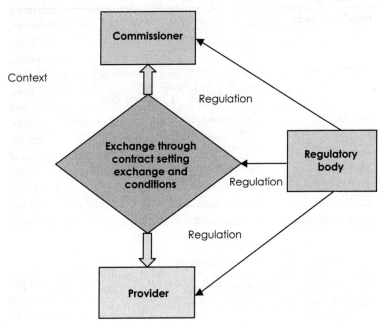

Context

Table 7.6
Variations in forms of contracts

Variable	Commentary
Object of contract	This can include services provided, such as preventive, clinical, support and administrative/managerial work.
Type of contracting	There is a difference between contracts which are a) adversarial, low trust, detailed, strictly monitored and legally binding, and b) based on mutual obligations and high trust, longer term, less detailed and may not be legally binding.[34] Contracts can also be used in leasing, concessions and build-lease-operate and transfer arrangements.
Type of exchange/ payment	The type of exchange which would be closely related to a) the contract, would be based on a (loose or tight) service definition b) the system of payment, such as performance-based

Table 7.6 continued

Table 7.6 continued

Variable	Commentary
Regulatory body	This body, which is responsible for regulating the contract, may have different degrees of independence from the commissioner.
Commissioner	The commissioning body could include agencies (centralised or decentralised) with diverse arrangements for financing and autonomy.
Provider	The contracted provider of services could be any form of provider such as the public sector, NGO or private-for–profit.
Market/non-market based context	Contracts can be founded in a market context and through competitive tendering. Alternatively, they may be agreed through non-market mechanisms.

Source: Derived from Collins and Green.[35]

related to the role of the private sector and new forms of public sector operation is the issue of market competition in which contracting can be one of the mechanisms. We now turn to examine this.

3.4.5 Market Competition between Service Providers

This has emerged as an important factor in relations between providers. One element of the neo-liberal approach to health systems is to encourage choice between service providers and efficiency in provision through the development of market competition. We refer here to those situations in which these decisions involve providers who compete with one another and are rewarded with incentives. To explain how these markets operate, we need to draw on the forms of funding analysed in Chapter 4.

Figure 7.3 shows instances of market competition involving users, private providers and insurers. Relationship A is where users choose their provider from among various competing private providers and pay a fee which is paid at the point of service delivery. Relationship B is where the user makes a prepayment to the provider who takes responsibility for all those forms of health care stipulated in the formal agreement it makes with the user. In this case, the provider is often referred to as a Health Maintenance Organisation. Relationship C is also a form of prepayment but is through a third party private insurer. User makes agreements with private insurers who register selected and competing private providers. Users can choose among competing

Figure 7.3
User choice and service provision in private health care markets

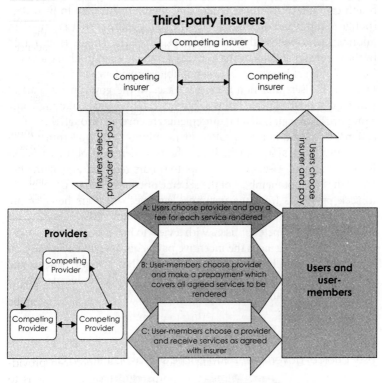

but registered providers for services in the agreement between the user and the insurer.

The workings of these forms of markets can lead to a range of inter-related problems; provider profit can be put ahead of health care need, the asymmetry of knowledge between the provider and user can lead to the provision of unnecessary care, adverse selection may be practiced (for example, the insurer is only interested in healthy members) and the market does not take account of the externalities of health interventions. Markets are not good at producing public goods and often reproduce the forms of social and economic inequality in access and utilisation of health care.

Neo-liberal reforms in health systems have sought to involve the public sector in markets leading to competition within and between the public and private sector providers. These reforms have been based on the separation of purchasers and providers. One form of this was practiced in the UK NHS in the early 1990s; the users paid the public purchaser through taxes and the purchaser then put out a series of health care interventions to tender and these are awarded to providers (public and private) depending on price and quality. The users are then informed as to where they should seek care. The choice is exercised by the purchaser and not by the user. In the public sector in China, another form of market operates between public providers, as suggested in Figure 7.4. Users and non-users pay taxes to the government, part of which are used to allocate funds to public sector hospitals, although only a proportion of their budget requirements are covered through these allocations. Users and non-users also pay premiums to the government-run health insurance systems which pay the providers part of the costs following treatment. Users may also opt to (or are required to) pay the full fees if they are not members of the scheme or consider it too problematic to seek payments from the insurance agencies. All users however are able to choose their provider even though they are in the public sector. The providers compete for users with a view to increasing income. A key element in this scheme is the incentive payments operated by some hospitals and received by the hospital staff when they increase patients and incomes. As we noted above, this results in supplier-induced demand and unnecessary care.

Figure 7.4
User choice, government and public sector hospitals in China

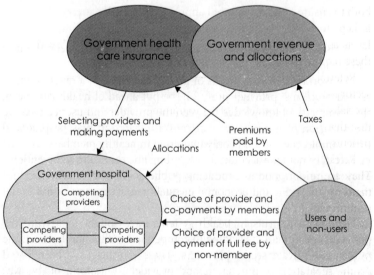

3.5 Referral System

Referral systems are a mechanism within service delivery whereby patients enter the system at a particular point (usually the primary level) and are referred through it, as necessary, to access the appropriate level of skill and resources for their particular needs. A well-functioning referral system allows a mix of (a) widely dispersed (and hence accessible) basic care which can both deal with the majority of basic health problems and can recognise when more specialised services are needed, and (b) a smaller number of facilities in which higher levels of expertise are concentrated and to which patients are referred by the previous provider. There can be several levels of referral; the most common is that of three levels (primary—clinics or health centres, secondary—district level hospitals and tertiary—specialist regional or national hospitals). The picture can be more complicated with the addition of further services. For example, the primary level may include a further level such as a dispensary which would refer to a health centre and hospitals may refer to further specialist services such as cancer hospitals. There may also be referral to agencies outside the health system. In high-income countries, for example, there may be a network of housing and social care agencies that become involved in the care of a patient.

A well-functioning referral system provides not only for patients to move up the system, but also for their referral back to the lower levels for continued care (see Figure 7.5). It should also provide a mechanism both to ensure a patient-centred approach (in which patient information is kept together for future use) and for continued learning for lower levels as they receive feedback on patients they have referred. Both of these require good information flow in both directions.

Referral systems can also cross between types of provider. The private sector may, for example, be able to refer cases to the public sector where specialist skill is required. TB programmes, for example, may recognise that private practitioners are involved in the diagnosis and care of patients but encourage referral to public centres of excellence.[37]

Referral systems make sense according to the values in this book. They are an important ingredient of efficiency; they mean that patients are treated at that level in the system that is the most appropriate in terms of location, skills and technology required. This is good for the patient; it is also good for the provider who treats according to the skills and technology available. It is also more efficient in terms of resource use. They are also important for the right to health and equity; they allow those who live in rural areas and in locations away

Figure 7.5
Referral system

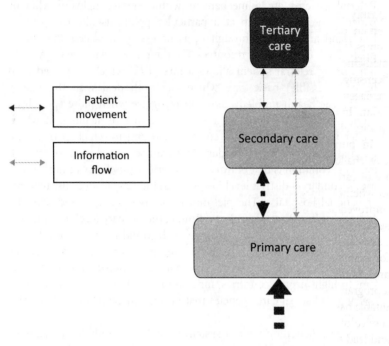

from the urban-based referral hospitals an opportunity of access to higher levels of health care.

However, managing referral systems can be difficult. They are highly demanding in terms of user and provider acceptance, information and transport to the point that, in many countries, the officially recognised system is poorly implemented. Problems can abound; information systems (including patient records) do not exist, there is a lack of feedback back to the primary level after the patient is treated at a higher level, patients show a lack of confidence in the quality of care and therefore avoid the lower levels of the system through what is known as bypassing. A study of the referral system in two rural health districts in Niger[38] points to lack of enthusiasm for referral by patients (due, for example, to costs involved of transporting ill-patients to the hospital and maintaining them while there) and staff in the health centre who '... *appear reluctant to refer because they see little added value in referral and fear loss of power and prestige*'. Some systems may attempt to discourage bypassing by the use of fees for non-referred patients using secondary and tertiary care.

3.6 Quality of Care

Quality in service delivery describes the extent to which it possesses certain positive characteristics that meet approved outputs and outcomes.[39] This is a large area and covers processes such as evidence based medicine, peer reviews, quality assurance programmes, inspection and licensing, accreditation, ensuring professional standards and supervisory management.[40] In Chapter 3, we also looked at the general area of regulation. In this section, we shall limit our analysis to relating the issue of quality of care to equity and sustainability.

In pursuing polices to improve quality, policymakers face difficult challenges and tensions. In themselves, policies to improve quality of care appear highly laudable. Yet, there is always the concern as to whether improvements in the quality of care through, for example, improved staff skills, new systems and better technology, can be made sustainable in low resource settings. In addition, there are two important issues around equity. First, programmes to improve quality of care in, for example, a group of health facilities covering a particular catchment area, need to consider the equity aspects of quality. A key issue in such a programme is surely whether the improved quality is offered on an equitable basis within the catchment area. Is there a tendency for improved service quality to be taken advantage of by richer elements in society and lead to greater inequity? Second, does investment in quality of care in one area of service delivery lead to disinvestment or neglect in other areas? For example, in the aftermath of a civil war or natural disaster, governments have to set priorities as to how to renovate a health delivery system. When resources are very scarce does the government focus on improving quality in the existing facilities or seek to expand coverage where it does not exist or is of very poor quality? Achieving high levels of quality in certain areas such as tertiary hospitals can leave secondary and primary care under-resourced and with low quality. Those advocating for wider coverage make the important point about the inequity of a focus on quality for a few whilst there are some with no or very low quality services. Those advocating for a focus on quality make the important points that low quality services are ineffective and that quality improvements may require focus in a small number of services followed by diffusion throughout the system. Trade-off decisions such as these are ultimately ones of applying values and the relative importance policymakers—on behalf of society—place on providing a spread of access to care throughout the population (an equity imperative) or focusing quality (through, for example, improved medical technology) for an element of such services.

4 Values, Inter-sectoral Action for Health and Health Service Delivery

In this section, we review the key values we set out in Chapter 2 in relation to IAH and service delivery. This draws on issues we raise in this chapter but also requires us to recall the analysis of financing, governance, policymaking, planning and management covered in previous chapters. We will also introduce new issues relating to utilisation of health services, the fragmentation of service delivery and the role of public sector provision.

4.1 Right to Health and Equity

Three issues emerge in relation to this value; the social and economic injustice underpinning the broad inequities in health, developing access and utilisation with a view to equity and last the fragmentation of service provision and the role of the public sector.

4.1.1 Social and Economic Injustice Underpinning the Broad Inequities in Health

The health needs of a country should be the primary influence on IAH and health service delivery. This is why we have depicted the desirable health system in Chapter 2 as a flow of action which stems from health need and results in improved and more equitable health. Low-income countries face major health challenges as a result of poverty and their demographic profile which have led to common epidemiological profiles of high communicable disease (particularly TB, AIDS and malaria). However, the more recent superimposition of non-communicable diseases such as heart-related disorders and diabetes together with increasing recognition of long-standing problems, such as mental illness, on to the existing profile of communicable diseases has led to a double burden of disease. New diseases such as strains of influenza also represent major challenges as do the re-emergence of diseases such as polio. Such challenges are not restricted to health issues where there are biomedical challenges—such as that of finding a cure or vaccine for HIV or the growing multi-drug resistance of TB. Areas in which there is considerable technical knowledge, such as maternal health, also constitute a major challenge for low-income countries, as they seek to find ways to ensure the health system delivers proven services for pregnancy and childbirth.

Figure 7.6 suggests the future global changes expected to occur in health and health need. This places an onus on the health system

Figure 7.6
Ten leading causes of burden of disease for the world

2004 Disease or injury	As percentage of total DALYs	Rank		Rank	As percentage of total DALYs	2030 Disease or injury
Lower respiratory infections	6.2	1		1	6.2	Unipolar depressive disorders
Diarrhoeal diseases	4.8	2		2	5.5	Ischaemic heart disease
Unipolar depressive disorders	4.3	3		3	4.9	Road traffic accidents
Ischaemic heart disease	4.1	4		4	4.3	Cerebrovascular disease
HIV/AIDS	3.8	5		5	3.8	COPD
Cerebrovascular disease	3.1	6		6	3.2	Lower respiratory infections
Prematurity and low birth weight	2.9	7		7	2.9	Hearing loss, adult onset
Birth asphyxia and birth trauma	2.7	8		8	2.7	Refractive errors
Road traffic accidents	2.7	9		9	2.5	HIV/AIDS
Neonatal infections and other	2.7	10		10	2.3	Diabetes mellitus
COPD	2.0	13		11	1.9	Neonatal infections and other[a]
Refractive errors	1.8	14		12	1.9	Prematurity and low birth weight
Hearing loss, adult onset	1.8	15		15	1.9	Birth asphyxia and birth trauma
Diabetes mellitus	1.3	19		18	1.6	Diarrhoeal diseases

Source: Reproduced from WHO. 2008 with permission from WHO.[41]

[a] This category also includes other non-infectious causes arising in the perinatal period apart from prematurity, low birth weight, birth trauma and asphyxia. These non-infectious causes are responsible for about 20% of DALYs shown in this category.

to recognise these changing needs and restructure service delivery as appropriate.

Figure 7.6 sets out health needs as defined and measured in a biomedical way. Most lay people however will have their own perceptions of health needs derived from personal experience and the wider environment. This leads to expectations about how a health system will respond to such self-determined health needs, which may differ from biomedically defined health needs. Given the limited resources available for any health system, prioritisation between different health needs (and their different interpretations) is necessary as has already been discussed in Chapter 5.

The current inequity in health status in societies is determined by social and economic injustice. Better education, better housing, better income lead to better health status. It is here that health-related advocacy needs to take the lead in pressing for IAH to meet the socio-economic injustices. These same injustices also have an impact on access to health services. This is where policies of IAH and health services delivery need to combine to act against the social and economic injustices that lead to poor access to health services. In short, inequity in health needs and risks is one element of, and consequence of, a broader range of social, political and economic inequality. Community social, political and economic relations also affect the level of effectiveness and differential utilisation of health service provision.

4.1.2 Utilisation and Equity

Universal coverage, as a policy goal in a health system, seeks to arrive at a situation in which all health system members have the same opportunities of access to a similar and complete range of quality services, at an affordable cost and that meet their health needs.[42] By equity we refer to equal utilisation of health care services in accordance with health needs. Any attempt to realise this key value faces major obstacles. For example, getting to a health facility can be a problem of not only transport but also loss of earnings. People may feel unable to pay for any direct or indirect costs to be paid in the facility. They may feel badly treated by the providers and that the services are culturally inappropriate to them and possibly of poor quality. The wider context of social inequality needs to be taken into account; utilisation is affected by factors such as income, gender, age, location and race. Box 7.3 draws on research undertaken in several countries; it underlines the different determinants of inequity and the interrelationship between them.

The analysis in this chapter has already noted the advantage of developing integration in health service delivery as a means to improving

---

**Box 7.3 Health care and determinants of inequity
in various countries**

Research has looked at the determinants of inequity in a range of countries and has underlined issues such as wealth, ethnicity, and gender. Five examples of research are:

Lopez-Cevallos and Chi (2010)[43] summarised their research in Ecuador by noting: *"Adjusting for various predisposing, enabling and need factors, a significant negative relationship was found between household economic status (as measured by assets and consumption quintiles) and utilization of preventive and curative services. The same was true for use of antiparasitic medicines. Further, indigenous ethnicity was found to be a significant negative predictor of health care utilization, regardless of economic status."*

Sousa et al's (2010)[44] research into unsafe abortions in Mexico also summarised the following "... *the probability for poor women (of having unsafe abortions) with less than 5 years of education and indigenous origin is nine times higher compared with rich, educated and not indigenous women. We also find marked geographical inequities as women living in the poorest states have a higher risk of having an unsafe abortion."*

Uzochukwu et al.'s (2009)[45] study of adherence to anti-retroviral (ARV) treatment that has been subsidised in southeast Nigeria concluded that *"While all patients clearly understood the need to take the ARVs throughout their lives, 75% of respondents were not fully adhering to their drug regimen. The main two reasons given for non-adherence were side effects and non-availability of drugs at the treatment centre. Being female, aged less than 35 years, being single, and having higher educational status (formal education) were significantly associated with non adherence."*

Referring to studies published in China, Tang et al. (2008)[46] point out the difficulties facing migrant women in China: *"Greater poverty, poorer living conditions, and inadequate or no access to essential antenatal and postnatal care for migrant women are probably major contributing factors to the very high maternal mortality rates in some cities for rural-to-urban migrant women: 48 deaths per 100,000 in Shanghai compared with 1.6 per 100,000 among resident women in 2005[47]; 42 compared with 18 per 100,000 for resident women in Beijing in 2004."[48]*

Claeson et al.'s (2000) study of child mortaility in India pointed out that *"... a girl in India is 30–50 per cent more likely to die between her first and fifth birthdays than is a boy; thus eliminating gender gaps in mortality rates would significantly reduce infant and child mortality overall."*

---

access. At the same time, the referral system allows for dispersed and accessible health facilities to be linked to more specialised health facilities. Contracting NGOs to provide health services where the government has not been able to expand its services can be important for widening access and equity. We also refer to the link between scaling up of services and equity.

An important issue in developing universal coverage is related to targeting; the application of particular policies or provision of services to specified groups rather than universally. Targeting may seek to focus service expansion to disadvantaged groups based on income, location, gender, ethnicity and age. Decisions as to which groups to target are value-driven and require discussion of the criteria to be used in such a choice.[49] Scaling up health services can also result in increasing inequities if service expansion does not consider equity.[50] Specific measures to increase greater coverage for underprivileged groups include targeted subsidies, user fee exemptions, targeted health care interventions, voucher schemes, social marketing and contracting NGOs to increase coverage in underserved areas.[51] Laudable as these specific targeting measures may be, it is important that they do not detract from, replace or contradict higher level and longer term policies designed to achieve equity and universality. There are two important and related policy considerations. First, targeting needs to be seen as part of, and contributing to, a policy of universal coverage and form part of the changes in health systems that we are advocating for in this book. These changes include fair health system funding based on developing collective prepayment systems, resource allocation with a view to equity, IAH, a proactive state system, health planning and management with a view to equity, greater health systems accountability and effective regulation of the private sector. Second, context is an important consideration. This recognises the interlinked nature of health with social, economic and political determinants; health and health care inequities are affected by, and form part of, a broader range of inequalities in society. Any attempt to reduce the inequities in coverage needs to be part of a broader strategy that impacts on the social determinants of health and forms part of a social strategy for greater equality and fairness in society. Working on these determinants and developing inter-sectoral strategies to tackle social inequality is important for improving access to health care and better health[52].

4.1.3 Fragmentation, Inequity and the Provider Role of the Public Sector

In this section, we examine heterogeneity and fragmentation in the health system and how it is related to inequity. On a number of occasions during this book, we have pointed to heterogeneity in the health system; funding can take various forms, the stakeholders are many and the providers cover a wide range of public and private providers. Three arguments could be put forward in favour of greater heterogeneity of health service providers. First, the proliferation of different organisational forms of service delivery can allow adaptation to different circumstances. There is no universal 'correct' form of service delivery but many different forms that fit the many different contexts. This heterogeneity represents a move away from monolithic systems of public sector provision, allowing more flexible and adaptive private organisations to operate. Second, it means the system may be able to take advantage of many different opportunities, groups and strengths and channel them to improve service delivery. Third, and more controversially, the diversity of providers allows for the operation of choice and the development of market competition.

Heterogeneity can, however, be a problem. It can be part of a broader fragmentation in the health system that leads to inequity. The heterogeneity may permeate the health system affecting the funding, planning, regulation, management and policymaking. The providers shown in Table 7.4 have different funding streams, offer services to different groups and have different levels of quality. An example of this can be seen in Africa and Latin America outlined in Box 7.4.

Box 7.4 Fragmentation of health systems and inequity

There are strong historical roots of fragmentation in LMICs and in the class, gender, geographic and racial inequality in health delivery. Colonialism in Africa during the 19th and 20th centuries was responsible for developing exclusive health systems that gave privileged access, particularly to the ruling elite. In some Latin American countries, the fragmented funding system led to the emergence of a tripartite system of service delivery; tax-funded health care mainly for the poor, social health insurance mainly for the organised working class and the middle classes and the formal private sector mainly for the upper classes through fee paying and/or private health insurance. Although the reality has been much more complex than this, it did form a basic framework around which fragmentation led to inequity. Fragmentation has also been linked to the implementation of neoliberal health financial reforms and the development of the private sector in Ghana, South Africa and Tanzania.[53]

There is a balance to be achieved between, on the one hand, universalism and equity of access to health services and, on the other, the benefits of diversity among the service providers. This balance can be facilitated by developing the capacity of the public sector in funding (and particularly through collective prepayment systems), health policymaking, strategic health planning, management and regulation to ensure that the diverse service providers work towards the overall goals of the system. It also requires that the public sector plays a major role in service provision. This forms the bedrock of a system of provision that should be geared towards the development of a universal system based on equity. It is on this foundation that greater diversity in service providers can be allowed on the condition that the activities of these providers are directed towards the overall goals of the system. The heterogeneity should be used to further these goals and not subvert them. We therefore argue against the neo-liberal approach which has supported an increased role in expenditure and provision by the private sector and make the case for a significant, and potentially predominant, role for the public sector in service provision. This position is based on the following reasons for emphasising the service delivery role of the public sector:

- The public sector has the potential to incorporate social objectives in service provision which lay the basis for improved coverage, equity and universality of health care. The public sector also has the organisational scope and presence to manage resources throughout a given territory and thereby is better placed to move towards universality of care.
- The public sector is better placed than other providers, through its ability to raise finance, to sustain service provision.
- Public sector provision contributes to a broader process and culture of social solidarity that is essential to meeting objectives of improved equity. The term *social solidarity* is often used in relation to funding and suggests collective forms of prepayment. It can also be applied to heath service provision where everybody in a community has potential access to the same health services. As we explained in Chapter 2, we are taking the objectives of the health system beyond the issue of health and underlining wider social cohesion based on equity.
- Public sector provision can emphasise the importance of collaboration rather than competition between service providers. Collaboration is important within and between health facilities and is epitomised in teamwork, resource sharing for improved efficiency, relationships of trust and referral between health facilities.

To complement the positive arguments in favour of a significant role for public sector service delivery, there are also concerns about private sector provision, particularly delivery through the private-for-profit sector. In this book, we have raised concerns over the association of user fees and private health insurance with private for profit provision and hence the shift towards inequity.[54] Box 7.5 provides further support to this analysis.

Box 7.5 'No comfort for commercialisers'

Research in 44 low- and middle-income countries examined the relationships between private/public expenditure and provision on the one hand and improved health outcomes (child mortality and healthy life expectancy) on the other. The results show 'no comfort for commercialisers' (idem: 13), although the authors correctly hold back from awarding causal status to the correlations found. These are:

- 'Countries with better health outcomes have significantly lower commercialization of health expenditure ...
- Countries that spend more of their GDP on private health expenditure do not display better health outcomes ...
- Countries that spend more of their GDP on health through public expenditure or social insurance do, however, have significantly better health outcomes ...
- Better care at birth is associated with more of GDP spent by government or social insurance funds on health care, but not with more private health spending/GDP ...
- Higher primary care commercialization is associated with greater exclusion of children from treatment when ill ...
- Commercialization of primary care is associated with greater inequality in rates of consultation for children when ill' (idem: 14–16)

Source: Derived from Mackintosh and Koivusalo. 2005.[55]

From the above, it is clear that we are arguing for a strong provider role for the public sector. Let us be clear however as to what we are not arguing. First, we are not suggesting that the private sector does not or cannot have any of these attributes. However, we consider that the public sector has a higher possibility of achieving these features and there are good experiences to back this up. Second, we are not arguing that the private sector has no role at all to play in service delivery. There are situations in which the private sector, particularly NGOs, can play an important role in service delivery. Third, we are not denying the failings of the public sector in many health systems. Consistent with our analysis throughout this book, but particularly in Chapter 3, we recognise that there are problems in the public sector which can impede this potential. However, these problems are not universal and, when they do occur, are not insurmountable. For this reason we emphasise in this book the importance of developing the values that underpin the health system and developing its capacity to move in the direction of realising these values. This capacity includes a strong role for the public sector in financing of health care, policymaking, planning, management and regulation alongside good governance, inter-sectoral action for health and service delivery.

4.2 Efficiency

We argue in Chapter 2 for efficiency to be seen as a core value focusing on the use of resources that need to be employed to their full potential to meet health system objectives. This raises issues concerning IAH and service delivery that have been discussed in different parts of this book. Chapter 3 discusses IAH and its importance in achieving equitable health gains and therefore accompanying health service provision. Chapter 5 analyses health planning and priority-setting and relating interventions to need. Also, the analysis of health programmes in the current chapter emphasised the integration of service delivery as improving efficiency while the tendency for prioritising national health programmes according to the availability of funding and not health need was criticised. The duplication of management and planning systems associated with some health programmes and projects together with any depletion of the general health services also lead to inefficiency. Also, an effective referral system is strongly associated with efficiency; patients are treated at the most appropriate level in the system. These discussions are all relevant to achieving efficiency in service provision. Efficiency is also about avoiding waste through inefficient management. Efficiency in service delivery is a major objective for any provider. At its bluntest, inefficiency reduces the resources available for services. We address efficiency in service delivery from two directions: first, we consider the efficiency of the public and private sectors and second, we refer to the public contracting of the private sector.

4.2.1 Public and Private Sector Efficiency

As we note in Chapters 2 and 6, private sector service provision has frequently been portrayed as more efficient than the public sector.[56] There are, however, problems with this perception.

First, we have argued that efficiency does not stand by itself as a value but is relevant in association with other values. Given our view of the objectives of the health system, we are concerned in looking for the least cost means to achieve goals of, among other things, improved health, equity and sustainability. Even if service provision by a private provider *were* less costly than its public sector equivalent, then we argue that the private sector provider has problems in securing both equity and sustainability.

Second, there is no conclusive evidence across a significant range of country health systems to confirm that private-for-profit provision is inherently less costly than the public sector in providing the same type of health services. This is not to suggest the opposite—that the public sector is more efficient. It is just not that simple. Stories of wasteful inefficiency and incompetence are to be found in both sectors. There are great variations in the efficiency and effectiveness of public and private agencies both within and between countries. The private sector also shows great variation both within and between for- and not-for-profit agencies.

Third, there are complex issues in conducting any comparison between the two sectors. Does the public sector provide (hidden) subsidies to the private sector and therefore tend to show the private sector in an efficient light? For example, private facilities may employ staff trained through in-service programmes in public facilities. Furthermore, public facilities may be allowed to run down as high cost/poor quality facilities as part of a tacit political project to increase service provision in the private sector and as such not reflecting their real potential for efficiency. Costs may be higher in public sector facilities because they are providing a more integrated and better quality of care, working with poorer/sicker patients who require more attention and lack the means of recovery from treatment. All these examples suggest the difficulties in making informative and fair comparisons of both the costs and outputs from the two types of providers in a way that leads to general conclusions about the relative efficiency of the two providers. More attention has to be paid to developing comparative methodologies that can furnish more reliable evidence for policymakers dealing with public and private provider responsibilities.

4.2.2 Public Sector Contracting and Private Sector Provision

Public contracting of the private sector has been seen, in many neoliberal health reforms, as a way to enhance efficiency. It is said to do this through various perceived advantages. The contract is seen as a predetermined means for implementing services, facilitating monitoring and competitive tendering and allowing for a greater specialisation of the purchaser function in defining need leaving the private provider to focus on the service function. Contracting the private sector can bring in specialised services in areas such as transport maintenance and cleaning that are not the focus and strength of health care organisations. It can also break-up the large public bureaucracies that traditionally combine the financing and provider functions. However, as we have argued above, research does not show a clear position on the superiority of the private or public sector as efficient service providers. A review of the literature on contracting out[57] primary health care services suggests that while it '... *has in many cases improved access to services, the effects on other performance dimensions such as equity, quality and efficiency are often unknown. Moreover, little is known about the system-wide effects of contracting-out, which could be either positive or negative'.* The study also emphasised the importance of the way in which the contract is designed and the context in which it takes place.

In addition to the points mentioned in the previous section, there are significant problems to be faced in assessing the efficiency and quality of public contracting of private providers. Transaction costs need to be calculated in any comparison with public sector provision. Questions also need to be asked about why differences in costs exist. For example, are lower private sector costs merely a result of lowering payments and benefits to the staff?

There are also questions concerning the appropriateness of contracting the private sector in many countries. Are there sufficient private sector companies to allow for competitive tendering? Will patronage and corruption infiltrate the contracting process? Does the public sector have the skills and systems to permit effective contracting?

Finally, there are further specific issues around contracting the private sector in the health system. For example, a private company may be specialised in cleaning offices and factories but they may not be specialised in *health facility* cleaning. Cleaning staff need to be part of a team operation focused on the patient—a situation which the changing and low-paid staff of a private company may not be in a position to appreciate. Inflexible contracts can also reduce the flexible operations needed in the health system. Primary health care provision requires a mode of flexible, sustainable and community focused operation that a time-limited and legally enforceable contract might find difficulty in meeting.[58]

There are no simple and generalisable conclusions from the above two sections about the relative merits of efficiency in the public and private sectors. As such, we emphasise the need to treat each potential case on its merits, recognising the complexity of making comparative judgements, considering the appropriateness of service delivery in its context and relating efficiency to considerations such as quality, equity and sustainability.

4.3 Participative and Accountable Decision-making

We argue for a balanced involvement of stakeholders in decision-making throughout the health system. This is based on both rights and instrumental reasons. We also argue in support of accountability; we particularly examine this for a DHA in Chapter 6. Community involvement is discussed in Chapter 3. Communities have the potential to understand inequalities and the determinants of health better than an institutionally segmented structure of the public sector. Of particular relevance is the involvement of communities in decision-making in priority-setting and the appropriateness of service provision. It is also important to monitor the quality of care delivered and ensure the accountability for services. In addition, there is an important role for the community in the actual delivery of health care[59] and community case management where village or community health workers take a part in service delivery.

Developing involvement and accountability are also relevant to inter-and intra-professional relations in service provision. This includes the authority exercised within professional hierarchies and the role of professional associations in ensuring quality and ethical behaviour by professional members, together with the authority exercised between professions such as doctors over nurses, and the professional autonomy claimed and exercised by professional members in the exercise of their professional work. This is a difficult area that needs balance to ensure two things. First, the role of professions in ensuring quality of care is important. Second, however, it is important to preclude using the idea of 'professional rights and autonomy' to avoid accountability for health care provided, employ excessive rigidity in the demarcation of rights to do certain health care interventions and/or to use professional hierarchies to exercise poor interpersonal relations in work.

Mechanisms to allow users to choose between alternative service providers within competitive markets can be seen as a form of user involvement. Arguments in its favour tend to take four interrelated forms.[60] First, it is suggested that by giving patients the freedom to choose their provider (as opposed to being told from whom they should receive health care), they have greater control over their health care. Related to this, the user may become more willing to monitor the provision of care, particularly when they pay directly a price for the care provided. Second, and linked to the above, providers only provide goods when there is an apparent demand for them. Third, markets may lead to an increase in service provision (through the motivation of a link between income and services) and make that supply sustainable. Fourth, markets change the incentives of health care providers who, it may be argued, strive for better quality (or perceptions of it) on the basis that good quality health care attracts more users and therefore income. They also supposedly have strong reasons for pursuing efficiency as lower costs result in higher profit.

However, these arguments can be challenged. There are costs associated with the working of the market which may reduce, rather than promote, efficiency including transactions costs and marketing. Economies of scale may also be sacrificed at the altar of competition. In some areas, there is no choice as there is only one provider. The quality of care for the individual patient may be compromised by the development of a culture of competition rather than cooperation between providers. Quality may also be interpreted as superficial and/or inappropriate perceptions by potential users (such as appearance of the facility, existence of high-technology equipment, willingness to provide [unnecessary] diagnostic services) rather than factors that respond to need. Market signals and profit motives can reduce health care need and equity to secondary considerations. Sustainability may be threatened by the shorter term considerations of private firms and the vulnerability of income streams for individual providers.

Underlying some of these counterarguments are more fundamental ones which relate to whether one sees user choice as a key driver or value for the health system. Choice can sound attractive partly because it responds to the (implausible) idea of individuals with free will and good information exercising judgement and selecting between providers. Ill people do have to make decisions on how to deal with their episodes of illness within health systems that offer a variety of health care providers. These decisions however are socially and economically conditioned by their historical and current circumstances and the characteristics of the providers in the system.

A distinction also needs to be made between user choice and general participation in decision-making. User participation and service accountability can be more meaningful as part of a collective community approach as opposed to the more individual approach suggested by market choice. Certainly a community-based approach becomes more powerful and relevant to common health problems and common contextual determinants of ill-health.

Stimulating choice in the health system and the associated market system introduces inequity. Better off people have more opportunities to take real advantage of choice. They have the means of transport to be able to use better quality health facilities that are further away. Where user charges are used for health care, then choice is a hollow word for the poor. It cannot be assumed that users and potential users have the (same) information on the quality of care in a range of health facilities to be able to make the choice. Wealthier and better educated individuals have better access to information that allows them to identify the genuinely better quality facilities.

It is also not that clear that choice is an important value recognised by health care users and certainly not so important as to mould health care delivery around it. It is likely that access and quality are more highly valued.

4.4 Service Provision and Longer Term Perspective

We argue that a balance has to be made between responding to present and future needs in the health system. Sustainability of IAH and health service delivery requires recognition of the second of these—the longer term perspective. It is about continuity of action for health and services that contribute to meeting the goals of the health system. However, sustainability is not an absolute value in itself; some actions and services should *not* be sustained as health needs and forms of intervention need to respond to change. Unfortunately, bureaucratic inertia and vested interests can lead to the continuation of unnecessary organisations and services.

Sustainability of service provision can be threatened in different ways. Private-for-profit organisations can move in and out of health care provision (and supporting areas such as hospital cleaning) depending on the (changing) rate of return on investment while small NGOs can appear and disappear depending on funding and the continued interest and survival of founder members. The public sector is also prone to poor sustainability as staff are subject to frequent transfers and service delivery is organised around time-limited projects. The unpredictable and time-limited nature of international funding also raises the problem of continuing service delivery once the international flow of funds is wound down.

Elsewhere in the book we point out ways in which greater appropriate sustainability can be given to the health system and thereby service delivery. These include orienting international funding more to health systems development, greater involvement of communities in local health decision-making processes and improving the management of health staff allowing them to perform over a longer time period in jobs. It could also be argued that contracting could take on a longer term perspective and more flexible forms.[61]

Despite its shortcomings, the public sector provides, we argue, a stronger potential for developing sustainability through its ability to raise finance and its organisational legitimacy. Whether it achieves this or not depends on the emphasis placed on strengthening its capacity to achieve sustainability. Having said this, we need to be aware of the difficulties faced by fragile states where social and political upheaval in conditions of poverty is not conducive to sustainability. This does, however, place an onus on developing the right balance and complementarity between shorter term assistance to meet emergency situations and longer term development of capacity for sustainable service provision.

5 Final Thoughts

This chapter has focused on IAH and health service delivery. These are the culmination of the working of financing, governance, policymaking, planning and management in pursuit of improved and more health; we argue that these have to be carried out in such a way as to allow for the progressive development of IAH and health service delivery.

IAH is viewed as including joint programmes, legislative and regulatory responsibilities (and similar bodies) together with health-related advocacy. We set out a range of activities associated with advocacy and underline its value base together with the skills and support needed of effective advocacy. Health service delivery was analysed around five key topics—health programmes, health projects, scaling up of services, public–private providers and the referral system. The analysis recognises the importance of integrating health care services, the cautious use of health projects and contracts, the problem associated with markets in service delivery and the importance of the referral system.

The IAH and health service delivery have been analysed in relation to our four key values. In order to advance rights to health and equity, we recognise the importance of policies directed towards universal coverage. These policies include targeting as part of a broader changes advocated in this book—fair health system funding, resource allocation for equity, inter-sectoral action for health, a proactive state system, health planning and management for equity, greater accountability and effective regulation of the private sector. We justify the important role to be played by the public sector in service provision but do not discount the role of other providers, particularly by NGOs.

We argue that efficiency needs to be seen in the context of the other values; it is about the least cost means to achieve goals such as improved health, equity and sustainability. Even where a private provider is less costly than a public provider, it may not be as productive in improving health, equity and sustainability. We also take note of the absence of clear comparative evidence and the difficulties in such public–private comparisons. Generalised statements proclaiming the superior efficiency of the public or private providers are neither accurate nor helpful—each potential case needs to be assessed on its merits. We also need to understand the context in which service delivery takes place, appreciate the complexity of making comparative assessments and relate efficiency to considerations such as quality, equity and sustainability. We raise concerns about reducing participation to patient choice. Although both public and private sectors are subject to poor sustainability, nevertheless, we argue that the public sector has the greater potential for sustainability and there are specific changes which can be made for this to emerge over time.

We now turn to the final chapter in which we bring together the key messages developed in all the chapters so far and put forward a broad framework for developing health systems strengthening.

Notes and References

1. MSF is 'an international, independent, medical humanitarian organisation that delivers emergency aid to people affected by armed conflict, epidemics, healthcare exclusion and natural or man-made disasters'. See http://www.msf.org/ (accessed 21 May 2010).
2. See, for example, the discussion in Van Damme, W., Van Lerberghe, W. and Boelaert, M., 2002. 'Primary Health Care Versus Emergency Medical Assistance: A Conceptual Framework', *Health Policy and Planning*, 17(1): 49–60.
3. Commission on Social Determinants (CSDH). 2008. *Closing the Gap in a Generation: Health Equity through Action on the Social Determinants of Health. Final Report of the Commission on Social Determinants of Health*. Geneva: World Health Organization.
4. See Box 16.3 in Commission on Social Determinants (CSDH). 2008. *Closing the Gap in a Generation: Health Equity through Action on the Social Determinants of Health. Final Report of the Commission on Social Determinants of Health*. Geneva: World Health Organization.
5. Blas, E., Gilson, L., Kelly, M.P., Labonté, R., Lapitan, J., Muntaner, C., Östlin, P., Popay, J., Sadana, R., Sen, G., Schrecker, T., Vaghri, Z. 2008. 'Addressing Social Determinants of Health Inequities: What Can the State and Civil Society Do?' *The Lancet*, 372(9650): 1685.
6. Commission on Social Determinants (CSDH). 2008. *Closing the Gap in a Generation: Health Equity through Action on the Social Determinants of Health. Final Report of the Commission on Social Determinants of Health*. Geneva: World Health Organization.
7. Chapman, J. and Wameyo, A., 2001. *Monitoring and Evaluating Advocacy: A Scoping Study*. Actionaid; Coates, B. and David, R. 2002. 'Learning for Change: The Art of Assessing the Impact of Advocacy Work', *Development in Practice*, 12(3): 530–41; Shiffman, P. 2007. 'Generating Political Priority for Maternal Mortality Reduction in 5 Developing Countries', *American Journal of Public Health*, 97(5): 796–80.

8. This issue is explored in Shiffman, P. 2007. 'Generating Political Priority for Maternal Mortality Reduction in 5 Developing Countries', *American Journal of Public Health*, 97(5): 796–80.

9. Thiede, M.H. and Castillo-Riquelme, M. 2010. 'How Pro-poor are Infectious Disease Programmes?' *TropIKA Reviews*, 1(1): 1. Available at http://www.tropika.net/svc/review/Chinnock-20100602-Review-Pro-poor-interventions (accessed 18 August 2010).

10. Cavalli, A., Bamba, S.I., Traore, M.N., Boelaert, M., Coulibaly, Y., Polman, K., Pirard, M. and Van Dormael, M. 2010. 'Interactions between Global Health Initiatives and Country Health Systems: The Case of a Neglected Tropical Diseases Control Program in Mali', *PLOS Neglected Tropical Diseases*, 4(8): e798.

11. An argument can also be put about the need for control programmes to have basic services to ensure adequate case-finding. See Unger, J.P., d'Alessandro, U., De Paepe, P. and Green, A. 2006. 'Can Malaria Be Controlled Where Basic Health Services Are Not Used?' *Tropical Medicine and International Health*, 11(3): 314–22.

12. See, for example, Ekman, G.B., Pathmanathan, I. and Liljestrand, J. 2008. 'Integrating Health Interventions for Women, Newborn Babies, and Children: A Framework for Action', *The Lancet*, 372(9642): 990–1000.

13. El-Sadr, W.M. and Abrams, E.J. 2007. 'Scale-up of HIV Care and Treatment: Can it Transform Healthcare Services in Resource-limited Settings?' *AIDS*, 21(5): S65–S70.

14. Cavalli, A., Bamba, S.I., Traore, M.N., Boelaert, M., Coulibaly, Y., Polman, K., Pirard, M. and Van Dormael, M. 2010. 'Interactions between Global Health Initiatives and Country Health Systems: The Case of a Neglected Tropical Diseases Control Program in Mali', *PLOS Neglected Tropical Diseases*, 4(8).

15. Unger, J.P., De Paepe, P. and Green, A. 2003. 'A Code of Best Practice for Disease Control Programmes to Avoid Damaging Health Care Services in Developing Countries', *International Journal of Health Planning and Management*, 18(S1): S27–S39.

16. Atun, R., de Jongh, T., Secci, F., Ohiri, K. and Adeyi, O. 2010. 'Integration of Targeted Health Interventions into Health Systems: A Conceptual Framework for Analysis', *Health Policy and Planning*, 25(2): 106.

17. Rondinelli, D.A. 1983. 'Projects as Instruments of Development Administration: A Qualified Defence and Suggestions for Improvement', *Public Administration and Development*, 3(4): 307–327.

18. Rondinelli, D.A. 1983. 'Projects as Instruments of Development Administration: A Qualified Defence and Suggestions for Improvement', *Public Administration and Development*, 3: 307–27.

19. Korten, D.C. 1980. 'Community Organisation and Rural Development: A Learning Process Approach', *Public Administration Review*, 40(5, September–October): 497.

20. El-Sadr, W.M. and Abrams, E.J. 2007. Scale-up of HIV Care and Treatment: Can it Transform Healthcare Services in Resource-limited Settings?' *AIDS*, 21(5): S65–S70.

21. Mangham, L.J. and Hanson, K. 2010. 'Scaling-up in International Health: What Are The Key Issues?' *Health Policy and Planning*, 25(2): 85–96.

22. Johns, B. and Torres, T.T. and on behalf of WHO choice. 2005. 'Costs of Scaling up Health Interventions: A Systematic Review', *Health Policy and Planning*, 20(1): 1–13.

23. See, for example, Mangham, L.J. and Hanson, K. 2010. 'Scaling-up in International Health: What Are The Key Issues?' *Health Policy and Planning*, 25(2): 85–96.

24. See Gericke, C.A., Kurowski, C., Ranson, M.K., Mills, A. 2005. 'Intervention Complexity – A Conceptual Framework to Inform Priority-setting in Health', *Bulletin of the World Health Organization*, 83(4): 285–93.

25. See, for example, Mangham, L.J. and Hanson, K. 2010. 'Scaling-up in International Health: What Are The Key Issues?' *Health Policy and Planning*, 25(2): 85–96.

26. In franchising the funder contracts, a franchisor that has a unique and innovative form of service delivery to spread this model to other service providers. The support of the franchisee by the franchisor covers responsibilities such as quality assurance, supply of materials, capacity development and supervision. This process could help in improving the quality of care, scaling up of successful processes and allow for better value for users. This system is often used in international donor funding, although there is a potential for it to develop in the public sector. See IHSD. 2000. *Private Sector Participation in Health*. London: IHSD [available through www.eldis.org]. How effective these different forms of inter-organisational relations are for scaling up will depend on issues discussed in other parts of this book such as regulatory systems, allocation mechanisms and the effectiveness of inter-organisational relations discussed in Chapter 6.

27. See, for example, Mangham, L.J. and Hanson, K. 2010. 'Scaling-up in International Health: What Are The Key Issues?' *Health Policy and Planning*, 25(2): 85–96.

28. See, for example, Palmer, N., Mills, A., Wadee, H., Gilson, L. and Schneider, H. 2003. 'A New Face for Private Providers in Developing Countries: What Implications for Public Health?' *Bulletin of the World Health Organization*, 81(4): 292–297.

29. The breadth of this book means that we cannot go into all the areas that merit attention. The area of self and family care is one of them.

30. Bangladesh Health Watch. 2008. *Health Workforce in Bangladesh: Who Constitutes the Healthcare System? The State of Health in Bangladesh 2007*. Dhaka: James P. Grant School of Public Health, BRAC University, Table 2.1, page 8.

31. See http://www.chinacsr.com/en/2007/05/28/1359-public-private-partnership-aids-sino-german-friendship-hospital/ (accessed 20 August 2009).

32. Liu, X. and A. Mills. 2005. 'The Effect of Performance-related Pay of Hospital Doctors on Hospital Behaviour: A Case Study from Shandong Province', *Human Resources for Health*, 3: 11.

33. The issues of dual practice are discussed in Ferrinho, P., Van Lerberghe, W., Fronteira, I., Hipólito, F. and Biscaia, A. 2004. 'Dual Practice in the Health Sector: Review of the Evidence', *Human Resources for Health*, 2: 14.

34. Developed from Flynn, N. 1997. *Public Sector Management*. UK: Prentice Hall/ Harvester Wheatsheaf; McCoy, D., Buch, E. and Palmer, N. 2000. *Protecting Efficient, Comprehensive and Integrated Primary Health Care. Principles for Inter-Governmental Contracts/Service Agreements*. Durban: Health Systems Trust.

35. Collins, C. and Green, A. Draft discussion paper Public Contracting of Private Providers for Primary Health Care Services: Context, Sustainability and Accountability for EU Funded Concerted Action on 'Regulating private primary care for more sustainable, equitable and efficient health provision: Is contracting out the good solution for Central America?'

36. Macq, J., Martiny, P., Villalobos, L.B., Solis, A., Miranda, J., Mendez, H.C. and Collins, C. 2008. 'Public Purchasers Contracting External Primary Care Providers in Central America for Better Responsiveness, Efficiency of Health Care and Public Governance: Issues and Challenges', *Health Policy*, 87(3): 377–388.

37. See, for example. Deepak, K., Mirzoev, M., Green, A., Newell, J. and Baral, S. 2007. 'Costs of a Successful Public-private Partnership for TB Control in an Urban Setting in Nepal', *BMC Public Health*, 7(84).

38. Bossyns, P. and Van Lerberghe, W. 2004. 'The Weakest Link: Competence and Prestige as Constraints to Referral by Isolated Nurses in Rural Niger', *Human Resources for Health*, 2(1).

39. C.f http://www.euro.who.int/observatory/Glossary/TopPage?phrase=Q (accessed 27 April 2010).

40. WHO. 2003. *Quality and Accreditation in Health Care Services. A Global Review*. Geneva: WHO. WHO/EIP/OSD/2003.1

41. WHO. 2008. *The Global Burden of Disease* (2004 update) WHO, Geneva Fig. 27, p. 51. Available at http://www.who.int/healthinfo/global_burden_ disease/2004_report_update/en/index.html.

42. Gilson, L., Doherty, J., Loewenson, R., Francis, V. and with inputs and contributions from the members of the Knowledge Network. 2007. *Challenging Inequity through Health Systems, Final Report, Knowledge Network on Health Systems*; WHO. 2008. *The World Health Report 2008: Primary Health Care Now More Than Ever*. Geneva: World Health Organization.

43. López-Cevallos, D.F. and Chi, C. 2010. 'Health Care Utilization in Ecuador: A Multilevel Analysis of Socio-economic Determinants and Inequality Issues', *Health Policy and Planning*, 25(3): 209.

44. Sousa A., Lozano, R. and Gakidou, E. 2010. 'Exploring the Determinants of Unsafe Abortion: Improving the Evidence Base in Mexico', *Health Policy and Planning*, 25(4): 300.

45. Uzochukwu, B.S.C., Onwujekwe, O.E., Onoka, A.C., Okoli, C., Uguru, N.P. and Chukwuogo, O.I. 2009. 'Determinants of Non-adherence to Subsidized Anti-retroviral Treatment in Southeast Nigeria', *Health Planning and Policy*, 24(3): 192.

46. Tang, S., Meng, Q., Chen, L., Bekedam, H., Evans, T. and Whitehead, M. 2008. 'Health System Reform in China 1. Tackling the Challenges to Health Equity in China', *The Lancet*, 372(9648): 1493–1501

47. Zhu, L.P., Jia, W.L., Hua, J.Z. 2006. 'Study on the Situation and Policies of Health Care for Floating Pregnant Women in Shanghai'. *Chin J Reprod Health*, 17: 271–74 (as referred to by Tang et al. [2008: 1498]).

48. Shen, R.G., Yang, H.G., Li, H., He, F., Ding, H., Deng, X.H., et al 'Study on the Maternal Mortality Rate from 1995 to 2004 among Residential and Migrant Women in Beijing'. *Chin J Epidemiol*, 27: 223–25 (as referred to by Tang et al., 2008: 1498).

49. Green, A.T. 2007. *An Introduction to Health Planning for Developing Health Systems*, 3rd edition. Oxford: Oxford University Press.

50. Mangham, L.J. and Hanson, K. 2010. 'Scaling-up in International Health: What Are The Key Issues?' *Health Policy and Planning*, 25(2): 85–96.

51. Victora, C.G., Wagstaff, A., Schellenberg, J.A., Gwatkin, D., Claeson, M., Habicht, J.P. 2003. 'Applying an Equity Lens to Child Health and Mortality: More of the Same is not Enough', *The Lancet*, 362(9379): 233–41.

52. See Commission on Social Determinants on Health. 2008. *Closing the Gap in a Generation: Health Equity through Action on the Social Determinants of Health. Report of the Commission on Social Determinants of Health.* Geneva: WHO.

53. McIntyre, D., Garshong, B., Mtei, G., Meheus, F., Thiede,M., Akazili, J., Ally, M., Aikins, M., Mulligan, J.A. and Goudge, J. 2008. 'Beyond Fragmentation and Towards Universal Coverage: Insights from Ghana, South Africa and the United Republic of Tanzania', *Bulletin of the World Health Organization*, 86(11): 871–876.

54. This and other issues may be explored in Oxfam. 2009. 'Blind Optimism, Challenging the Myths about Private Health Care in Poor Countries', Oxfam Briefing Paper and the Discussion with the World Bank. Available at http://www.oxfam.org.uk/resources/policy/health/bp125_blind_optimism. html#responses (accessed 20 November 2010). See also McCoy, D. 2007. 'The World Bank's New Health Strategy: Reason for Alarm?' *The Lancet*, 369(9572): 1499–1501.

55. Mackintosh, M. and Koivusalo, M. (eds). 2005. *Commercialization of Health Care: Global and Local Dynamics and Policy Responses*. London: Palgrave Macmillan.

56. As noted above, these issues may be explored in Oxfam. 2009. 'Blind Optimism, Challenging the Myths about Private Health Care in Poor Countries', Oxfam Briefing Paper and the discussion with the World Bank. Available at http://www.oxfam.org.uk/resources/policy/health/bp125_blind_ optimism.html#responses (accessed 20 November 2010). See also McCoy, D. 2007. 'The World Bank's New Health Strategy: Reason for Alarm?' *The Lancet*, 369(9572): 1499–1501.

57. Liu, X., Hotchkiss, D.R. and Bose, S. 2008. 'The Effectiveness of Contracting-out Primary Health Care Services in Developing Countries: A Review of the Evidence', *Health Policy and Planning*, 23(1): 1.

58. McCoy, D., Buch, E. and Palmer, N. 2000. *Protecting Efficient, Comprehensive and Integrated Primary Health Care, Principles for Inter-Governmental Contracts/ Service Agreements.* Durban: Health Systems Trust.

59. This can be seen, for example, in the community directed interventions approach. See http://apps.who.int/tdr/

60. See World Bank. 2003. *World Development Report, 2004: Making Services Work for Poor People.* Oxford, UK: Oxford University Press. For a more comprehensive set of arguments for the operation of the market.

61. See McCoy, D., Buch, E. and Palmer, N. 2000. *Protecting Efficient, Comprehensive and Integrated Primary Health Care, Principles for Inter-Governmental Contracts/ Service Agreements.* Durban: Health Systems Trust—although this study focuses on inter-governmental relations.

8

Strengthening Health Systems through a Value-based Approach

We began this book with two central propositions—first, the importance of recognising and understanding the complexity and heterogeneity of health systems, and second, the need to recognise the effect that values have on the design and functioning of health systems. The first of these propositions required the development of a framework that differed from previous analytical frameworks. Our framework emphasises processes and their interactions. It also suggests the need for a holistic analysis of these processes. We hope that readers will have found this approach convincing and a useful complement to other frameworks.

We also hope that the analysis has demonstrated the importance of health systems—their intrinsic value and hence the importance of understanding their weaknesses and strengths in order to adjust their design to meet our social objectives. As part of this, we have also emphasised the role of the health system in working with other systems alongside their more conventional role of delivering health services—the development of a health rather than solely health care agenda.

The processes that we have identified as central to the health system are governance, financing, policymaking, planning, management and IAH and health service delivery. It also requires us to view them as interlocking and operating within a broader context.

However, the other major thrust of the book has been its emphasis on the importance of values in the design and the operation of the processes and the system as a whole. Concerning this second proposition, we have laid out the values that we believe should permeate health systems—the right to health and equity, efficiency, participative and accountable decision-making and the need for a long-term perspective. As such, we are clear that there can be no technocratically neutral 'best' design for a health system. We repeat our own vision of a good health system as *one that has access to a level of resources commensurate with the national level of income and uses these resources in the most efficient way to ensure an equitable and maximised level of health which is sustainable over the long term and which empowers the health system members in areas concerning their health and contributes towards wider social cohesion and mores.*

We end this book by doing two things. First, by way of a summary we bring together the key messages from the preceding chapters and relate them to the values and our interpretation of a good health system. Second, we recognise the gap that exists between such an ideal health system and the current reality in LMICs. As such, we challenge the reader, whatever his/her role within the health system, to reflect on their own values and position and consider actions that they can take to strengthen their own health system. We suggest three key actions that are needed to embark on such strengthening of health systems in the direction of the values championed in this book—assessing the situation, developing strategies of change and working the context and developing advocacy coalitions.

1 A Value-based Health System

In Chapter 2, we outlined and argued for our guiding values for a health system and our expectations of a good health system. We recognise that as is the nature of values, not all readers will espouse these values, but we hope that the explicit laying out of these will at least spark readers into considering their own desired values for a health system even if they are not persuaded to our own view. Subsequent chapters sought to give meaning to these values and the notion of a good health system by analysing the principal processes in the health system. We have also explored the interrelation between the different health system processes. The key messages related to these processes are as follows.

Governance is about power, authority and responsibilities. Good governance refers to those relations that are consistent with the values of the health system and promotes its objectives. The foundations of our interpretation of good governance lie in a proactive state that takes the strategic lead in the health system and seeks to promote equity, account-ability, decentralisation, inter-sectoral action for health, participatory governance, ethical conduct, effective regulation, and transparency and accessibility of information.

Financing is a critical underlying resource for health systems yet is very low in LICs compared to health needs. Different societies and states give different priority to the health system and collective financing for it. The level of finance generated affects the ability of the health system to operate. Furthermore, the way in which finance is raised reflects the dominant ideology and values and can have severe implications both for equity in terms of utilisation of services and the effects on patients and in terms of the efficiency of the system response to needs, given the incentives inevitably built into the different financing mechanisms. External funding, on which many health systems are reliant, can also have severe and distorting implications for the operation of the national health system. Our values point to the need to develop mechanisms of collective prepayment—taxes and social health insurance—as long as both are designed 'progressively'.

Policy-making and planning set the direction for the health system and its outputs in terms of service delivery and promotion of IAH. Both the processes and the resultant policies and plans need to be firmly rooted in the values underpinning the health sector. Such plans need to be achievable; as such, they need to recognise both the scarce resources available to a particular health system and the wider context, including the health, political and social environment. Policies and plans are ultimately made by actors who bring to the processes their values. Which actors are involved in these processes will therefore radically affect the nature of the policies and plans. These values need to be set alongside clear evidence of the likely effects of proposed policies and plans.

We define *management* as a *systematic process of mobilising, combining and using resources with a view to moving efficiently towards agreed objectives.* Managers need to consider the characteristics of management and we have argued for a style of management that is outward looking, based on fairness, proactive, innovative, problem-solving, flexible and evidence-informed. The specific 'public' and 'private' features of management need to be recognised together with its political and systemic character. Our analysis of management is a value-based approach which should run through the management of structures and processes, resources, culture and external linkages. We recognise the constraints on achieving this but challenge managers to seek and exploit unrealised opportunities.

The *IAH and health services* are the product of the above health system processes in pursuit of equitable health. We lay out a simple framework for IAH that consists of assessing health needs, developing strategies (consisting of joint programmes, legislative and regulatory action and health related-advocacy) and the monitoring of action taken (which feeds back into the assessment of health needs). In the delivery of health services, we argue in favour of integrating health programmes into the general health services, caution in the use of health projects and contracts and the importance of the referral system, but draw attention to the problems in using markets in service delivery and simplistic comparisons about the relative efficiency of the public and private sectors. In development of the values championed in this book, we argue in favour of universal coverage and a significant role for the public sector in service provision.

Our view of what constitutes a good health system is based on our analysis during the year 2010. Although we see our values as timeless, the specific *application* of these values to the health system processes will be affected by the context. This context will inevitably change. For example, health needs will change, new technologies will emerge, economic and political development will produce new winners and unfortunately losers, the power of nation states will vary and the political consciousness of the poor will hopefully impress itself on the world. Consequently, the specific analysis on how to develop values in a health system will need to change alongside the changing context, though the broad issues set out in the different chapters will still apply.

2 Strengthening the Health System

We have laid out our interpretation of the health system in full recognition that there will be readers who disagree with our values. Building on different values, they will produce different conclusions as to their interpretation of a 'good' health system. We look forward to continuing the debate with them. In contrast, there will be many (we hope) who agree with our values. The challenge for them (and us) is how to translate these beliefs into action. One fundamental message of this book is that all members of the health system have both a right and a responsibility to shape their health system; it should not be left to those with current power.

There is no simple and easily fashioned approach to health systems strengthening. A great deal will depend on the context. We suggest, however, three fundamental activities that we believe could lead to a strengthened health system. These are shown in Figure 8.1 as assessing the situation which leads on to developing strategies and then capacity strengthening. Running alongside these are what we refer to as 'working the context'. We explain each of these further below.

2.1 Assessing the Situation

The disparity between what exists now and what is needed in health systems can be daunting, although its degree and nature varies from country to country. We offer in Table 8.1 a simple value-focused checklist as a tool for organising this assessment; the four values are set out with, for each, four broad questions to guide the assessment. Of course, this represents only the beginning of an analysis—a more detailed analysis should be developed; however, what we present in Table 8.1 provides a starting point for subsequent action.

2.2 Developing Strategies for Change

Having conducted a basic assessment of the health system, the next step is to develop strategies for change. The political, social and economic context will affect how such change is formulated and implemented. Strengthening the health system involves doing things, and in such

Figure 8.1
The process of capacity strengthening

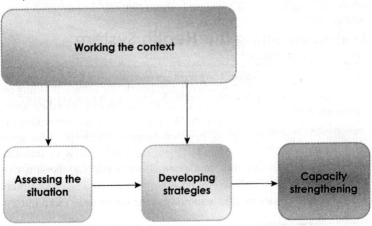

Table 8.1
Checklist of key questions for a value-focused assessment of a health system

Right to health and equity

What is the effect of the different funding mechanisms on the ability to pay for health care by, and the economic effects on, different groups?

What is the impact on equity of resource allocation mechanisms to different health facilities and areas of the country?

To what extent is equity on the policy agenda for policy-making and do health policies and plans express it?

What is the utilisation of health service by different groups and to what extent does it meet health need?

Efficiency

Are resources allocated to those areas of priority health need and used efficiently to achieve objectives at minimum cost?

Does the health system give adequate priority to inter-sectoral action for health?

Are decisions on resource use based on the best available evidence?

Does the organisation and delivery of health services respond to priority health needs

Participative and accountable decision-making

Is there a balanced involvement of health system members in decision-making in the health system and in particular are the needs of the disadvantaged adequately represented?

Is there transparency in how decisions are made and implemented in the health system?

Are decision-makers at all levels of the health system held accountable for their actions?

Are decision-makers transparent about sources of evidence for, and their values in decision-making?

Value: Long-term perspective

How is international funding incorporated into the longer term perspective of resourcing the health system?

How effective is strategic health planning in providing a long term perspective to the health system?

Are health staff given the appropriate security of employment to allow them to develop their work in the health system?

Is action taken to make the achievements of health programmes and projects sustainable?

ways, that are consistent with the values and are conducive to meeting the overall aims of the health system. Values need to permeate not just *what* is done, but *how* it is done; for example, participative and account-able decision-making needs to permeate the process of change itself. The decisions on the 'what' and 'how' of change need analysis and debate; there may be many different options. The values should point the poli-cymaking process in the direction of types of change.

The study referred to in Box 8.1, for example, suggests that in Sri Lanka an emphasis on in-patient care has been an important strategy in the relative success of the health system. Such a priority might or might not be appropriate to other country health systems. This contextualisa-tion is a major challenge of policy-making for health systems strengthen-ing. In developing strategies, there are opportunities for learning from the experiences of other countries through conducting a critical analysis of both positive and negative experiences and assessing the appropriate-ness to the context of other countries.

In order to achieve a degree of comprehensiveness in health systems strengthening, it is advisable to use some sort of tool for organising the range of options, prioritising and ensuring its comprehensive charac-ter. In Table 8.2, we give an example of this. This links the three levels

---

Box 8.1 Success in health and health care in Sri Lanka

A report on health and the health system in Sri Lanka by Save the Children raises issues regarding health system capacity. *The report (p. 6) clarifies that it "… does not discuss the health implications of Sri Lanka's internal conflict between the Liberation Tigers of Tamil Eelam (LTTE) and the Sri Lankan Gov-ernment, although we acknowledge that significant health effects exist."* How-ever, it argues that health status in Sri Lanka is generally superior to countries with a similar GNP. It suggests there are particular factors which explain this such as the status of women, political democracy and agreement on government social policies. Inter-sectoral action for health has been important; positive edu-cation and female literacy, nutrition, water and sanitation. The health system in the country has developed positive features. Relatively high levels of efficiency, productivity and utilisation are found in government health facilities. Good levels of equity in access to health care are secured through, for example, the location of health facilities and the tax-based funding and absence of user fees. Government commitment to finance in-patient care protects the poor against catastrophic expenditure and leads to low levels of maternal mortality. The health system has also built on, and developed complementarity between, the public and private sectors with the private sector primarily focusing on out-patient care and the public sector's in-patient care providing across most social groups.

Source: McNay et al. 2004.[1]

Table 8.2
Examples of levels and processes in capacity change in a district health system

Health system processes	Levels of capacity change[2]		
	Environmental	Organisational	Individual
Governance	Legislating for district autonomy in responsibilities, authority and resources	Creating an effective District Health Team	Ensuring individual staff have the means to raise concerns over health policies
Financing	Allocating national funds on an equity basis	Allocating district funding to sub-districts and health facilities on an equity basis	Developing awareness of the importance of equity
Policymaking and planning	Incorporating district health planning into the national planning system	Creating a system for district health planning	Ensuring staff are fully ware of district health policies
Management	Developing national career plans for health staff	Improving the system of supervision of district health staff	Developing staff skills
Inter-sectoral action for health and health service delivery	Funding activities for inter-sectoral action for health Creating awareness in national health programmes of the systemic impact of their activities	Developing cross sectoral bodies to develop policies	Developing among staff an interpretation of health based on the social and economic determinants

of capacity set out in Chapter 2 and used in Chapter 6 to the health system processes by providing examples of what could be done when strengthening a district health system. This simple framework has three levels. First, there is the immediate environment related to the objective of health systems strengthening; in a health district, for example, we would consider the broader issues in the health system that have an impact on the capacity of the district. This would include factors related to the five systems processes—such as the allocations coming into the health district for financing. The organisational level refers to a range of management and planning systems operational at the district level and the capacity to work inter-sectorally. The individual level refers to the current skills and cultural norms held by district health staff.

The usefulness of such an approach is that it provides a system-wide perspective and allows prioritising areas of capacity strengthening along-side linking the different areas. Such prioritising would need to be based on an assessment of the performance of the district system and recognise consultation among interested stakeholders. Recognising the links between the cells in Table 8.2 is also important in any process of change. To improve skills in, for example, financial management raises the question as to whether the staff have the authority to make decisions using their new skills, their level of technical supervision, their accountability, the existence of appropriate management systems, etc. It also requires those responsible for change to consider not only the *intended* consequences but also the *unintended* consequences—both favourable and unfavourable. Negative unintended consequences can thwart or outweigh the achievement of desired results. For example, the introduction of individual performance bonuses for health staff might result in increased productivity in those areas subject to the bonuses. However, teamwork, among other things, might suffer.

There are dilemmas to be faced in the process of change. We have already pointed to this in fragile states where trade-offs have to be made between actions now to deal with emergencies and building for the future. We also point to the challenge of absorbing change. Organisations with the strongest capacity may similarly have a greater ability to generate new resources and change than those with less capacity—leading to greater not less disparity. Funding change can also be a dilemma. International funding for health systems strengthening may attempt to impose agendas for change that do not meet the perceived needs of national planners for health systems strengthening. Thus, funding opportunities instead of needs determine what is done. In addressing these dilemmas, realistic compromises are required; however, in making these, recognition of the value base will provide guidance to the decision-maker.

2.3 Working the Context

Once again, we return to the importance of the context and the role of political coalitions in progressive change. Context explains many of the reasons why health systems are weak in the first place. It also affects the way in which policies of strengthening are formulated and implemented.

The context, however, is neither immutable nor static. Its historical character means that it is constantly widening and restricting opportunities for change. The context is, to a large extent, the product of individuals and groups in society (including the health system) and simultaneously provides the opportunities and restrictions for change. By 'working' the context, we mean knowing the options and what to do and what not to do according to the context and where appropriate attempting to widen these options and create policy space.

The changes outlined in this book will affect the interests of stakeholders in different and complex ways. For example, strengthening the regulatory capacity of the state over private health facilities might be favoured by some private groups who want to improve the legitimacy of the private sector and rejected by other private providers who foresee a decline in their rate of profit. Also, members of the medical profession may reject the devolution of government health care to local government seeing their future career path disrupted by local political control. Expanding the access to health care through new funding sources and new services raises questions as to which groups will gain and which groups might see their privileges cut. Ideologies around the role of the state and interpretations of liberty will similarly affect the calculations of individuals and groups.

We have argued at several points in this book about the importance of developing support coalitions. We have seen how groups and coalitions can support a specific health cause; so they can, to a wider extent, support the strengthening of the health system itself. The politically contested nature of change suggests the need for those who pursue change to work together. Support among a wide range of social and political groups needs to be created to promote the progressive strengthening of the health system. Advocacy coalitions can be developed and merged with other progressive groups in support of strengthening the health system. These coalitions can conduct research into the working and impact of the health system, analyse options for change, and develop platforms for strengthening the health system. They can develop health awareness and action among community groups, support changes in the bias of representation and access in the health system, support additional financing for health, campaign for the allocation of resources to meet health need and back increases in the supply of qualified and appropriately remunerated staff. Underlying this needs to be similar (or compatible) values and a confidence that the health system *can* be improved. International experiences can be important in providing that confidence and highlights the relative success of government polices on health and health care in Sri Lanka. In Chapter 5 we also saw the success of a particular policy coalition in Thailand in the promotion of an equity focused set of changes in the health system. These coalitions can also take on an international dimension, learning from progressive movements in other countries and linking up with organisations such as the Peoples Health Movement.[3] Table 8.3 suggests how different stakeholders in the health system can play an important role in contributing to the cause of a strengthened health system.

We do not underestimate the immensity of the challenges faced. But we also believe there are opportunities for change. The balance between these will depend on the context. Some will live and work in situations where there are good opportunities to introduce progressive change while others may live and work in societies that reject in voice and/or action the values upheld in this book. At one extreme, health system members may consider that to continue residing and working in societies and health systems based on strong discrimination, political threats and the lure of speculative profit and/or corruption is unacceptable. Societies and health systems can also provide political space in order to advocate for progressive change for improved and more equitable health. This

Table 8.3
Stakeholders and their role in strengthening a health system

Stakeholders	Examples of constructive contributions to strengthening health systems
Politicians	Provide the legislative framework to allow for regulation of service provision and also provide the framework for inter-sectoral action for health
Ministry of Health policymakers	Develop health system wide planning to give a strategic direction to the health system
Professional groups	Move beyond restricted notions of medical care to a more inclusive approach to health that recognises social inequalities and determinants of health
Ministry of Finance policymakers	Provide the financial backing to ensure resources for an effective health service provision by the public sector
Internationals funding agencies	Pool funding to allow improved nationally led priority-setting for the health system
Researchers	Focus applied research activities on key areas that identify and analyse options for change
NGOs and CBOs	Advocate for improved inter-sectoral action for health and widening access to health care

is where the political skills of analysing the strength of constraints, the feasibility of overcoming these same constraints and taking progressive action are so important. Political judgement is required in knowing the extent to which agreement is sought or change is imposed, the balance between quick and gradual implementation, interpreting the opportunities for change in the political context and measuring the extent of change according to its political support and opposition.

It is on this note of politics that we wish to finish. The values we express in this book are not some abstract thoughts; rather, they are held (or not) by, and impact on, the lives of, people. They are not immutable but can be the subject of change through, for example, education, advocacy and research. Values are contested and form part of a political process at local, national and international levels. The health and health care we have is more than just the sum of technical skills and technology, important as these may be. They are about the dominant political values in the health system and how they lead to, or detract from, a good health system.

Notes and References

1. McNay, K., Keith, R. and Penrose, A. 2004. *Bucking the Trend. How Sri Lanka has Achieved Good Health at Low Cost: Challenges and Policy Lessons for the 21st Century.* London: Save the Children Fund.
2. See UNDP. 2008. *Practice Note: Capacity Development.* New York: United Nations Development Programme.
3. See http://www.phmovement.org/

Index

ability to pay, 123, 128
academic researchers, 59
access to health care, 35, 133,
    142–143, 294, 317, 320–321
accountability, 17, 24, 28–29, 44, 48,
    65, 72, 77–79, 82–83, 86–87,
    89, 96, 101, 103, 107, 112–115,
    138, 147, 156, 218, 229, 236,
    249, 274, 294, 304, 313, 319
    action to improve, 79
    case of international funding and,
        79
    of civil society organisations, 28–29
    decentralisation and, 82–83, 86,
        173
    degree of sustainability, 79
    democracy and, 87
    of DHA system, 221, 226–227
    diverse forms of, 78
    effectiveness of, 77–78, 108
    generalised, 139
    of GHIs, 28
    of IAH activities, 267
    importance of information,
        113–114
    as precondition for promoting
        efficiency, 44
    of private sectors, 79
    of public sectors, 79, 217
    stakeholders in, 78
    values associated with, 210
accountable decision-making, 44,
    47–48
    effects of financing, 146–148
    in service delivery, 300–303

actors, 3–4, 7, 16, 47, 121, 126,
    189–190, 200, 211, 313
    accountability of, 77
    advocacy by, 263–264, 266
    definition, 58
    dispersal within health system,
        105
    evidence and, 181, 184, 186
    examples of, 59
    GHIs, 28
    governance, role in, 42
    international, 136, 163
    interrelationships between
        members, stakeholders and, 57
    objectives held by, 53
    policy and planning process,
        role in, 92–94, 106, 156–157,
        160–164, 167, 179
    priority-setting process, role in,
        173
    role of networking, 178–179
    values held by, 49
advocacy, 7, 28, 55, 57, 61–62, 111,
    146, 148, 193, 200, 216, 259,
    263–267, 292, 312, 314, 320,
    322
    groups/organisations, 58–59, 102
    NGOs, 184
Africa, 10–11, 132, 223, 238
aid, 24, 29, 74, 135, 139, 144, 191,
    231, 269
aim of the health system, 74, 142,
    175, 215, 263
allocation capacity of health system,
    76

involvement of stakeholders or
health system members,
175–180
planning spiral, 165–166
policy advocates, 5, 94, 179, 184,
264
policy agenda, developing, 168
policy analysts, 5, 23, 94, 179
policy attention and policy
implementation, case studies,
169
policy capture, 189
policy community, 178
policy evaluators, 94, 179
policy evaporation, 189
policy facilitators, 93–94, 179
policy implementers, 94, 179
policy leaders, 3, 93, 177–179, 183
policy makers, 93, 172, 179, 265
political capacity of health system,
76
priorities, 168–174
processes for, 163–175
professional planner, role of, 167
rationality of, 164–168
rights-based agenda for, 171
role of evidence, 180–186
setting priorities, 168–174
'stages heuristic' conceptualisation,
165
stages of, 164
value-driven, 186–188, 197–199
politically manipulated state, 74
politicians, 59
politics, 7, 11, 14, 23, 49, 104,
107, 187, 189, 294, 299, 303,
320–322
of collaboration, 248–249
decentralisation in political context,
86–87
of decision-making, 115, 122, 167,
210
of DHA, 220, 226–227
empowerment and, 53
of financing mechanisms, 134,
136, 139, 149, 276

of full employment, 53–54
of health decision-making, 60
of IAH, 90–95, 260–261
impact on national health systems,
29, 31, 34–36, 41, 63
of policymaking, 161, 164–165,
168, 177–179, 209, 313
political accountability, 78
political authority, 72–75
political capacity, 76, 104, 315
political coalitions, 15, 51, 64, 92,
216, 261, 319
political correctness, 111
political determinants of health
services, 13
political governance, 51, 71
political interdependence, 26–27
political lobbying, 263–264, 266
politically manipulated state, 74
political nature of management,
215–216
political participation, 97, 100–101
political patronage and
manipulation, 77, 211–212
of process for prioritisation, 169,
171–173
regulation, in political context,
109–112, 262
of supplies managements, 242
values associated with, 51, 107
poverty, 96, 115, 126, 290, 304
Poverty Reduction Strategy Papers
(PRSPs), 98, 162
reduction strategies, 141, 187
President's Emergency Plan for AIDS
Relief (PEPFAR), 135
preventive services, 56
Primary Health Care (PHC)
movement, 12–19, 30–31
'community' participation, 16–17
comparison with neo-liberal
reforms, 25–26
development of health services,
15–16
equity principle, 12–14
principle of Alma Ata, 14–15

World Health Organization (WHO),
  2, 53, 90, 126, 134, 140, 187
  Commission on Macroeconomics
    and Health, 29
  Commission on Social
    Determinants, 261

constitution of, 45
definition of a health system,
  54
World Health Report, 31, 37, 237

Zambia, 108

About the Authors

Charles Collins currently holds an honorary post at the Liverpool School of Tropical Medicine at the University of Liverpool, UK. He has worked in Colombia at the Escuela Superior de Administración Pública and Universidad del Valle, and at the (now) Nuffield Centre for International Health and Development, University of Leeds, UK. He has also worked in countries of Asia and Africa on a short-term basis.

Andrew Green holds an honorary professorial appointment at the University of Leeds from which he retired in 2012. He has worked in a number of countries in Asia and Africa on a short- and long-term basis, including as Head of Planning for the Ministry of Health in Swaziland. He also worked as a health planner in the British NHS for two years before joining the Nuffield Centre for International Health and Development at the University of Leeds which he led for many years and where he researched and taught in the fields of health policy and planning.